Communication Development During Infancy

Communication Development During Infancy

Lauren B. Adamson
Georgia State University

DEVELOPMENTAL PSYCHOLOGY SERIES

Series Editor: Wendell Jeffrey, UCLA

Book Team

Executive Editor *Michael Lange*
Developmental Editors *Kassi Radomski and Ted Underhill*
Production Editor *Gloria G. Schiesl*
Visuals/Design Developmental Consultant *Marilyn A. Phelps*
Visuals/Design Freelance Specialist *Mary L. Christianson*
Marketing Manager *Steven Yetter*
Advertising Coordinator *Mike Matera*
Production Manager *Beth Kundert*

WCB Brown & Benchmark
A Division of Wm. C. Brown Communications, Inc.

Executive Vice President/General Manager *Thomas E. Doran*
Vice President/Editor in Chief *Edgar J. Laube*
Vice President/Marketing and Sales Systems *Eric Ziegler*
Director of Production *Vickie Putman Caughron*
Director of Custom and Electronic Publishing *Chris Rogers*

Wm. C. Brown Communications, Inc.

President and Chief Executive Officer *G. Franklin Lewis*
Senior Vice President, Operations *James H. Higby*
Corporate Senior Vice President and Chief Financial Officer *Robert Chesterman*
Corporate Senior Vice President and President of Manufacturing *Roger Meyer*

Brown & Benchmark's Developmental Psychology Series

Cover design/image by Marilyn A. Phelps

Copyedited by Rebecca Mills Burgart

A Times Mirror Company

Library of Congress Catalog Card Number: 94–72184

ISBN 0–697–14590–5

Printed in the United States of America by Wm. C. Brown Communications, Inc., 2460 Kerper Boulevard, Dubuque, IA 52001

10 9 8 7 6 5 4 3

To Wally

CONTENTS

PREFACE

Until recently, only a few pioneers ventured into the preverbal domain to observe infants interacting with their caregivers. Their writings provided others with a clear and compelling introduction to the whys and ways of investigating communication before speech. Now scores of scientists have followed in their footsteps, transforming the area of early communication development from a scientific frontier to a cultivated research field. Armed with sophisticated methodological tools, they are clustering around specific phenomena to debate issues at the core of developmental psychology. Cries, smiles, gestures, and words are providing access to early experiences. Intricately patterned social interactions are revealing capacities for shared moments and enduring relationships. Exchanges about objects are imparting information about the emergence of intentional and conventional actions.

To newcomers, the crowded landscape of early communication development may be a bit disorienting. Many of its most fascinating sights can now only be reached through volumes steeped with specialized parlance. Many of its most illuminating discussions are situated within dense debates. My aim in writing this book is to help clear the way to these most interesting vantage points. From the onset, I imagined that it would be read by advanced undergraduates and beginning graduate students in psychology, education, and communication. I also hope that it will be of interest to professionals in speech–language pathology, pediatrics, and clinical psychology, as well as to academically inclined parents of young children.

The first three chapters provide historical, conceptual, and methodological preludes to our review of contemporary research. In the first, I explain why the study of infants as communicators is so timely. In the second, various definitions of communication and development are presented, along with an overarching sketch of the terrain that we will explore. In the third, a brief methodological orientation is provided. Then we embark on our tour of the recent literature. I have organized it into four sections, dividing it with four light lines that cross each infant's developmental course. In Chapter 4, we focus on shared attentiveness during the period from birth to the biobchavioral shift that occurs during an infant's second month. In Chapter 5, we consider the intricate episodes of interpersonal engagement that occur between the onset of smiling at 2 months and the beginning of object fascination at 6 months. In Chapter 6, we follow changes in communication that occur as 6- to 15-month-olds begin to converse with their caregivers about objects and events in their immediate environment. Finally, in Chapter 7, we take note of the emergence of symbolic communication, including the first stirrings of language.

As you read through these chapters, I suggest that you consult the list of references. It is filled with examples of exemplary scholarship that can take you deeper into the details of infant communication. Moreover, it contains recommendations about paths forward into early childhood, with its miracle of language, and bridges into neighboring domains of emotional, social, and cognitive development during infancy.

Many people contributed directly to the preparation of this book. Roger Bakeman, who has been the best of collaborators for over a decade, worked with me on beginning this book, sharing his ideas about infants and, especially in Chapter 3, his wise words about research methodology. My colleagues Patricia Spencer, Mary Ann Romski, Carolyn Mervis, Amy Lederberg, and Jeffrey Cohn graciously read an earlier version of the manuscript and provided extremely helpful comments. Barbara Dunbar generously shared her ideas about infants with communication disorders, and Rose Sevcik tutored me on nonhuman primate communication. I am also grateful to Donna Borkman Reed, who read the manuscript with her astonishing eye for detail, and to Duncan McArthur, who turned my sketches into figures. I want to thank as well the many graduate students at Georgia State University who read and commented on drafts of this text.

I am also fortunate to have had several other sources of support as I struggled with this book. First, I am grateful to my first guides into infancy research, T. Berry Brazelton and Edward Tronick, for providing me with powerful working models of insightful and compassionate researchers. Second, during the writing of this book, I was the appreciative recipient of research support from the National Institute of Child Health and Human Development's program project grant to Georgia State University's Language Research Center and from the faculty research initiative program of Georgia State University.

Finally, I lovingly acknowledge my family. I am grateful to Daniel and Thomas for sustaining my fascination with and delight in parent–child communication. And I thank Wally for listening, applauding, commenting, and caring. It is a pleasure to dedicate this book to him.

CHAPTER

1

The Communicating Infant

An Historical Introduction

CHAPTER OUTLINE

For the past two decades, developmental psychologists have joined with colleagues from disciplines as diverse as anthropology, ethology, linguistics, pediatrics, psychiatry, and speech–language pathology to study early communication development. Together they catalog how infants express themselves, and they speculate about how infants understand our messages. They ponder the significance of such seemingly simple acts as a newborn infant's selective attention to her mother's voice, a 10-month-old baby's glance at his father before crawling toward a novel object, and a toddler's attempt to gain attention by touching a friend's toy. They convene at international conferences to discuss infant crying, and publish articles to document the nuances of speech perception, the emergence of pointing, and the use of first words. They write review articles and book chapters summarizing the extensive literature about early parent–infant interactions. In short, by almost any index of academic enthusiasm, scientists now consider communication development during the first 18 months of life an electrifying topic.

In this first chapter, we focus primarily on the reasons why scientists currently find communicating infants so compelling. To explain their fascination, it is useful to examine the history of how developmental psychologists have regarded communicating infants. This longer view will establish two important points. First, the facts about early communication capture scientific interest only when they are placed within a theoretical sphere. Second, the theoretical spheres of developmental psychology—like those of all sciences—are more like soap bubbles than like steel orbs. That is, as they rise (as science progresses), some spheres expand, while others contract or even burst. And, as the following brief historical account will demonstrate, sometimes spheres may join together, bringing previously separate contents into a startlingly new configuration.

The Confused Infant

The intensive study of early communication development is of recent vintage. Earlier scholars, of course, knew about infants' cries, smiles and coos, and babbles and gestures. Moreover, these familiar phenomena were introduced into the scientific record at psychology's beginnings. For example, Charles Darwin (1877) devoted an entire section in his celebrated "Biographical Sketch of an Infant" to specific observations of the development of communicative means. Both Arnold Gesell (1945) and Nancy Bayley (1969), creators of two of the first widely used standardized tests of infant development, included several items related to communication. Periodically, an insightful developmentalist like the psychoanalyst René Spitz (1957) would write eloquently about the theoretical significance of nonverbal acts such as the 2-month-old's smile and 15-month-old's head shake 'no'. But primarily, the roots of today's interest in infant communication taper out rapidly, reducing to a rare reference by the early 1960s.

There are several related reasons why developmental psychologists have tended to ignore infants' communicative acts. For one, these acts' very familiarity may have led to their being overlooked. As the path-breaking Gestalt psychologist Wolfgang Köhler (1940) once noted in his essay entitled "Ways of Psychology," people often find it difficult "to wonder" and "to be startled" when they study a familiar phenomenon. Yet Köhler, like the ancient Greeks, thought this was "the primary condition that leads to inquiry" because "in a realm where hardly any occurrence is ever *quite* new, few questions about the genesis of things are likely to be asked" (pp. 6–7). Thus, given scientists' tendency to want to explore frontiers for new facts, they often fail to probe for "hidden facts" in areas close to home.

A second reason why the study of infant communication has such a short history is that infants have traditionally been cast in a marginal role in psychological theories. All too often an unelaborated image of infants was presented to serve as a preface to a grand theory of adult functioning. Such images can be a powerful deterrent to research, so much so that Robert Emde, a prominent student of Spitz, once chided his fellow child psychiatrists for ignoring "day-to-day reality" to cling to "theoreticomorphic myths" in which "that baby is like my theory" (Emde & Robinson, 1979, p. 98).

Usually, these myths have been about what infants cannot do. Indeed, the very term *infant* is derived from the Latin for *without speech*. One type of myth depicts unorganized infants who begin development without ways of structuring their activities. Consider, for example, William James's famous claim that newborns are "assailed by eyes, ears, nose, skin, and entrails at once" and so feel all is "one great blooming, buzzing confusion" (1890, Vol. 1, p. 488). Young infants are in such a state, according to James, because they are not yet able to attend selectively to some sensations and to ignore others. A second sort of myth contains disengaged infants who lack the basic capacity to be aware of their environment. A classic version of this myth can be traced to Sigmund Freud (1958/1911), who suggests that very young infants hallucinate satisfying objects.

The Competent Infant

Understandably, images of unorganized and unaware young infants did little to entice scientists to take a closer look. Nevertheless, during the early 1960s, unprecedented curiosity arose about the beginnings of human development. In part, this interest was prompted by extensive technological and societal changes. For example, medical advances dramatically increased the survival rate of critically ill and premature newborns, raising new questions about how biological insults might affect the course of early development. Educators, increasingly concerned about the effects of poverty on learning, raised difficult questions about the outcome of early experiences. Parents, seeking to reform childbirth procedures and facing a growing need for alternative childcare, asked for more information about newborns' experiences and first relationships.

In addition, psychologists were propelled toward infants by forces deep within their discipline. A new theoretical mood (or *Zeitgeist*)—often identified as the Cognitive Revolution—was sweeping the human sciences (see Baars, 1986, for personal accounts). At the heart of this movement is a desire to understand the inner processes hidden behind behavior. Within this movement, infants were seen as [with]holders of crucial information about fundamental or primary human experiences.

As soon as researchers began to question them, infants started to give surprising answers. Contrary to the theoreticomorphic myths about newborns, these infants appeared strikingly competent. Emde and Robinson (1979), in an extensive review of research on newborns, remarked that researchers had essentially started to study "a new species" who was "active, stimulus-seeking, and creative in the ways he begins to construct his world" (p. 74). Far from being unorganized, infants' actions right from birth seem to be patterned, predictable, and above all, functional.

This astonishing characterization of competency gained rapid currency. By the early 1970s, enough excellent work was available to compile a volume of over 1300 pages, *The Competent Infant*. Here, hundreds of fascinating studies were abstracted in celebration of an infant who "from his earliest days . . . is an active, perceiving, learning, and information-organizing individual" (Stone, Smith, & Murphy, 1973, p. 4).

Methodological Contributions

It is unusual for a new field of study to be fruitful so quickly. In large measure, such abundant productivity was made possible by adopting sophisticated research methods from closely related areas. For example, experimental psychologists had already developed a rich store of procedures for studying perception, learning, and memory in nonhuman animals which could be modified to suit young infants' response capacities. For example, Robert Fantz (1958) transformed a simple two-choice stimuli paradigm into an elegantly simple technique for probing young infants' preferences. In this paradigm, infants inform us which of two stimuli they prefer (such as two pictures of a human face, one with the features in their proper place and one with scrambled features) by consistently looking longer at one picture than at the other.

The power of techniques like Fantz's is that they provide a standardized way to ask nonverbal infants an endless stream of questions. Each researcher does not need to puzzle anew over how to communicate with infants to get a clear answer. Moreover, researchers gain confidence that they are interpreting infants' answers correctly when they use a technique refined by repeated use, and they gain even more confidence when two such techniques converge toward the same answer.

Ethology, the biological discipline devoted to the study of animal behavior, which was founded in the 1940s by Konrad Lorenz and Niko Tinbergen, also provided a wealth of inspiration. Ethologists argued forcefully that the function of behavior patterns might best be understood if animals are observed in their natural settings. Furthermore, they provided compelling support for their position, offering plausible explanations for behavior patterns as diverse as the mating rituals of the male three-spined stickleback (Tinbergen, 1951) and the mother-following efforts (or *imprinting*) of greylag goslings (Lorenz, 1970/1935). In the 1960s, the psychoanalytically trained psychiatrist John Bowlby (1969) argued persuasively that the ethologists' perspective might help us understand how human infants develop attachment relationships with their caregivers, and he inspired many researchers (e.g., Ainsworth, 1967; Wolff, 1966) to document what transpires between human caregivers and infants in everyday contexts.

Heuristic Theories

Sophisticated research methods did much to stimulate the gathering of new facts about infants. But new facts, even about infants behaving in ways that were previously thought impossible, soon lose their luster unless they find a theoretical sphere. Developmental psychologists have long held as their primary goal the understanding of the *process* of human development. This understanding entails not only the description of what *is* (i.e., the facts of systematic change) but also an explanation of why the facts are as they are. Thus, a theory that explains development is a crucial part of the scientific process.

If a theory is a good one, it does more than extend facts into the realm of explanation. It also inspires the search for new information. It anticipates the empirical world, acting as a *heuristic* device that guides the investigator into interesting territory. Central to a theoretical heuristic are both the compelling questions it raises about phenomena and the general image it paints of what lies ahead.

Of course, not all theories are equally heuristic. Some may steer people away from exploration; others may initiate a voyage that takes an unexpected turn. Within the area of developmental psychology, Jean Piaget's theory of cognitive development is a superb example of a heuristic theory that has led researchers into uncharted waters. Moreover, Piaget's theory was one of the (many would say, *the*) primary motivations for the new interest in infants' cognition that swept psychology in the 1960s.

From an historian's point of view, it is interesting to note the chronology of events here. Works about infants constitute a small, albeit very important, part of Piaget's published corpus, which started in 1907 with a paper about an albino sparrow and grew unabated until his death in 1980 (see Chapman, 1988, for a detailed and incisive intellectual biography). Piaget's primary research on infancy was based on observations of his own three children. These were collected in the late 1920s to early 1930s and presented in three books originally published in French between 1936 and 1945. Yet, although he was recognized as an international scholar by the end of the 1930s, his trilogy about infants was not translated into English until the 1950s and early 1960s. Moreover, it was not until 1963, with the publication of John Flavell's detailed overview of Piaget's work, that many developmental psychologists became aware of their scope and richness. (For an excellent, brief introduction to Piaget's child psychology, see Ginsburg and Opper, 1988).

Piaget's Sensorimotor Infant

Initially, developmental psychologists who read Piaget's work on infancy were most impressed by the hidden facts of infancy he described. His observations included astonishing details about the emergence of specific behavior patterns such as the development of visually guided reaching at around 4 months of age (see pp. 157–165 in *The Origins of Intelligence in Childhood,* 1963/1936) as well as startling examples of young infants acting as if objects do not exist if they are not currently being sensed (see the first chapter of *The Construction of Reality in the Child,* 1954/1937).

Such dramatic findings gradually lured developmental psychologists to examine the grand theory of cognitive development that had led to Piaget's amazing discoveries. They soon learned that Piaget's main interest in infancy stemmed from his idea that the origins of human intelligence lay in organized, adaptive sensorimotor actions, not in symbols (which he thought emerged late in the second year of life) or in logical reasoning (which he thought was first evident only years after birth). Moreover, his research questions were those of a *genetic epistemologist* (a biologist/philosopher who studies the development of knowledge) rather than of a traditional child psychologist: As infants interact with the environment, how do they organize their actions? How does this organization change so that their actions become increasingly adaptive? As this organization changes, how too does an infant's understanding of reality—of objects, space, time, and causality—change? Further, how does the capacity to represent (literally, re-present) action—to use symbols to stand for or signify actions—emerge over the course of infancy?

In answering these questions, Piaget made three claims that deeply challenged traditional myths of unorganized and disengaged young infants. Piaget's first claim was that human infants—like all living organisms—are capable of organized acts that they actively regulate in order to adapt to their environment. In the case of human newborns, these acts are qualitatively different from the adaptive acts of adults or even of 2-month-olds or 2-year-olds. Nevertheless, these early action patterns, which Piaget called reflex *schemes,* are well-suited to development. As a newborn interacts with her environment, her current actions closely resemble her previous actions. But, because the circumstance of each occasion is never quite like that of prior occasions and because the infant actively tries to adapt her schemes to suit the occasion, slight change occurs each time a scheme is used. The infant gradually develops more adaptive ways to interact with the environment through this process of the self-regulation of actions.

Piaget illustrated this claim with detailed observations (1963/1936, pp. 25–27, Obs. 2–6). For example, he recorded that his son, Laurent, sucked his fingers immediately after birth and that as soon as his mouth contacted his mother's nipple, he began to suck. Moreover, he noted that Laurent practiced sucking without anything in his mouth just for the sake of sucking, and that he modified his sucking pattern so that he could suck on novel objects such as his pillow and Piaget's finger. Piaget also illustrated how creative modifications of a scheme might form qualitatively new action patterns. For example, he provided extensive examples to demonstrate how, during the second and third months of life, Laurent and his two siblings each altered the sucking reflex scheme to develop a repertoire of acquired sucking habits that included tongue protrusion, saliva bubbling, and lip smacking.

Piaget's second claim was that as infants gradually change the organization of their actions, they also gradually develop the capacity for intelligent action. To Piaget, intelligence lies not only in specific actions but also in the way different actions are related to each other and to objects in the environment. To Piaget, *intentionality,* the ability to establish goals for actions before actually acting, is the hallmark of intelligence. In his theory, he relates the emergence of intentionality to the gradual changes in the structure of infants' activity.

Initially, infants are unable to act intentionally because they can perform only one scheme at a time, and they do not relate their actions specifically to objects. But, over the course of the first months of life, they develop a number of schemes that they can tailor to specific objects. For example, they can reach for an object, move an object by kicking it with their leg, stroke an object with their hand, and so forth. Then, at around 9 months of age, they begin to coordinate these object-related schemes in a temporal sequence. Such coordination, Piaget argues, allows them to perform one scheme *in order to* perform another scheme.

To illustrate this developmental sequence, Piaget provided well-selected vignettes. For example, he illustrated the first dawning of intentionality with the report that when his daughter Jacqueline was 11 months, 22 days old, she

> lets fall a celluloid swan from its swinging nest. Unsuccessful in her attempts to pick it up, she immediately displaces it with her feet and brings it nearer to her. (1963/1936, p. 224, Obs. 129)

Within Piaget's theoretical sphere, Jacqueline's action reveals her newly emerging capacity for intelligent activity. She now forms a desire ('I want to pick up my swan again') before she acts, and she is able to employ a different act, a foot movement that she had made many times in the past, as a means to fulfill this desire.

To Piaget, Jacqueline's actions reveal an important step in cognitive development, the emergence of intentionality. Moreover, he saw great significance in the fact that this step took place in the middle of infancy. It meant to him that our capacity for intentional action is neither innate nor is it dependent on the acquisition of language that marks the end of infancy. In addition, it strengthened his conviction that intelligence emerges as an infant actively interacts with objects and constructs increasingly adaptive structures of actions.

Piaget's third claim was that the ability to use symbols arises at the end of infancy, only after a year and a half or so of sensorimotor activity. His overall view of the emergence of symbolic thought is much like his view of the emergence of intentionality: the capacity to form symbols depends upon an infant's organization of actions. In this instance, the infant structures his actions such that one scheme can stand for another. In other words, one action can be a symbol for or re-present another action. Structuring actions in this way is extremely complex and assumes a lengthy period of development. But once it is achieved, the infant possesses a qualitatively new way of interacting with her environment since she can relate current actions to those far in the past and way in the future.

According to Piaget (1962/1945), when 18-month-old infants begin to be able to form symbols, this ability is revealed throughout their activity, including how they imitate, play, and use language. For example, the child can say "Moo" to recall or communicate about the activities involved in experiencing a cow, mimic silly antics of a friend who is no longer present, and pretend to drink milk from a doll's empty bottle.

In summary, Piaget argued that infants continually change the organization of their activity as they perform action patterns. Different organizations support different levels of cognitive accomplishments. Furthermore, by infancy's end, these accomplishments include the ability to perform intentional actions and the capacity to use symbols.

Expanding the Piagetian Sphere

By the 1970s, developmental psychologists began to appreciate fully that behind Piaget's astonishing observations of infants lay a formidable theory rich with contentions about the essence of human development.

Many developmentalists found his views convincing and followed his lead to locate the center of development in the transforming structures of the infant's sensorimotor activities.

This new theoretical view lent an unprecedented amount of order and range to our understanding of infants' development. For example, Robert McCall (1979) drew an impressive picture of the developmental stages that occur during infancy from what he called a modified Piagetian perspective. The theme for each stage was set by a fundamental cognitive attribute that could be discerned throughout a range of domains, including an infant's notion of objects, attention, exploration and play, imitative abilities, vocalizations, memory, and social behavior.

Gradually, however, developmental psychologists' confidence in such orderly normative pictures of development began to wane. As psychologists began to feel more comfortable viewing infants from a Piagetian perspective, they also began to notice other phenomena that Piaget did not often mention. One particularly troubling concern was that Piaget might have focused so tightly on infants' developing activities that he may have disregarded some essential qualities of infants' environment (see, e.g., Gibson, 1988) and, in particular, their social environment (see, e.g., Bruner, 1972; Kessen, 1979; Newson & Newson, 1975).

Jerome Bruner (1983c) captured this concern well in his engaging autobiography, *In Search of Mind*. By the time Bruner became interested in studying how mind begins, he had already made numerous pathbreaking contributions to the study of cognition, perception, and education which had led him to appreciate Piaget's theory. It is therefore interesting to note that he prefaced his story about his turn toward developmental psychology with reflections on his "complicated relation with Piaget" (1983c, p. 142).

Bruner began with an unequivocal acknowledgment of his enormous debt to Piaget. He then, however, quickly lamented the way Piaget isolated "little intellectuals" so that they were "detached from the hurly-burly of the human condition." To Bruner, Piaget's child appeared to be "a calm child and a lone one" (1983c, p. 139). Bruner also saw the world of Piaget's child as "a quiet place" where "he is virtually alone" in

> a world of objects that he must array in space, time and causal relationships. He begins his journey egocentrically and must impose properties on the world that will eventually be shared with others. But others give him little help. The social reciprocity of infant and mother plays a very small role in Piaget's account of development. And language gives neither hints nor even a means of unraveling the puzzles of the world to which language applies. (1983c, p. 138)

This image of "quietism" clearly troubled Bruner, who suspected that there must be a "richer picture behind mental growth" (p. 142), one that included aspects Piaget did not consider.

The limitations of Piaget's vision were noted as well by social and developmental psychologists in England who were trying to understand "the integration of a child into a social world" (Richards, 1974c). For example, John and Elizabeth Newson published a provocative essay in 1975 in the *Bulletin of the British Psychological Society* in which they began with Piaget's standpoint. They praised it for highlighting both the way infants actively interact with the environment and the way infants' overt activities are related to later-developing symbolic functioning. Like Bruner, though, they then chided Piaget for considering only solitary infants interacting with inanimate objects.

Thus, many developmental psychologists began to consider the implications of placing infants within a social context by questioning competent infants. They were not alone in these considerations. Again, just as their previous movement to the study of infants' intelligence was in tune with a general turn toward cognition, their new interest in early social interactions meshed well with a rising contextualism that was being heatedly debated within cognitive psychology. Within this emerging Zeitgeist, difficult questions were raised about the relation between "cognition and reality" (Neisser, 1976; cf. Neisser, 1967) and how everyday social contexts influence cognitive development (e.g., Bronfenbrenner, 1979; Donaldson, 1978).

The Communicating Infant

When psychologists began to consider infants in their everyday contexts, they started to discover astonishing interpersonal facts. Infants continued to appear remarkably competent; now they also seemed to be engaged and engaging communicators who are embedded in a responsive and rich social world.

Several qualities of infants-in-context were particularly striking. First, human infants appeared "surprisingly *socially* active almost from the moment of birth" (Newson & Newson, 1975, p. 276) as they eagerly sought out and responded to other people. Moreover, from a functional point of view, the primacy of their social interest made good sense as a beginning point for development. After all, even if human infants are initially active and organized, they are nevertheless born in a state of profound immaturity; their very survival depends on their caregivers' actions (Bowlby, 1969).

Second, the organization of exchanges between young social infants and their caregivers appeared intricate and finely tuned. By comparison, the interaction between infants and inanimate objects at the same point in development seemed simple and faltering. For example, at 2 months of age, infants often engage with their parents in sustained face-to-face conversations of smiles and gleeful vocalizations even though they are not yet able to reach accurately for an object they see and desire (Brazelton, Koslowski, & Main, 1974).

A further intriguing quality of infants' actions in a social context is that they often seem both responsive and initiative. What an infant does can be affected by his partner's actions and vice versa. Such *bidirectional influences* (Bell, 1968) mean that any adequate model of early infant social interactions must consider not only how infants are socialized but also how they act as socializers who subtly alter their own context. The eminent developmental psychologist, Harriet Rheingold, made this point well in a classic essay in which she argued that it is crucial that researchers recognize that an infant

> modulates, tempers, regulates, and refines the caretaker's activities. He produces delicate shades and nuances in these operations to suit his own needs of the moment. By such responses as fretting, sounds of impatience or satisfaction, by facial expressions of pleasure, contentment, or alertness he produces elaborations here and dampening there. (Rheingold, 1969, p. 785)

Infants' communicative acts now appear to be powerful ways of affecting the environment. Moreover, communicative skills are central to parenting. To gratify an infant's needs, parents must understand nonverbal expressions and react in ways that their infant can appreciate.

The final quality of infants' actions in social context that we will consider is perhaps the most obvious and, at the same time, the most difficult to characterize. This is the quality of *meaningfulness*. This quality has two aspects. First, infants' actions always seem meaningful to human observers. Even when we might readily agree that the infant cannot possibly have meant what we think (as, for example, when we react to a sleeping infant's smile with a comment like "He's enjoying his dream" or "She's thanking me for holding her"), we cannot resist interpreting these acts within our own frame of meaning. Moreover, the human gloss that caregivers provide for infants' actions influences their own reactions to the infants. Such interpretations are an integral part of the social relationship.

Secondly, caregivers continually embed infants into a world of *cultural meaning*. As adults care for human infants, they bring with them a uniquely human repertoire of language, social rituals, and well-honed strategies of problem solving. They are "curators of meaning" (Trevarthen, 1988, p. 68) who, through everyday social interaction with infants, guide them into a realm of collective meaning.

We will often notice these basic qualities of infants-in-context when we discuss recent research on early communication development in Chapters 4 through 7. For our purposes here, it is important to note that when a contextualist perspective was adopted, questions relative to Piaget's major claims about the development of regulated, intentional, and symbolic action spewed forth. For example, recall that Piaget claimed that young infants actively regulate the organization of their actions as they attempt to interact adaptively with their environment. When the interaction occurs with another person, particularly a caregiver who has his or her own goals in mind, the possibility for mutual regulation and a shared organization arises. How do the infant and caregiver negotiate a structure of shared activity? Do caregivers impose organization on the infants' activities? Further, do infants' experiences during moments of mutual regulation with their caregivers help them to develop ways to regulate their own actions?

Similar kinds of issues arose relative to Piaget's claims about the development of intentions. Recall that Piaget thought the capacity for goal-directed activity developed quite late in infancy because it depended on the infant's ability to coordinate different actions. One example we considered was his daughter's attempt to use her foot to move a toy swan closer to her hand so that she could then pick up the swan. From a sociocultural perspective, two new aspects of becoming intentional are apparent. First, well before infants might form clear intentions on their own, other people might provide them, glossing infants' actions (for example, a foot movement) with both words ("You want the swan, huh?") and actions (movement of the swan into the baby's hand). Moreover, other people may even act as if babies had such intentions before they were able to form them on their own. Second, two people may share intentions. This realization raises difficult questions about how infants develop the ability to communicate with other people so that they might reach common goals.

Finally, a sociocultural perspective has provoked a far-reaching reexamination of Piaget's claim about the way infants develop symbols such as words. Recall that Piaget argued that the formation of symbols was a remarkable cognitive feat, one accomplished only after infants organized their actions so that one act might stand for another. Viewing infants as communicators features a second aspect of this achievement: infants come to use actions that are *socially conventional*. That is, their actions are meaningful not only within their own system of action but also within a cultural system of actions. The words they make their own and the topics they communicate about are not fundamentally their own. Instead, they are appropriated from the human environment and gain infants entrance into a collectivity of cultural accomplishments that transcends the mind of any single human being.

The Empirical Study of Early Communication Development

Abstract reflections such as these about the implications of the interpersonal facts of human infancy captured the imagination of scholars from several disciplines and drew them together to study early communication development. It was soon apparent that our knowledge was sorely limited. Traditional theoretical approaches provided scant hints about communication prior to language and, although basic information about when infants could perform communicative acts such as cries, smiles, coos, and words was available, there were remarkably few accounts about how these acts emerged and how they were used.

The emerging scholarly interest in early communication development fortunately found places within the scientific community. Without institutional legitimization and support, even the most exciting of new views may not flourish. Moreover, attributes of the first generation of researchers in an area often linger, coloring the style and tone of subsequent work on a topic.

One particularly important place for the first studies of communication development during infancy was the Center for Cognitive Studies at Harvard and its surrounding sites, which included settings for the study of language development (see Kessel, 1988) and communication processes (see Bullowa, 1979). In the late 1960s, Bruner drew to this center an exceptionally talented group of researchers from several disciplines and countries to do the pioneering studies on early infant social interactions that form the basis of much of the work we will consider in the following chapters. He clearly facilitated groundbreaking encounters. One participant, the noted British social psychologist Martin Richards, recalled how, during the summer of 1966, "people from several different backgrounds" were engaged late into the night in "talk, argument, discussion, and excitement" about mother–infant interaction and how, during the next summer, the collective "cry was for data" (in Bullowa, 1979, p. 61).

About This Book

This cry for data about early communication has been amply answered in the past 25 years. New methods of data collection and analysis have greatly increased both the precision and the scope of descriptions of communication during infancy. However, these data have done little to quench debates about the implications of early communication. No single model has merged with or displaced Piaget's theoretical sphere. Rather, the data have provided continual fuel for lively discussions and debates about fundamental issues related to the beginnings of human development.

This twin state of being data-filled and discussion-rich makes the study of early communication development a challenging area for students new to developmental psychology. My aim in this book is to act as a tour guide who provides commentary about the field's major theoretical issues and views of specific empirical highlights. The next two chapters provide a general overview of the territory. First, we consider what developmental researchers mean by the terms *development* and *communication*. During this preliminary exercise, we meet three theorists, Lev Vygotsky, Heinz Werner, and Roman Jakobson, whose images have oriented contemporary researchers toward interesting aspects of early communication development. Then, in Chapter 3, we consider what it means to study communication development as a science, and we describe several methods that have contributed to this study. In the remainder of this book, we trace the development of communication up until the second half of the second year when children, by dint of their emerging mastery of language, are no longer infants. Along this path we consider, in Chapter 4, newborns' first moments of shared attentiveness; in Chapter 5, 2- to 6-month-old babies' intense engagement with other people; in Chapter 6, 1-year-old infants' involvement with both people and objects; and finally, in Chapter 7, toddlers' first use of communicative symbols, including words.

CHAPTER

2

Theoretical Foundations for the Study of Communication Development

CHAPTER OUTLINE

Research on early communication development is potentially boundless. Without an overarching plan of study, it is easy to be overwhelmed by the variety and richness of infants' actions in a social context. Of course, certain acts such as smiles and first words stand out as candidates for inquiry, and specific situations such as a mother calming her crying infant or two toddlers sharing a toy seem particularly promising focus points. But even when common sense seems to dictate what phenomena merit attention, it provides little guidance concerning either how to relate these specifics to general claims about communication development or how to explore them further to gather more telling information. To achieve these ends, scientists formulate theoretical models and research methods.

At the close of Chapter 1, I noted that the field of early communication development is now discussion-rich and data-filled. This is in part because scholars from several different disciplines have found phenomena of interest in the area. In this chapter, we consider several views of development and of communication that scholars brought with them as they started to study infants. These views are then used to draw a rough sketch of the developmental course of communication that will orient our review of current research.

Definitions of Development

In psychology, introductions to the study of children and of development are often equated so that, for example, the content of courses titled *child psychology* and *developmental psychology* overlap extensively, varying at most in how much of the life cycle is considered. This practice makes the concept of development seem relatively unproblematic. Yet, when this term is used by scientists, it is loaded with powerful allusions that have been the subject of continual debate (see, for example, the three volumes titled *The Concept of Development* [Harris, 1957; Stevenson, 1966; Collins, 1982] which record lively interdisciplinary discussions from conferences held at the Institute of Child Development [previously Welfare] at the University of Minnesota).

One main reason why developmental psychologists are so interested in the concept of development is that they have seen its power in biology, especially in embryology. There, the use of developmental notions has succeeded in ordering phenomena into systematic sequences of growth and in describing overarching trends in these sequences. Scholars across the behavioral sciences (and even in the humanities; see e.g., DeWitt, 1957, and Heaton, 1957, for applications in literature and in history, respectively) have been tempted to organize their own observations in a similar manner. However, as we will see, some theorists now worry that making such parallels is not without conceptual dangers.

Development as a Predictable Sequence

We can parcel out two ways in which developmental psychologists have typically used the word *development*. The first way restricts the label only to the substance or material of developmental phenomena and emphasizes how specific entities (be they new behaviors, accomplishments, or neuronal organizations) emerge in an orderly sequence. Charles Spiker, for example, urged that *development* be "used to name those changes in behavior that normally occur with an increase in the chronological age of the child" (1966, p. 41).

Infancy is an excellent period for such a simple developmental analysis. Strikingly new action patterns emerge regularly and often. Furthermore, it is possible to specify not only the order of emergence but also to approximate when each act typically emerges. I have done just

TABLE 2.1 Milestones of Early Communication Development

Milestone	Average Age	Typical Range
	(in months)	
Eyes open	0	
Eye-to-eye contact	2	
Social smile	2	
Coos and goos	2	
Laughs	4	
Squeals, raspberries, growls, yells, etc.	4	
Canonical babbling (e.g., [bababa])	7	
Comprehends a word	9	
Comprehends 10 words	10.5	
Variegated babbling	11	
Onset of pointing	12	
Comprehends 50 words	13	
Produces first word	13	9 to 16
Produces 10 words	15	13 to 19
Produces 50 words	20	14 to 24
Produces word combinations	21	18 to 24

this for communication development in Table 2.1, where I outline a sequence of milestones, each with a typical age of onset.

Using the term *development* to describe such a sequence rarely provokes warnings, although several cautions are in order. First, we need to remember that many judgment calls are made when such a neat list of milestones is drawn up. Researchers in the area of early communication development often dispute what acts are important enough to be considered milestones. Further, they often challenge its details, especially the association between act and age.

The dating of an act certainly depends on how one defines the act, and here is the first rub. Consider, for example, the behavior pattern labeled *pointing*, whose onset is presented as 12 months of age in Table 2.1. This age is derived from studies in which researchers record when infants first intentionally extend an index finger to direct a partner's attention toward an object (see Chapter 6). However, researchers also note that infants begin to extend their index finger months before and that adults often have no difficulty following such points to locate the object of the infant's interest. If this more lenient definition were used, pointing would have appeared considerably earlier in our list of milestones.

Second, we need to be careful not to overinterpret the correlation between age and act. The key developmental claim of lists such as that in Table 2.1 is that the sequence of acts is invariant, not that the link between each behavior and a specific age is determined. One reason to soften the significance of chronological age norms is that they are merely averages. The amount of variation across normally developing infants (i.e., those who meet established norms by passing standard milestones without undue haste or delay) may be quite large. For example, notice in Table 2.1 that although some infants have a 50-word vocabulary at 16 months and some at 20 months, all have likely begun to use symbolic gestures before they can produce so many words.

Yet another reason to be careful about interpreting age norms is that, especially early in the life cycle, the emergence of many acts depends heavily on nervous system maturation. The maturational clock begins to tick at the moment of conception, not at birth, an event that usually occurs 38 weeks or so after conception but may occur at 28 weeks or even earlier. Thus, if an infant is born prematurely and the emergence of an act depends largely on a certain degree of neural maturation, then he is likely to perform that act at the same age since conception as his full-term peers. That is, he would meet this milestone at the same conceptional age as his peers but appear delayed in terms of chronological age. For example, both full-term infants and those born after 30 weeks gestation are likely to begin to smile approximately 46 weeks after conception, when the premature infant is officially almost twice as old. In Chapter 4, we will consider how the displacement of the event of birth in the predictable sequence of communicative milestones may present unique challenges. For now, we need only note that the sequence of events, and the time interval between events, may prove more interesting from a developmental perspective than the age of onset for any one event.

Moreover, we should resist reducing development to lists of milestones. If we do, we might well miss important variations that any adequate developmental account should incorporate. For example, we might miss that a large minority of infants never crawl or that others may produce whole phrases ("I–want–juice") before uttering a single word ("juice"). We might also overlook events that occur between milestones. While such events, by definition, are not recorded as the culmination of a developmental process, they may nevertheless be crucial to the process of formation that precedes the emergence of a celebrated achievement such as the first step or the first word.

Finally, we must be careful not to assume that the typical sequence derived from the study of one group of children necessarily applies to other groups of children. The generality of even well-documented sequences such as the one presented in Table 2.1 is limited by sampling. If a researcher were to study a sample of children from a time or place different from those used to determine the norms, it is certainly conceivable that the age norms would vary. It is even possible that the sequencing of acts might vary as well. However, this is an empirical question to be answered, rather than a logical necessity to be asserted.

Even with all of these cautions firmly in mind, it may be difficult to resist the clarity of reducing development to a list of predictably sequenced acts. Such a list is a fine place to begin gaining a sense of how infants' communication changes over time. But it is only a beginning, and as we just saw, a beginning that is itself built upon several assumptions about what is and is not relevant to early communication development.

Development as a Systematic Pattern of Change

A second way the term *development* is used emphasizes the formal properties of change. This usage is far more controversial—and interesting—than the restrictive definition that we just considered. Here the notion that behavioral development occurs when new phenomena emerge in a sequence is retained. In addition, two related claims about the abstract pattern of relation between specific points in the sequence are made.

The first claim is that the relation between points in a sequence is lawful. In other words, later points in some sense may be seen as derived from, the result of, or an elaboration upon earlier points. The law might entail a statement of the structural relation between specific actions. For example, we might note that two earlier acts (such as grasping an object and looking at an object) become incorporated into a single subsequent act (such as visually guided reaching for and grasping of an object). Or we might state the relation in terms of functions. For example, we might note that infants substitute one form of communication (e.g., a word) for an earlier emerging form (e.g., a point) to accomplish the same aim (e.g., singling out a particular object from a range of possibilities). The key point is that a list such as that presented in Table 2.1 is viewed not only as a sequence of discrete acts but also as the beginning point for an analysis of the laws or principles of developmental change.

The second claim is that development is inherently progressive. That is, a sequence of development courses towards a developmental end point; each step along the way leads toward this point and away from less developed stances. This connotation of the term *development* is deeply engrained in our vocabulary. For example, we often say that speech is an advanced mode of communication and that caregivers bring up a child.

The developmental psychologist Heinz Werner (1890–1964) did much to sensitize contemporary child psychologists to these abstract implications of the term *development.* Of particular importance is his *orthogenetic principle of development,* which he hoped would focus attention on the formal and progressive relation between developmental points. This principle states that

> wherever development occurs it proceeds from a state of relative globality and lack of differentiation to a state of increasing differentiation, articulation, and hierarchic integration. (Werner, 1957, p. 126)

As this principle indicates, development from Werner's perspective is characterized by directional changes in the organization of parts within a whole (increasing differentiation and hierarchic integration) as well as changes in the specific parts (increasing articulation). Unlike the definition proposed by Spiker that we considered earlier, Werner's view mentions neither the substance of a particular state nor the time frame of developmental change. Indeed, Werner (1948) purposely deleted such references because he thought that his principle might serve as a heuristic guide to the study of such seemingly unrelated topics as children, comparative animal behavior, psychopathology, and cross-cultural differences. In all of these fields, he argued, a developmentalist should seek to understand changes in organization over time. Werner himself proceeded to apply the orthogenetic principle in several areas of development, including an insightful analysis of symbol formation (Werner & Kaplan, 1963) that we will soon consider.

For the time being, however, we need to raise two cautions about the use of laws of development. First, principles such as Werner's are menaced by what William Kessen has called the "dragon of entelechy" (1966, p. 63). When a developmental course is laid out from start to finish, there is the tendency to view all states before the end point as if they are merely preludes to this end point, and so knowing the end point in advance may subtly redirect our attention in misleading ways. For example, in the case of language development, it may direct attention toward infants' vocal acts rather than toward infants' initial efforts to use symbolic gestures. Further, it might lead to a serious underestimation of how important nonverbal acts, such as facial expressions and manual gestures, continue to be, even after verbal language, the designated end point, is reached. Of even more concern is the possibility that knowledge of the end point may lead us to view the end point as the *cause* of earlier occurring states. For example, the simple statement that "infants babble because they will soon speak" implies that a final state causes an earlier one. Such a *teleological* implication (*telos* means end, goal, or completion in Greek) presents grave concern to scientists who seek efficient (rather than final) causes that occur before effects.

Second, it is important to acknowledge the status of principles like Werner's. As he argued cogently, such principles are heuristic guides that establish themes for research. They draw our eyes to interesting phenomena. However, they are not testable, nor do they predict specific developmental courses. Thus, for example, such principles may stimulate interest in certain nonobvious relations such as the functional link between a gesture and a word, but they do not specify this relation. That specification must await both the psychologist's empirical description and theoretical explanation of this relation.

In summary, the term *development* implies systematic changes over time. And, at least to developmentalists who subscribe to Werner's perspective, the lawful relation between points is as interesting as the details of each point.

Images of Communication

Specification of both the details and the lawful relations of development depends, of course, on what is being studied. In our case, we are considering an area that is notoriously difficult to define. Human communication is a complex process. It involves both the coordination (*communion*) of people and the flow (*transmission*) of information between them. Moreover, when partners differ greatly in their ways of communicating as do, for example, an infant and a caregiver, it also involves *education* in that each may lead the other to a new understanding of the means and process of communication. Further, human communication can be accomplished by acts as diverse as a gesture of one's hand, an expression on one's face, a smell, a shift of posture, a turn of gaze, a sigh of despair, and, of course, a word. These acts may serve a multitude of functions such as promising, requesting, declaring, and disputing, and they may focus on an endless variety of topics, including objects close at hand and deeply guarded secrets.

Given the range and complexity of communication, it is not surprising that reasonable scholars disagree about what constitutes "genuine" or "full-blooded" communication (Johnson-Laird, 1990). On the one hand, some psychologists claim that "one cannot *not* communicate" (Watzlawick, Beavin, & Jackson, 1967, p. 51). All behavior can have message value to a social partner, and so any behavior—even that produced to indicate a lack of desire to communicate—constitutes communication. Other psychologists argue that it is more useful to speak of communication only when some sharing occurs. For example, Richards wrote that he finds it valuable to consider communication "something beyond interaction. It is not simply a two-sided modification of behavior or responsiveness to signals, but involves notions of mutuality, reciprocity, and intersubjectivity" (1974a, p. 123). Still other researchers add that the process of genuine communication involves intentionality or the construction of internal representations (see, e.g., Johnson-Laird, 1990).

It is ultimately fruitless to try to resolve such definitional disputes. Indeed, it may be useful to embrace the range of definitions in order to formulate different ways of looking at a process as rich and multifaceted as communication. I adopt such a strategy here by discussing not one but three complementary images of communication.

The first image emphasizes the interpersonal coordination or *communion* that occurs during communication episodes. The importance of sharing ongoing experiences and affective expressions will be most clearly drawn in this view. The second image highlights the *transmission* of information between two people during communicative events. It will provide us with a plan for describing the diversity of topics and functions that communication may serve. The final image focuses on the inherent asymmetry that exists between a preverbal child and more sophisticated communicative partners in a way that portrays communicative episodes as a setting for *education*. This view is particularly helpful in orienting us toward how caregivers guide infants as they learn how to use conventional means of communication such as words.

Communication as Communion

The first image that we will consider is a simple diagram of three overlapping circles representing *mother, child,* and *object*. (See Figure 2.1.)

Werner and Kaplan (1963) drew this figure to depict what they call the *primordial sharing situation*. In their theory of symbol formation, this situation was the beginning point of the developmental course that leads to symbols. In many ways, their theory of symbol formation is similar to Piaget's theory which we discussed in the introduction. Like Piaget, they thought that the emergence of symbols during the second year of life was prepared for by events much earlier in infancy. And, like Piaget, they thought that infants develop new capacities as they interact actively with their environment. But, as their diagram of the primordial sharing situation makes clear, Werner and Kaplan's view of the infant in context is radically different from Piaget's view of the young scientist experimenting with objects.

The most obvious difference is that Werner and Kaplan consider other people as a crucial aspect of the infants' early symbol-nurturing environment. Indeed, in their diagram, another person literally overlaps with the infant. This intersection of infants and others adds three important considerations to Piaget's account of the early development of symbols.

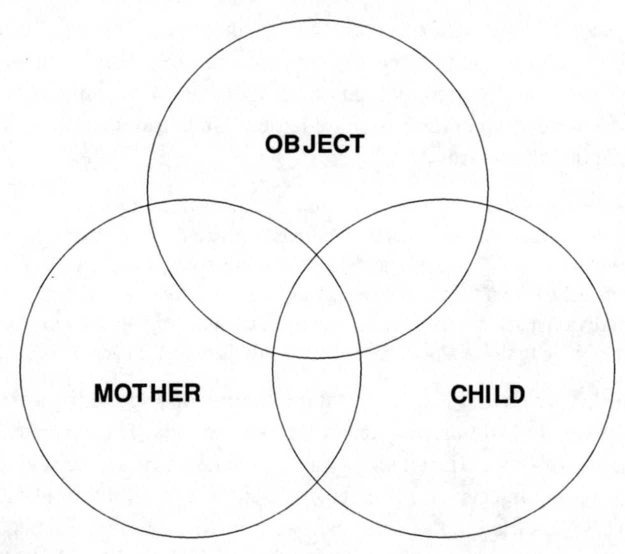

FIGURE 2.1
Communication as communion: Werner and Kaplan's primordial sharing situation.

First, Werner and Kaplan's account explicitly includes early social interactions as part of the process of symbol formation. In Werner and Kaplan's words, the ontogenesis of " 'communicating' messages *to* the Other" begins within "early forms of interaction which have the character of 'sharing' experience *with* the Other" (1963, p. 42). The transition from sharing to communicating occurs, in accord with Werner's orthogenetic principle, through the increasing differentiation of the components of the first interactions. That is, as infants begin to appreciate the boundaries between their experiences with objects and with people, they also begin to develop the capacity to use symbols to communicate with other people about objects. Thus the symbol emerges as a fourth component of the primordial sharing situation. It was termed the *fourth moment* (i.e., constitutive element) by Werner and Kaplan, which emphasizes its developmental source in the global, undifferentiated instances of sharing objects that occur between caregivers and infants.

Second, it is important to note that the primordial situation provides a meeting place for inanimate objects and people at the beginning of communication development. Perhaps the most interesting aspect of the diagram is the three-way overlap of adult, child, and object. Even in this first global state, there is, in Werner and Kaplan's view, sufficient reason to distinguish this triadic situation from dyadic ones where the infant interacts only with a person or with an object. This triadic situation is important to include because it is the one region that contains the seeds of referential communication that, by definition, contains both a communicative partner and a shared topic of communication. Thus, Werner and Kaplan wrote

> It is worthy of note that within this primordial sharing situation there arises *reference* in its initial, nonrepresentational form: child and mother are now beginning to contemplate objects together—however slightly these objects are detached from the child's self. Thus, the act of reference emerges not as an individual act, but as a social one: by exchanging things with the Other, by touching things and looking at them with the Other. (1963, p. 43)

Third, Werner and Kaplan highlight the importance of the affective as well as the sensorimotor aspects of infants' actions. They asserted that "the *sharing* of objects is not simply a secondary condition helpful to the learning about objects or symbols but is rather of vital significance" (1963, p. 71). Although they did not dwell on what sharing entails, they did make two suggestions about what a full analysis must include. They noted that during early interactions, infants' actions are *affective* as well as sensorimotor and that an important aspect of early development might be missed if this emotional quality were not included in analyses. Moreover, they recognized that moments of early sharing are *intimate* ones. Early communication with a caregiver allows a rapport and emotional depth unavailable during interaction with inanimate objects or even with well-meaning acquaintances.

As we will see in our discussions of communication as transmission and as education, intimate sharing may allow human infants access to a wealth of information that they could never gather on their own. Such intimacy is currently being discussed using the term *intersubjectivity*. Many researchers (Newson & Newson, 1975; Trevarthen, 1979, 1988) have consciously selected this term over the simpler term *interpersonal* in order to emphasize that intimacy involves the meeting of two minds and the sharing of meaning. As Colwyn Trevarthen notes, although intersubjectivity

> is not a graceful word . . . it does specify the linking of subjects who are active in transmitting their understanding to each other. The relating is 'interpersonal', but we need to penetrate the psychological process by which conscious intending subjects relate their mental and emotional processes together. (1979, p. 347)

To summarize the discussion so far, the three interlocking circles of Figure 2.1 provide an image of early communication episodes that elaborates the idea that communication involves communion or intersubjective coordination. In particular, it draws attention to the intimate, affect-filled, interpersonal context of early communication.

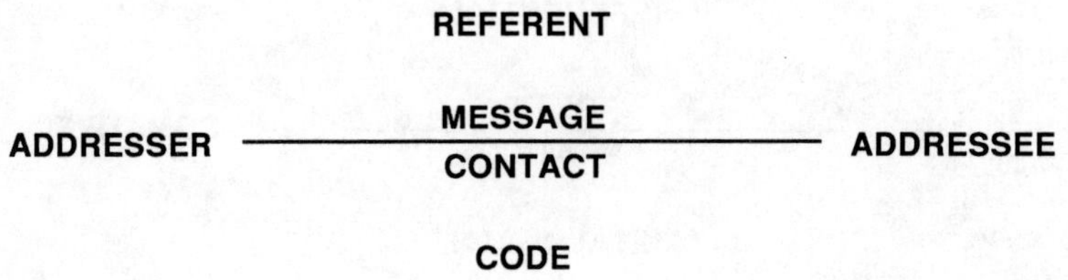

REFERENT

ADDRESSER —— MESSAGE / CONTACT —— ADDRESSEE

CODE

FIGURE 2.2
Communication as transmission: The six structural facets of Jakobson's speech event.

Communication as Transmission

In addition to coordination between people, communication involves the transmission of messages. One classic way to image this transmission is to draw a simple diagram of two communicative partners (a transmitter and a receiver) connected by a channel along which information may flow. This very schematic image was once widely used by scientists who sought to calculate how much information flows between participants (e.g., Shannon and Weaver's mathematical view of communication, 1949; see Lyons, 1977, for a detailed historical account). The same general strategy can help us sketch an image of the sorts of messages that infants and their partners may convey.

Two simple diagrams that I (Adamson, 1992) have found helpful in illustrating the diversity of messages that caregivers and infants can convey were drawn by the acclaimed linguist, Roman Jakobson (1896–1982). Jakobson presented his two-part image in a famous essay called "Linguistics and Poetics" (1960), which he wrote to celebrate language's scope, its capacity to be used "to convey not only information about the physical world, but also to establish social relations, to give vent to emotions and to create art" (Stankiewicz, 1983, p. 24; for general introductions to Jakobson's theory, see Holenstein, 1976; and Waugh, 1976).

In the first of Jakobson's related figures, the structure of a speech event with six facets is drawn. (See Figure 2.2.) Jakobson describes the diagram in the following way:

> The *addresser* sends a *message* to the *addressee*. To be operative the message requires a *context* referred to ("referent" in another, somewhat ambiguous, nomenclature), seizable by the addressee and either verbal or capable of being verbalized; a *code* fully, or at least partially, common to the addresser and addressee . . . ; and, finally, a *contact,* a physical channel and psychological connection between the addresser and the addressee, enabling both of them to enter and stay in communication. (1960, p. 353)

At this point, Jakobson's image is compatible with the image of Werner and Kaplan that we just considered, even though they were

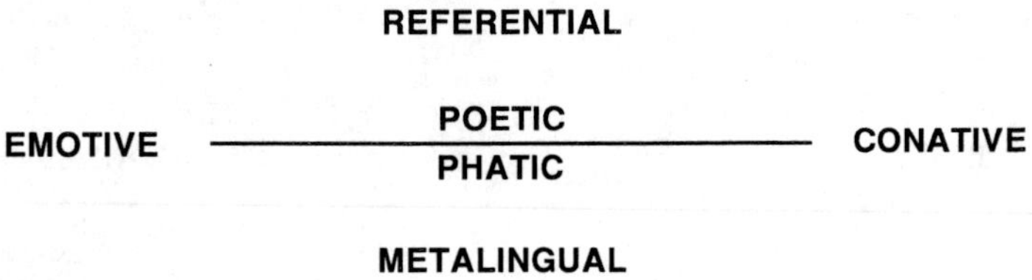

REFERENTIAL

EMOTIVE	POETIC ——— PHATIC	CONATIVE

METALINGUAL

FIGURE 2.3
Communication as transmission: The six functional facets of Jakobson's speech event.

drawn for different purposes. This similarity might be dismissed as a mere coincidence prepared for by obviousness. But it is most likely not; recall that Piaget did not place the infant in relation to both people and objects. Rather, it is likely a reflection of Jakobson and Werner's shared intellectual debt to the Viennese psychologist Karl Bühler who discussed language in terms of three fundamental relations: "one person communicating—another person being communicated to—the things being communicated about" (Bühler, 1982/1933, p. 147).

Jakobson (unlike Werner and Kaplan) also followed Bühler's lead in linking the structural components of a communicative event to the function of the messages that can be conveyed. The key to this link is *attention*. As two people focus together on a certain point in the speech event, they share a common view of what this event is about. As attention shifts to a different place in the event, so too does the function of a communicative event.

This is a tricky theoretical move which is easier to appreciate visually than verbally. Thus, Jakobson (like Bühler) drew a second diagram, which he suggests be overlaid on his first diagram. (See Figure 2.3.) In this second diagram the various functions that a speech event might serve are arrayed such that each corresponds to a facet of the speech event.

Jakobson's second diagram adds two ingredients to our view of infant–caregiver communication. First, it makes clear that there are several functions that can be served. There is considerable variation in both the number and the names contemporary researchers give to these functions (see Chapter 6). Nevertheless, Jakobson's list is worth considering at this point to gain a fuller appreciation of the types of messages that infants will gradually come to convey and to comprehend.

As can be seen in Figure 2.3, Jakobson noted that when an addresser focuses primarily on herself, she produces a communicative act (e.g., saying, "I am confused") that serves the *emotive* or expressive function. When she focuses on the person she addresses (e.g., "Do you get my basic point, or do you need further information?"), her communicative act serves a function that Jakobson called *conative* (i.e., expressing and striving; not to be confused with implying or connotative). When she focuses on objects in context ("The topic is really difficult"), the *referential* function is served. These three functions are often included in analyses of communicative functions.

In addition, Jakobson noted three functions that are important during infancy which have sometimes been overlooked. The first is called the *phatic* function. Here an addresser focuses on the contact between herself and her listener in order to establish, prolong, or discontinue communication ("Hello, anybody home?"). Sheer communion is primary. Jakobson regarded the phatic function as the first one acquired by infants, a contention now well confirmed by studies of early caregiver–infant interactions that show how the modulation of attention between partners is of focal concern (see Chapters 4 and 5).

The second function is called *metalingual*. Here the addresser focuses attention on the mode of communication itself. The metalingual use of communication occurs when, for example, a caregiver provides the name of an object ("That's a *doggie*"), or a quizzical toddler seeks the name of a familiar object ("What's–dat?" accompanied by a point toward a picture of an apple in a book). Jakobson suggested that "any process of language learning, in particular child acquisition of the mother tongue, makes wide use of . . . metalingual operations" (1960, p. 356) such as the request for or presentation of labels (see Chapter 7).

The third function is called the *poetic*. This function is served when the addresser focuses on the shape of the message itself as when, for example, she asks why we always say "arts and sciences" rather than "sciences and arts." Especially before words dominate, infants often seem to delight in transforming the medium itself. For example, M. M. Lewis compared an infant's babbling to a work of art, a joyful manipulation of the medium of language so that "almost from the very outset the practical and the aesthetic functions of language develop side by side" (1936, p. 69; see also Chapter 7).

A second important ingredient highlighted in Jakobson's sketches is attention. Jakobson (1960; see also Waugh, 1976) thought that the way in which we make speech serve the different functions diagrammed in Figure 2.3 is that we selectively highlight different facets of the speech event diagrammed in Figure 2.2. In other words, we selectively attend to different parts of the event in ways that mark this aspect for our partner. Of course, in most conversations, such marking occurs with great flexibility and complexity. Moreover, as Bruner explained in a tribute to Jakobson, marking occurs continually:

> Marking is everywhere evident, even in the initial decision whether to speak or to stay silent, and then in how and what we *select* as the elément of an utterance, and how we then *combine* the elements. They, the marked aspects, are choice points in the system. (1983a, p. 90)

This view emphasizes the importance of *shared attention* to early communication development. As Bruner noted in his book *Child's Talk,* which he dedicated to Jakobson, "The problem of how reference develops" can be restated as "the problem of how people manage and direct each other's attention" (1983b, p. 68). More generally, the problem of negotiating shared attention may be an important issue in developing an understanding of how infants come to appreciate the variety of functions that communication may serve.

In summary, Jakobson's twin diagrams of the structure and the function of speech events provide us with images that emphasize the variety of messages that early communication may convey and the importance of mutual or shared attention in transmitting different messages. They provide a complementary view to Werner and Kaplan's image, adding an elaborated consideration of the variety of communicative foci and functions to its view of caregivers' and infants' intimate sharing of affective–sensorimotor activities.

Communication as Education

The third image of communication we will consider focuses attention on the mechanism of developmental change. In Chapter 1, we considered Piaget's theory, which stresses how children's active attempts to interact adaptively with the environment provide an important impetus for change. We also noted that, in addition to this process of self-regulation, a process of mutual regulation might promote and guide change. The general notion is that when infants interact with caregivers (as opposed to inanimate objects), they gain access to a human environment (replete with human tools such as language and other social ways of being) that surrounds and permeates human dialogues. Moreover, they gain the assistance of people who, because they are further along the developmental course, may act as guides into this larger cultural realm.

Many scholars now use an abundance of metaphors associated with education to talk about the asymmetrical roles of infant and adult. The infant is said to act like a *cultural apprentice* (Miller, 1981; Rogoff, 1990); the caregiver is referred to as a *tutor* (Bruner, 1972; Wood, 1989), a *master* (Miller, 1981), and a *guide* (Rogoff, 1990). Moreover, these scholars characterize transactions that occur as a *teacher* continually calibrates his *lessons* to suit the needs of an ever-changing, eager *pupil*.

The writings of the Russian psychologist Lev Vygotsky (1896–1934) often provide the inspiration for these images of education. Vygotsky was born the same year as both Piaget and Jakobson and 6 years after Werner, and he shared with them a common intellectual foundation in European psychology as well as a fascination with our capacity to form symbols. His unique contribution was to attempt a sociohistorical theory of the development of "higher mental processes" that might explain "the mechanism by which culture becomes a part of each person's nature" (Cole & Scribner, 1978, p. 6). Tragically, Vygotsky died of tuberculosis at the age of 36, well before his theory was fully formulated. But his writings, particularly a translated volume of essays entitled *Mind in Society* published in 1978, are now highly valued by developmental psychologists as a provocative sketch of a "story of the embeddedness of the developing mind in society" (Kessen, 1979, p. 820).

In his writings, Vygotsky painted images with words. For example, in the following passage from *Mind in Society,* he illustrated clearly how children's actions gain human meaning because other people understand them as meaningful and communicate this meaning back to the child:

> From the very first days of the child's development, his activities acquire a meaning of their own in a system of social behavior and, being directed towards a definite purpose, are refracted through the prism of the child's environment. The path from object to child and from child to object passes through another person. (1978, p. 30)

Vygotsky did not refer to young infants when he provided examples for this image, but it readily lends itself to their situation. Consider, for example, what happens when a 5-month-old infant produces a squeal within earshot of a parent while looking at a twirling mobile. In middle-class American culture, the probability is high that the parent will respond to the squeal as if it were a word appropriate to the ongoing event. For example, a father might laugh and say, "Telling the toy to turn, huh?"

Vygotsky's image highlights two aspects of such a commonplace occurrence. First, even though the infant probably did not intend to say something about the toy, the father reacted to his squeal as if it were a sensible communicative act. In short, he interpreted the act as if it were a meaningful statement about the object or about the infant's action relative to the object. The baby is not merely vocalizing and watching the mobile; the baby is acting within a social world in which these acts make *human sense* (Bruner & Haste, 1987).

Second, in this image, the father not only drew the infant into a social world; he reflected to the infant a specific cultural–historical view of this world. He acted as *a curator of culture* (Trevarthen, 1988), as someone who resides in a specific society that the infant is poised to enter. His response to his son's actions is therefore fundamentally cultural, and not individual, in origin.

In our example, the father's actions might strike us as unremarkable because he drew upon the same cultural reservoir that we are also immersed in. Like us, he speaks English, considers twirling mobiles to be amusing toys, and believes that young infants might benefit cognitively from watching them. But there are clearly cultural alternatives to these specific acts and beliefs. A member of another culture would surely draw on another reserve of collective acts and commitments when interpreting the infant's squeal. Perhaps she might hear it as a call for protection (after all, a mobile is a common object only within some cultural contexts) and respond immediately with a calming sigh and close body contact.

In addition to Vygotsky's word image of infants and objects situated with culture-providing adults, he provides additional images of the educational process that leads children towards a fuller understanding of their culture. Two of these are particularly provocative. The first image provides us with a moving image of how children learn. In the first frame, a child and a teacher are performing an act together; in the second frame, the child is performing this act on her own. Vygotsky described these two situations in the following, oft-quoted passage:

> Every function in the child's cultural development appears twice: first, on the social level, and later, on the individual level; first, *between* people (*interpsychological*), and then *inside* the child (*intrapsychological*). (1978, p. 57)

For example, at first a year-old infant may point to an apple and the mother may nod and say "apple." The labeling of an object is a shared act. Six months later, the same infant might spontaneously say "apple" when he sees the apple, even if another person is not connecting the word to its referent. Using Vygotsky's words, in the first frame, the infant is able to experience the human use of language even though this function is still a "bud" or "flower" of the "fruits" of human development (Vygotsky, 1978, p. 86).

Vygotsky provided a second provocative image for the process through which a shared act is transformed into an individual achievement. Often when children interact with a more sophisticated person, they are able to act in ways they are not yet able to on their own. According to Vygotsky (1978), at such times they enter a *zone of proximal development*. Within this zone, a caregiver essentially schools the child in the ways of their common culture, although he or she may be unaware of being an instructor. Good learning—learning that nurtures development—is most likely to occur in this zone as the adult constructs finely calibrated *scaffolds* that support the young child's actions (recall the example above where the adult provides the word for an object that is the focus of shared attention) and thus "sets in motion a variety of developmental processes that would [otherwise] be impossible" (Vygotsky, 1978, p. 90; see also Cole, 1985).

In summary, Vygotsky's sketch of children within society highlights for us how early communication may serve to educate infants about cultural tools, including powerful modes of collective symbolization such as language. It also helps us recognize the obvious asymmetry between infants who act as eager apprentices and skilled adults who willingly act as their teachers.

A Schematic View of Early Communication Development

Communication is such a multifarious process that it can be conceptualized in many different ways. Typically, when faced with several theories, psychologists will argue for one. But as we just saw in our brief discussions of the three views of communication proposed by Werner and Kaplan, Jakobson, and Vygotsky, different theories can also sometimes provide complementary views of a single process. Granted, if we focused on specifics, we might well find major points of contention. But for our purposes, it is helpful to smooth out points of friction and compile a composite view of a communicative event that lets us appreciate communication as communion, as transmission, and as education.

Once again, it is helpful to begin with a sketch of this view. In Figure 2.4, I have drawn a schematic of a communicative event. Notice first that it retains the basic format of Werner and Kaplan's sketch of the primordial sharing situation with its three circles, one for the *child,* one for her *adult* partner, and one for *objects*. I have then added to it three elements—a line, a triangle, and a dotted circle. First, drawing from Jakobson's image, I have added a line for the contact or *channel* that connects the infant and her partner. Second, I have inserted a triangle for the *message*. My aim here was to depict how the message is central to communication as it touches each partner as well as the objects and events around them. Third, I have tried to indicate where the *code* or conventional symbolic system lies relative to other elements of a communicative event, using the dotted circle that lies over the plane of the other elements. Finally, inspired by Vygotsky's theory, I explicitly noted that this arrangement of elements is all embedded within the sphere of *culture*.

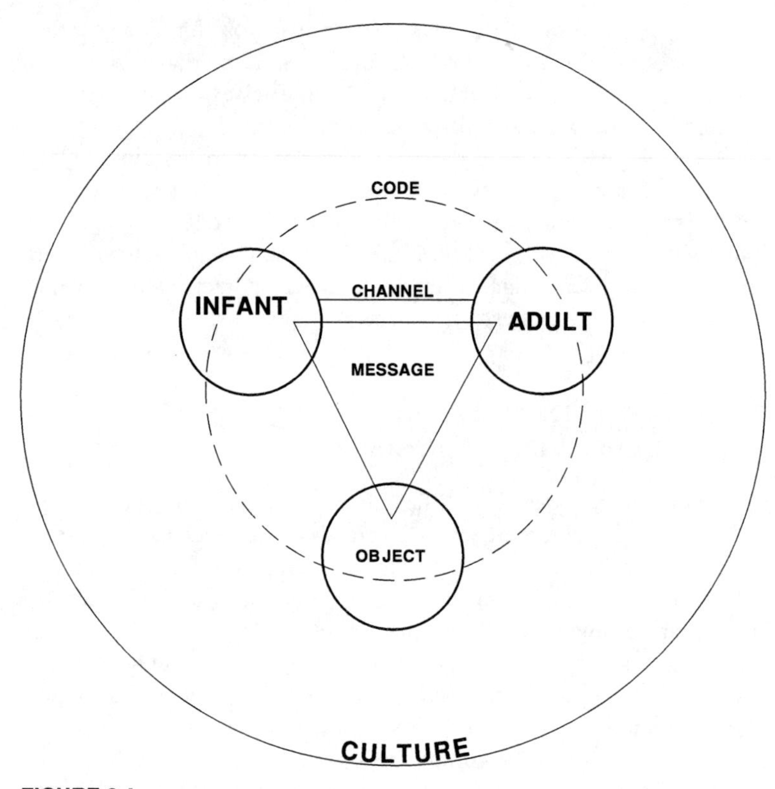

FIGURE 2.4
A schematic representation of a communicative event during the final phase of early communication development.

Four Phases of Early Communication Development

Figure 2.4 is but a skeletal view of a communicative event. It is surely an anemic reflection of any actual moment of communication. However, as a simplified view of an enormously complex event, it may be a valuable organizational aid. In particular, it can help us keep in mind the components of early communication as we trace its dramatic developmental course through infancy. In planning this book, I often stared at this image, pondering how different arrangements of and emphases on its elements might characterize different developmental phases. I ended up with four related arrangements, one each for the four periods or phases of communication development during infancy.

In the first period, *shared attentiveness,* two overlapping circles, one for the newborn infant, the second for the caregiving adult, are emphasized (see Figure 2.5 and Chapter 4). This period begins at birth

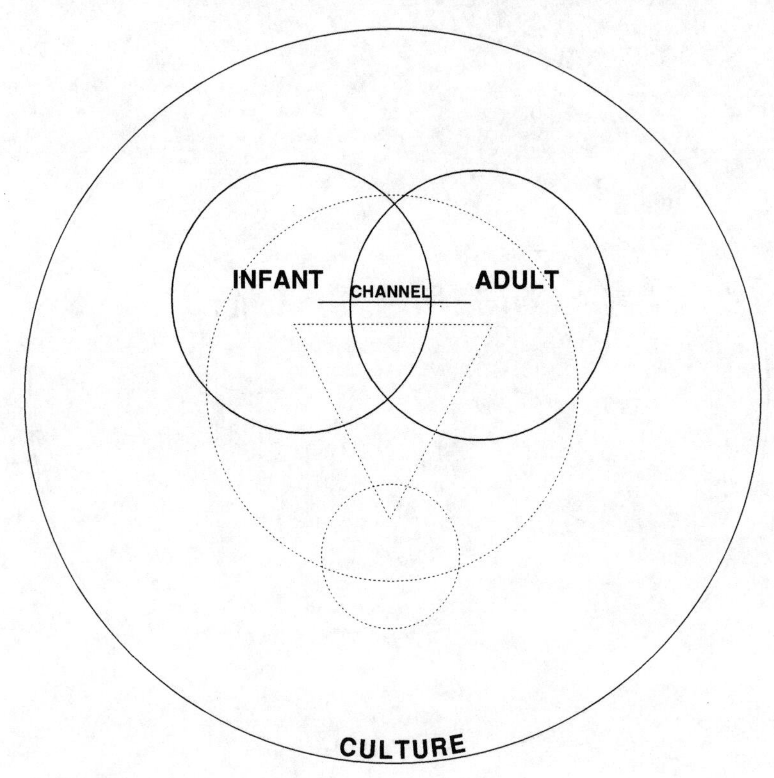

FIGURE 2.5
Shared attentiveness: The first phase of early communication development.

(and perhaps, before); it ends when the full-term infant is about 2 months old. Other elements are in the background, informing the adult but not highlighted during communicative events.

In the second period, *interpersonal engagement,* these circles are differentiated to indicate that the two participants can now focus attention on each other, on the communicative channel that links them, and on the intimate messages that flow between them (see Figure 2.6 and Chapter 5). The primary topics of communication are interpersonal ones as the infant and his partner share displays of attention and affect. This period begins at about 2 months of age, marked by the onset of social smiling and eye-to-eye contact. It draws to a close at about 5 to 6 months as the infant begins to shift attention outward toward objects.

In the third period, *joint object involvement,* infants begin to communicate with others about objects. The circle that stands for objects is now included within the communicative path (see Figure 2.7

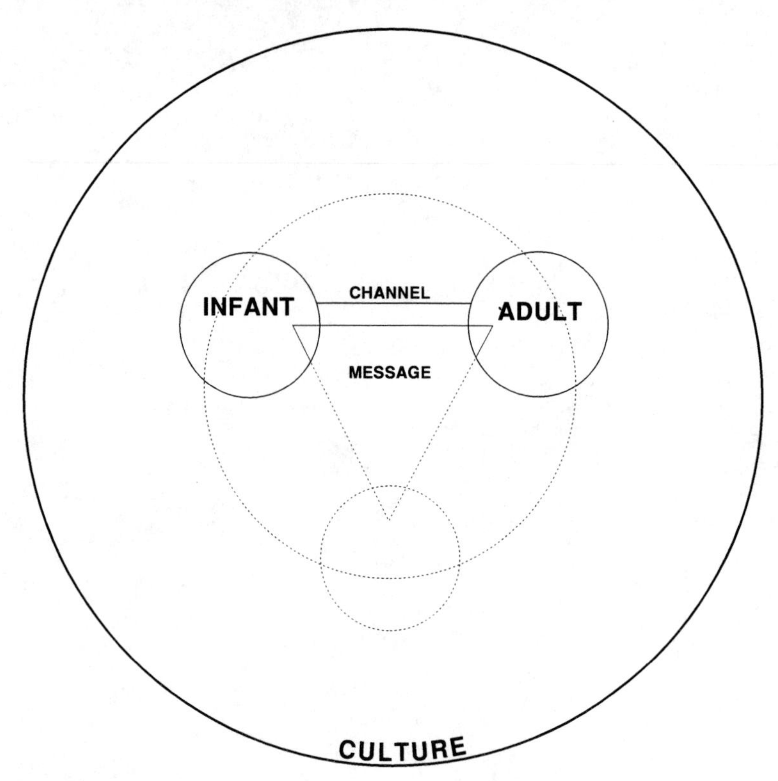

FIGURE 2.6
Interpersonal engagement: The second phase of early communication development.

and Chapter 6). Participants can now share attention to objects (a function that we will call *reference*), and they can ask each other for assistance when dealing with objects (a function that we will call *request*). Moreover, when infants and their partners communicate about objects, the ever-present cultural surround of communication is sometimes explicitly marked in the way objects are managed. This period begins at about 6 months of age. It has no distinct ending, although by the middle of the second year, the objects that are shared become increasingly more distant from the immediate here and now of the communicative episode.

In the final period of infancy, *emergence of symbolic communication,* the circle for the code stands out in relation to the other elements (as shown in Figure 2.4 and discussed in Chapter 7). At this point in development (which typically begins at about 13 months of age), the communication between toddlers and their partners becomes increasingly routinized and

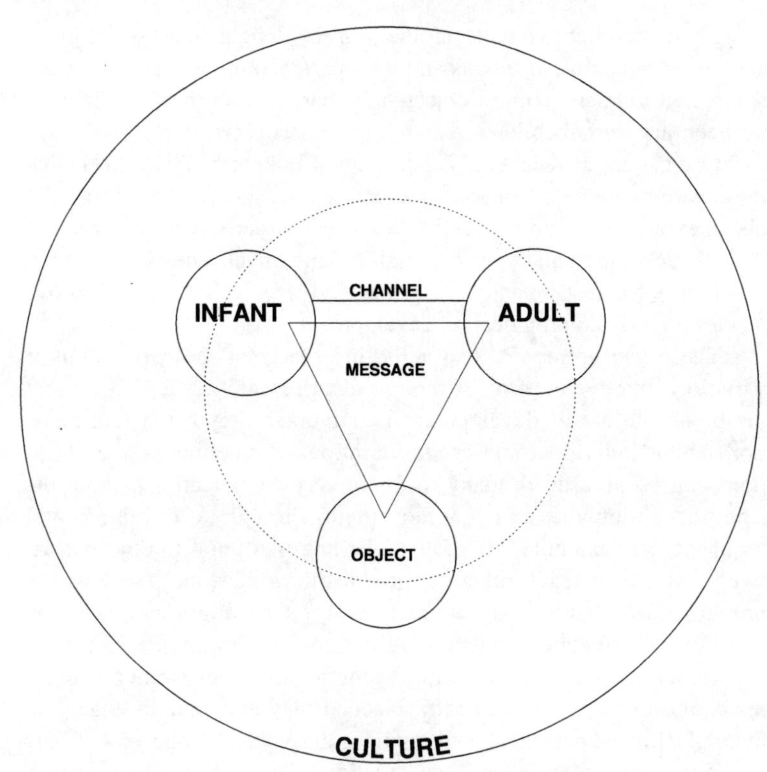

FIGURE 2.7
Joint object involvement: The third phase of early communication development.

ritualized as they repeat and expand upon their culture's repertoire of ways to interact. Especially noteworthy is the emerging focus on words and other socially shared means for conveying messages. These first words often overlap with a person's ongoing actions and often refer to objects that are literally right at hand. Nevertheless, communicative events during this phase can be characterized using essentially the same arrangement that we drew to characterize a communicative event between children and adults.

Themes and Variations

In Chapters 4 through 7, we will use the four images shown in Figures 2.4 through 2.7 to suggest themes for our selective review of contemporary research on communication development during infancy. For each period, we will first ask what is currently known about infants, both as expressive and receptive communicators. Then, as suggested by each respective image, we will concentrate on occasions when newborns and caregivers are attentive to each other; on the delight-filled social interactions of 3-month-old infants and their partners; on play periods when adults and toddlers explore objects together; and on the first dialogue between just-verbal children and their parents and peers.

One can argue (see, e.g., Adamson and Bakeman, 1982, 1991) that these various moments of shared attentiveness, social interaction, joint object exploration, and first verbal conversations are points along a predictable developmental course that all infants travel. They are, in short, key points for researchers to explore, and they define *the normative themes* of early communication development.

These key points are also a starting place for the exploration of variations in development. Although most researchers anticipate that the broad outline of development is universal, they often find questions about individual and group variations compelling. These questions can be phrased in many different ways. One can ask about the significance of the *rate* of movement through a developmental sequence. For example, do infants who begin to point to objects relatively early also reach other communication milestones, such as the production of first words, relatively early? One might also be interested in the effects of variations in the *quality or quantity* of certain experiences on later behavior. For example, do babies who experience relatively high rates of face-to-face social play at 3 months engage in more gleeful and persistent conversations during the second year of life?

A third type of question about variation focuses on *group differences*. Here the researcher groups individuals according to certain criteria and then compares across these groups. This strategy is especially important in establishing what constitutes the normative course of development. It is crucial that this course be drawn wide enough to respect variations across cultures as well as variations that occur within a particular culture. It is also crucial to remember that comparisons are, of course, two-way. In the study of early communication development, children who are following the normative course of development are often thought of as the *standard* (or, in the language of experimental psychology, *control*) group to which others are compared. Since researchers usually begin their research close to home, they may unwittingly mistake what children in their own cultural group do as the center of the developmental course.

Yet another approach to variation involves looking beyond the "normal" limits of the developmental path to trace the development of infants who are in some definable way *atypical*. Just as dramatic variations in a musical score often reveal new strains of a dominant theme, so too may major departures from normative themes. This claim will be illustrated in Chapters 4 through 7 when, at the close of our discussion of a specific phase of communication development, we ask how the phase's themes are varied by infants who are at risk for problems during this phase of communication development. In Chapter 4, we ask how prematurity might affect shared attentiveness; in Chapter 5, we consider how maternal depression might affect interpersonal engagement; in Chapter 6, we examine how infants with autism share objects with caregivers; and in Chapter 7, we describe how toddlers with hearing impairments acquire their first language.

CHAPTER

3

A Scientific Stance toward Infants

CHAPTER OUTLINE

At this point the reader who wants to know how infants communicate may experience some impatience. In the previous two chapters, we focused primarily on conceptual matters, especially the ideas proposed by grand theorists such as Piaget, Werner, Jakobson, and Vygotsky. Their ideas position us to appreciate the substance or facts of infant communication. In the remaining chapters of this book, we do indeed take a more empirical view of the infant's path from crying newborn to word user. But, before we embark on this course, there is one additional preliminary matter to attend to. This matter is science, and more specifically, how the researchers who study early communication development come to know what they claim to know.

Adopting a Scientific Stance

The studies on which this book is based fall mainly within the modern scientific tradition. One of the more dramatic developments of the last few centuries has been the immense flowering of the scientific enterprise, replete with an elaborate and international network of organizations and institutions. This development has occurred primarily within liberal democracies (Butterfield, 1957), which is hardly surprising given the necessarily anti-authoritarian spirit of scientific work (scientists bridle at being told that the earth occupies the center of the universe when they think that observations suggest otherwise). Yet a scientific spirit, as manifest in a desire to understand, predict, and perhaps control the surrounding world, can be detected in almost any historic age; consider the astronomical uses of many ancient monuments. Moreover, such a spirit is manifest at the beginning of human life as well, during early infancy.

Consider a description which Piaget gave of his 12-month-old daughter:

> For the first time Jacqueline is in the presence of the well-known toy consisting of chickens set in motion by a weight. A certain number of chickens are arranged in a circle on a wooden ring and the front of each chicken is connected by a string to a heavy ball placed on a lower plane than the ring: thus the slightest movement of the ball sets the chickens in motion, and they knock with their beaks against the edge of the ring.
>
> Jacqueline, after examining for a moment the toy which I put into action by displacing it gently, first touches the ball and notes the concomitant movement of the chickens. She then systematically moves the ball as she watches the chickens. Thus convinced of the existence of a relationship which she obviously does not understand in detail, she pushes the ball very delicately with her right index finger each time the swinging stops completely. (Piaget, 1954/1937, Obs. 149, pp. 309–310)

This is not formal science, of course, but it conveys a nascent scientific stance. Jacqueline observed a phenomenon which, earlier in her development, she might have found mystifying or, more likely, simply ignored. She formed an hypothesis as to the cause of the movement, tested that hypothesis, and, in this case, observed results consistent with it.

At 12 months of age, Jacqueline could hardly be expected to be articulate about the intelligence of her actions, but then adult scientists are not always articulate about the principles that guide their research either. Jacqueline investigating causality, young children acquiring their first language, and adults engaging in scientific inquiry all illustrate the widely held developmental principle that the ability to perform an action precedes the ability to think about and articulate whatever principles guide that action. Essentially all infants come to understand physical causality and acquire language, and some adults do scientific work, but they are alike in their almost exclusive focus on understanding within context so that the demands of the immediate situation can be met. Infants no more need to know formal grammar to speak than scientists need to know philosophic underpinnings and first principles to do science.

Nonetheless others can, and have, discerned a number of commonalties in the ways in which scientists work (see e.g., Kuhn, 1970; Pepper, 1942; Popper, 1968, for treatises about the history, philosophy, and logic of science). An understanding of these commonalties can be useful for a number of reasons. First, as already suggested, there are some fascinating parallels between infant activity and more formalized scientific investigation. In addition, because many issues concerning human infants call forth strong opinions, there are sound reasons why a book such as this is based on certain sorts of investigations (e.g., self-consciously scientific studies) more than on others (e.g., unsystematic observations and speculations). It is worthwhile to have in mind the characteristics of such investigations, both for one's own understanding and when discussing these topics with friends and colleagues.

To appreciate the strengths of a scientific stance toward infants, it is helpful to consider its primary qualities. To do this, I will invoke the STEP model (a mnemonic device formulated by my colleague, Roger Bakeman), which highlights the *skeptical, testable, explanatory,* and *public* nature of scientific work.

A *skeptical* attitude is the essence of science. All conclusions remain tentative, and ideally it is the scientist's duty to search diligently for discomforting and disconfirming evidence with which to challenge theories and conclusions that are currently in favor. Often a closed mind is easily recognized. We have probably all had the experience at one time or another of arguing a point with a person who overwhelmed us with facts, yet left us convinced that no counter facts would ever change that person's position. At other times, an opinion can be so pervasive in a culture that bias escapes recognition.

Something of this sort happened in American psychology, especially during the first half of the twentieth century, with regard to infants' abilities generally, including their perceptual and communicative abilities. Consider the oft-cited and influential comment of James (1890) noted in Chapter 1 to the effect that infants initially experience little more than one great blooming, buzzing confusion. His assertion was so consistent with the strong environmental bias that was common throughout late-nineteenth to mid-twentieth century American thought that it was rarely challenged. Newborns who have yet to experience the world could not possibly possess innate organizing abilities and so, until appropriately experienced, their perceptual world could only be confused and somewhat overwhelming.

Given the benefit of hindsight, it may seem surprising that this belief was taught and accepted as fact. One need only hold an hours-old infant and observe her alerting to one's face, following the movement of one's head, or turning toward one's voice to realize that her sensory world must be filled with interesting sights and sounds from the very beginning. Such an experience has surely been available to mothers for millennia. That James's comment would be taught as fact by otherwise intelligent scholars serves as a cautionary tale; an example of the failure of skepticism.

Still, the notion that newborns lack organizing abilities is eminently *testable,* which is the second element of the STEP model. Testability of ideas both propels scientific work and lets us distinguish scientific from pseudoscientific discourse. A simple test can determine whether an argument is based solely on belief and so not open to scientific discourse. One needs only to ask what pattern of facts would cause its adherents to abandon or to substantially modify their position. If none can be named—if no data can be imagined that would falsify the proposition under consideration—then we have left the realm of science.

In the instance of newborns' sensory experiences, it is easy to identify data that would falsify the notion that they experience only confusion at birth. Organized behavior patterns relative to visual and auditory experience have been repeatedly observed and reported, and as a result, an earlier conclusion is now viewed as an error, rather than a fact.

At other times, gathering information with which to challenge currently held ideas is far more difficult than merely pointing to overwhelming counterevidence. More often than not, scientists must first determine how to structure their ways of observing phenomena in order to gather the sort of evidence that can be used to put flawed notions to rest or to bolster sound ones. Indeed, although sometimes scientists are chided for overexercising their proclivity to amass data for its own sake, one of the great strengths of the scientific enterprise is its attention to and accumulation of methods that are used to produce volumes of data concerning phenomena of interest.

Given appropriate data, testing ideas can seem relatively easy. The *explanatory* quality of scientific discourse, however, is more difficult to achieve. In general, scientific explanations describe plausible mechanisms or reasons for the phenomena under discussion.

Scientific explanations vary markedly in both form and breadth. They may be quite inchoate. For example, Piaget's daughter, Jacqueline, initially acted as if she assumed that the toy chickens moved of their own volition, much as she herself did. Only later did she entertain the *theory* that, as the ball moved, it pulled the chickens with it. Such a theory may lack the mathematical refinements of formal physics (indeed, it may not have had any status independent of Jacqueline's ongoing actions), but it includes at a rudimentary level some notion of a mechanism responsible for the movement observed. Conversely, scientific explanations may be all-encompassing.

Consider, for example, the enormous scope of Darwin's (1859) famous proposal that a mechanism of natural selection explains the evolution of species, of Piaget's (1971/1967) claim that the process of adaptation is responsible for development both of species and of individuals within a species, or of Skinner's (1938) contention that a law of operant conditioning can account for much of what organisms do. However, most explanations of early communication are neither as nascent as a young infant's nor as far reaching as a grand theorist's. For example, in Chapter 4, the finding that 2-month-old infants do not yet babble is explained in terms of their physical characteristics, and in Chapter 5, the observation that adults exaggerate their facial expressions when they interact with 3-month-olds is explained in terms of infants' positive reactions to such silly displays.

In all cases, be they sweeping principles related to an entire domain or modest accounts for a specific phenomenon, explanations are the goal, the *raison d'être,* of science. Thus, as one reads scientific literature, it is important to go beyond descriptions to ask, What explanations or reasons are offered for the behavior described? Are mechanisms presented? Are they plausible and supported? These are rigorous tests for scientific discourse, although they are often honored in the breach.

Whatever else, scientific discourse and the details of scientific work are *public*. This is not to say that anything made public is scientific—only that there is a forthrightness to scientific life. People who keep details of their investigations private, or who will not show others their data when asked appropriately, or who will not divulge the reasoning behind a conclusion, cannot expect their work or their conclusions to be taken seriously as science.

Adopting a scientific stance is not always easy, especially when the focus of interest is infants. In many cultures, for example, controversy over important topics is to be avoided instead of embraced. Asking whether cherished beliefs and intimate personal experiences coincide with the results of scientific studies takes intellectual courage. Furthermore, skepticism and an open mind are harder to maintain the more personal and more emotionally involving the topic is.

Ways of Observing

Infants involve us all, centrally and emotionally, individually and as a species. This is one reason why studying them can be so challenging, and why, by way of inoculation, it is important to be aware of the characteristics of a scientific stance toward their study. With these characteristics in mind, we now consider three particular scientific strategies—naturalistic observation, systematic observation, and experimental manipulation—that have contributed considerably to an understanding of infants' communication development.

Naturalistic Observation

Human beings are born with a nervous system remarkably well-adapted to scrutinizing the world and detecting regularities. These perceptual abilities are hardly unique to humans (see Gibson, 1979), but human minds use them in unique ways to develop, refine, and occasionally abandon complex and elegant models for how the world works and why persons behave. Whether self-consciously scientific or not, broadly defined, such activities exemplify naturalistic observation.

At its best, naturalistic observation combines a keen eye with an informed and skeptical mind. Consider the following example, in which Darwin summarizes information from a diary which he had kept years earlier, primarily concerned with the expressive development of his infant son, Doddy:

> When our infant was only 4 months old I thought he tried to imitate sounds; but I may have deceived myself, for I was not thoroughly convinced that he did so until he was 10 months old. At the age of 11½ months he could readily imitate all sorts of actions, such as shaking his head and saying 'Ah' to any dirty object. . . . When 5½ months old, he uttered an articulate sound 'da' but without any meaning attached to it. When a little over a year old, he used gestures to explain his wishes; to give a simple instance, he picked up a bit of paper and giving it to me pointed to the fire, as he had often seen and liked to see paper burnt. At exactly the age of a year, he made the great step of inventing a word for food, namely, *mum*, but what led him to it I did not discover. And now instead of beginning to cry when he was hungry, he used this word in a demonstrative manner or as a verb, implying 'Give me food'. (1877, pp. 291–293)

A number of issues are raised in this brief excerpt from Darwin, including the age at which infants are capable of imitation and the order in which their means of communication develop. For present purposes, however, the point of this brief quotation is how well it exemplifies a probing mind at work.

Naturalistic observation, as the Darwin excerpt shows, can be immensely appealing. It is also both potentially enriching and disturbingly problematic. Often we are more convinced and compelled by what we believe our senses tell us or by a single anecdote than by careful scholarship or tedious weighing of evidence. Yet, even though nearly all of the ideas and findings discussed in this book can trace their parentage back to naturalistic observations, rarely are such observations alone enough.

Naturalistic observation is sometimes identified with *qualitative* research (as opposed to *quantitative* research), which is a modern term for the centuries-old endeavor of humanistic studies. At its best, qualitative interpretation (of texts, transcripts, videotapes, observations, etc.) can represent a lively and informed sensibility. There is a profoundly important, creative aspect to naturalistic observation. Ideas are often inspired by a surprising observation or rooted in the intense scrutiny of a phenomenon. There is much merit in total immersion: in participating as well as observing; in experiencing subjectively the object of one's study.

However, since the quality of naturalistic observation depends so much on each observer's talents, it tends to fluctuate widely. Darwin was not alone in keeping a diary of his infant's development. Earlier in this century it became fashionable for scientists to log their own infants' development, and what had been a trickle of baby diaries threatened to become a flood (Dennis, 1936). Their intent was to learn more about normal infant development, but their diaries are largely discounted today as a reliable source of information. Part of scientific skepticism is a keen awareness that too often observers, including or perhaps especially ourselves, are far too likely to see what we want to see, what we *know* is there. As a result, scientists often go to elaborate lengths to protect observations from their own biases. Further, they often accept other scientists' observations, including those of such perceptive naturalistic observers as Piaget and Darwin, only after they have been verified and replicated by others.

Systematic Observation

Usually, naturalistic observation involves observing phenomena as they unfold spontaneously. That is, naturalistic observers rarely intentionally manipulate the events that they observe, although they may be quite active participants in them. Thus, the baby diaries mentioned earlier are an excellent example of what is usually understood by naturalistic observation. The baby diaries also present, in stark form, the central concern which most investigators have about relying on naturalistic observations alone, a concern with observer *bias*. Human beings, even with the best of intentions, have a fascinating tendency to see what they expect to see. Recall Wilhelm von Osten, the German mathematics teacher, who early in this century became convinced that the horse Clever Hans could answer simple arithmetic problems by tapping his hoof the correct number of times, sincerely unaware that *he* signaled Clever Hans when to stop by raising his head expectantly (see Sebeok & Rosenthal, 1981, for various reflections on this classic error).

Over the course of the past century or so, investigators have developed a number of ways to reduce substantially the possible influence of bias in scientific studies. One evidence of this is the movement from naturalistic to *systematic observation,* from qualitative narrative to quantitative measurement. Systematic observation is at heart a measurement system for behavior (see, e.g., Bakeman & Gottman, 1986). It has proved especially useful for studies of nonverbal organisms, including human infants.

Chief among the many merits of measurement is the insulation it can afford between data and personal bias. Measurement, because it allows a common metric, provides greater objectivity to observations. It allows us to discount the personal qualities of the measurer and to expect reproducible results from trained professional observers under similar circumstances.

Quantification has its pitfalls, of course. For example, measuring instruments necessarily limit what phenomena are considered. But during certain phases of a scientific investigation, the appeal of precision outweighs the problem of scope. It is difficult to judge qualitative interpretation without also judging the interpreter's wisdom and astuteness. In contrast, the data that result from systematic observation are seldom acclaimed or discounted based on the observer's personal attributes.

Consider the phenomenon of neonatal *states of arousal,* which we discuss in Chapter 4. Naturalistic observation (which usually is a necessary precursor to systematic observation) convinced investigators that newborns were almost always in one (or transitioning between two) of a small number of states that characterize an infant's current biobehavioral organization. There is some disagreement concerning the exact number of states and their definitions, but most lists include crying, inactive or quiet alertness, drowsiness, quiet or deep sleep, and REM (rapid eye movement) or active sleep.

This list of codes along with their definitions constitutes a behavioral *coding scheme,* a behavioral yardstick, if you will, and is an essential component of systematic observation precisely because it allows behavior to be measured in a relatively objective way. The second essential component is the observer, the one who uses the coding scheme to record the behavior of interest.

Human coders are, of course, different from other sorts of measuring instruments such as thermometers and litmus paper. They sometimes sense whether the investigator, for some arcane theoretical reason, would rather have *hot* than *cold* recorded. So it is important to keep behavioral coders scrupulously blind as to desired results. However, like thermometers and other purely mechanical recording devices, observers need to be calibrated against some standard. In other words, it is necessary to be sure that different coders make essentially similar judgments and to demonstrate that they code reliably throughout a study.

In sum, a clearly defined coding scheme used by blind and reliable coders to measure and hence quantify behavior defines the essential aspects of systematic observation. As you will see in the remaining chapters, this methodology has been used productively and widely in studies of infants' communication. Sometimes investigators with similar interests may use the same coding scheme such as the one defining newborns' states of arousal presented earlier. This allows for comparability of results from different laboratories and encourages the accumulation of findings, which is often regarded as a hallmark of scientific activity.

Even when different coding schemes are used, as is appropriate for different phenomena and different interests, techniques of systematic observation provide a solidity and an acceptance that often escape findings based on naturalistic observation alone. The ideas that drive the investigation may well arise during naturalistic observation. However, the confirmation or justification for those ideas is often provided by the far less bias-prone procedures of systematic observation.

Experimental Manipulation

When children first start using language, they often overextend the meaning of a new word, and so all four-legged animals might be called *doggie*. Similarly, the word *experiment* is often overextended by students who refer to all scientifically motivated studies as experiments, no matter whether those studies are strictly observational or actively experimental. Yet the distinction is worth making because it emphasizes a crucial difference in the conclusions that these two approaches can afford.

The usual textbook statement claims that conclusions about the causes of behavior cannot rest on correlational or observational studies, but require experimentation. In an experimental study, the investigator intervenes and manipulates the situation in some way. Experimental procedures, rather than the subjects themselves, determine the sorts of situations or treatments to which subjects are exposed; if different subjects receive different treatments, subjects are randomly assigned to their respective treatments.

For example, imagine that we observe young babies who have moving mobiles hanging above their cribs. We note that they tend to be intrigued by these mobiles, using as evidence the fact that they often stare intently at them for many minutes. We also notice that they especially seem to enjoy these mobiles (as gauged by smiles and coos) when their parents jiggle the mobile each time they emit a coo or wave their arms. This notion occurs to us: babies might like mobiles best when they have a social partner to share them with.

To test this notion, we might systematically observe parents playing with their infants and mobiles, and record all instances of infants' smiles, coos, arm waves, and various other specified infant behaviors, all instances of the mobile moving, and all instances of specific parental behaviors such as mobile jiggles and baby tickles. Using these data, we might then attempt to determine whether infant smiles and coos are more likely to occur at certain times. Do their rates elevate primarily when parents direct their own smiles and tickles toward the baby? Or, is infant smiling and cooing most likely when parents couple their jiggles of the mobile to some action on the part of the infant? For example, if the mother jiggles the mobile whenever her infant waves his arm, does the baby predictably react with a smile and coo?

Appropriate analyses of such observational data could be informative. But in the end, they would not be as convincing as a simple experiment. For any observational study, no matter how systematically done, the suspicion always lingers that associations between observed behaviors (such as the associations between infant arm wave, parental mobile jiggle, and infant smiles and coos hypothesized above) may be due to a behavior unrecorded in the current study. This is often called the *third variable problem* (Simon, 1971), a shorthand phrase that reminds us of the weak causal inferences that observational studies allow.

By way of contrast, consider how an appropriate experimental study might proceed. (This study is based loosely on one done by Watson, 1972; see also Chapter 5). Imagine that we place two 4-month-old infants in adjacent cribs. Each has a mobile above the crib, but the mobiles are yoked, so that when one moves, the other does also. We then attach a ribbon between the mobile and the foot of one of the infants so that when she kicks, both mobiles move. Thus the experience of the two infants with the mobile will be identical; both will receive the same amount of stimulation and at the same time. But only one will experience *contingent stimulation;* that is, only one of the infants will see the mobile move in response to her kicks.

Assume that we use this procedure with several pairs of infants and record the amount of time each infant smiled and cooed relative to the amount of time the mobile moved. In some cases the infant whose foot controlled the mobile might smile and coo less than the other infant, and in some cases, more. Using the appropriate statistical analysis, we can determine if controlling infants smiled and cooed significantly more than their not-in-control partners. If we determine that indeed they did, we would conclude that in general, contingent stimulation causes more smiling and cooing in infants of this age than noncontingent stimulation. As part of the experimental procedure, infants were randomly assigned to either contingent or noncontingent conditions. Thus the experimental procedures assured that infants differed in only one key respect: whether the stimulation they received was contingent or not. This renders unlikely that the difference in smiling and cooing between the two groups of infants was due to a third, unmeasured variable, and so a strong causal conclusion is warranted.

True, experimental studies may not tell us much about the importance or frequency of behaviors in the unmanipulated world, and sometimes experimental circumstances may be decidedly unnatural. How many parents, for example, tie ribbons between their infant's foot and a mobile? Nonetheless, studies like the one just described can alert us to the importance of contingent stimulation and can establish unambiguously a causal link between it and infants' pleasure. Further studies based on systematic observation can then determine how often infants who represent different groups (such as premature infants and full-term infants, or baby girls and baby boys) experience contingent stimulation, and under what circumstances, in their unmanipulated lives.

The Interplay between Observation and Experimentation

Despite their differences, observational and experimental studies share many features. Moreover, they can, and often do, work best when researchers link these two types of studies together so that they complement each other. Design and measurement are key features of both kinds of studies. *Measurement* usually references the dependent variable in a study, the phenomenon which the investigator hopes to explain or account for. *Design* usually deals with the independent variables, those factors which the investigator thinks may affect or explain the dependent variable.

The design may be simple and may incorporate either experimental or nonexperimental variables. For example, a researcher is designing a study when she randomly divides subjects into those who receive drug A instead of drug B, or divides subjects into males and females. Measurement can be simple too. For example, a researcher might determine the weight of infants, or calculate what proportion of time they smiled or laughed. Sometimes, however, a particular procedure, usually one that is somewhat more complex than the simple examples just given, becomes sufficiently standardized and widely enough used to be called a *paradigm*. (Note that paradigm in this sense refers to a local procedure, not a global way of thinking as in Kuhn, 1970.)

Such paradigms are often immensely useful both in observational and experimental scientific studies. They allow for standardization across laboratories and accumulation of results within a field in the best tradition of normal science. A number of such paradigms have advanced studies of infants' communication development.

Three examples of influential paradigms will help to display the benefit of shared procedures. The first, and simplest, is the *coding scheme for infant states* mentioned earlier. Such a coding scheme can become a standard measuring instrument, used by many investigators. It is up to the investigator, then, to elaborate the design, thereby determining the effect which various factors such as infants' health status or the time of day have on infants' states.

A second example of a useful paradigm involves the process of *habituation,* the tendency for responses to decrease in strength (to attenuate) when a person is exposed repeatedly to the same stimulus, and then to increase again (or dishabituate) when he or she is exposed to another, apparently different stimulus (Rovee-Collier, 1987). The habituation paradigm has proven especially useful in studies with infants, who otherwise cannot tell us when they think one display is different from another. How, for example, might you tell if a 2-month-old infant can tell the difference between two drawings of a face, one with eyes and nose properly placed and one with scrambled features? Although they certainly cannot tell us verbally, their answers can be discerned using the habituation paradigm. When one display (say, the scrambled face) is presented repeatedly, an infant's attention continually decreases. Then, when a new display (the regular face) is presented, one of two patterns of attention may be noted. The infants' attention may remain depressed, or it may raise to its initial interest level. In the first case, we infer that the infants see no difference between the scrambled and regular face; in the second, we infer instead that they, like us, noticed the difference. The habituation paradigm thus provides a general way for determining what kinds of stimuli infants discriminate.

A final example of a widely used experimental procedure is the *still-face paradigm* (Tronick, Als, Adamson, Wise, & Brazelton, 1978). In this paradigm, adults are asked to face their infants as if they were going to interact socially, yet remain still-faced. This is, of course, a highly unusual situation since parents in our culture find it nearly irresistible to make faces and vocalize when they see a baby (see Chapter 5). Nonetheless, Tronick and his colleagues placed 2- to 5-month-old infants in infant seats and asked mothers to sit facing their infants without reacting to them in any way.

It is instructive to consider briefly why Tronick and his colleagues formulated such a seemingly odd paradigm because their reasoning illustrates the benefits of an interplay between observational and experimental approaches to research (see Chapter 5 for a more extended discussion). Typically, individual investigators have a particular methodological bent, leaning toward a preference for observation or for experimentation. However, most research arcas are nurtured by the convergence of these approaches so that observational insights can be verified by well-controlled experimental findings. This productive interplay between experimental and observational work has long enriched infant studies.

During the 1960s, a few psychologists interested in early relationships began to train their attention on a mundane social event common to many cultures, including our own. During spare moments, young infants, especially those between 2 and 6 months of age, play with their caregivers by engaging in animated and pleasurable dialogues of smiles and coos. Interest in this phenomenon rose quickly, as several scholars wondered what it might reveal about human infants' cognitive and social capacities. The initial task was to gain a fuller view of the phenomenon. To this end, the behavior of infants and caregivers was extensively described, using carefully refined systematic observational methods. Based on these observations, many researchers, such as T. Berry Brazelton (Brazelton et al., 1974; Brazelton, Tronick, Adamson, Als, & Wise, 1975) and Daniel Stern (Stern, 1974), were tempted to conclude that infants were actually active partners in such early interactions and could, for example, appreciate the rudimentary turn-taking structure of such play ('I smile'–'You smile') in a way that foreshadows verbal conversation.

Still, no amount of describing videotapes of mother–infant interactions could counter a skeptic's contention that perhaps skillful mothers carry the entire weight of the conversational structure (see, e.g., Kaye, 1982a). By anticipating momentary pauses in their infants' activity, mothers might unconsciously fill in the gaps, so to speak, giving the deceptive appearance of genuine turn taking. Probably no amount of observation, no matter how carefully and systematically done, could address this doubt. Some sort of intervention or manipulation is required.

The still-face paradigm seemed well-suited to the issue. The adult is available for interaction but, by being unresponsive, violates the fundamental turn-taking regularity of infant–adult social interaction. Tronick and his colleagues (1978) found that young infants detect this violation and often seem to try to entice the mother to engage in play. During the first moments of a still-face session, infants typically orient toward their mothers and smile broadly. When they receive no answer to their apparent greeting, their smiles rapidly fade, their brows furl, and they may look away or yawn. Then infants attempt additional greetings while monitoring their mother's [non]reaction closely.

The infants' reactions during the still-face paradigm provide compelling evidence that infants can share responsibility with mothers for the conversational structure they jointly create. They act as if they expect their mothers to take a turn, and when their mothers do not act as expected, they attempt to entice her to comply. Of course, they are not fully skilled at eliciting a response (an older child might, for example, tease a response by making a funny face), but they certainly do not appear to be passive puppets who look animated only because their mothers are exquisitely skilled conductors.

The still-face paradigm began as an experimental procedure honed to address a question derived from studies that use systematic observational procedures. More recently, it has been varied and refined so that it might generate data relevant to additional questions. For example, a study's design might include different experimental groups so that questions concerning the effects of different infant or adult characteristics might be probed. Moreover, researchers may formulate new measurements (for example, infants' physiological arousal or pattern of limb movements) that they think might be particularly relevant to a specific question.

We will return to these matters later on, but for now we wish only to highlight the kinds of contributions which both observational and experimental studies can make to the study of infants' communicative abilities. It seems unlikely that any amount of systematic observation would have revealed infants' reactions to unnaturally still-faced mothers (although nature may provide rare but informative cases; see Adamson, Als, Tronick, & Brazelton, 1977, and Chapter 5). An experimental manipulation was required. Yet the naturally-occurring events that inspired the manipulation were themselves carefully documented by observational methods. Clearly, neither systematic observation nor experimental manipulation should be regarded as superior, or more scientific. Both can, and usually do, work together, hand in glove, to advance our understanding.

In this chapter we have discussed the general characteristics of science, as well as some specific paradigms that are useful when studying infants. In the remaining chapters, as we concentrate primarily on the results of the scientific study of early communication development, it will be important to remain aware of these scientific underpinnings and procedures. Such alertness will help you retain sight of how researchers puzzle over methods that will let them reach conclusions. Further, it will help you form your own evaluation of our current understanding of communication development during infancy.

CHAPTER

4

Shared Attentiveness

CHAPTER OUTLINE

During the first phase of development, communication between infants and adults primarily involves establishing contact and sharing moments of mutual engagement. In Chapter 2, this phase was symbolized with an image centered on two overlapping circles, one representing a newborn and the other, an adult caregiver (see Figure 2.5). Unlike the images drawn for later phases, these circles are merged to emphasize that both participants are simultaneously involved in each communicative act. Moreover, although objects and the cultural surround are drawn, they remain in the background.

This image of shared attentiveness can help organize our review of recent research about communication during the first two months of life. In the first section of this chapter, we concentrate primarily on the edges of the infant circle to view newborns as expressive communicators. Given the overlap of the newborn and caregiver during communicative acts, we will consider as well the adults' crucial contributions to infants' nascent communicative acts.

In the second section, we focus on the infant circle from a different angle in order to describe newborns as receptive communicators. Our primary interest here is the newborns' experience of the sounds and sights of human communication. Once again, however, we will inevitably see their partners who intuitively modify the newborn's stimulus world so as to enhance the newborn's appreciation of the social world.

In the third section, we look directly at the overlap of infant and caregiver to consider how such different partners can each contribute to the opening of a communicative channel. In the final section, we abstract from the current literature this phase's most dominant theme—the biobehavioral preparation of human newborns for social communication. Then we consider the especially revealing variation of this theme that occurs when an infant is born prematurely.

Newborns as Expressive Communicators

Expressiveness is the human newborn's most central behavioral talent. Compared to neonates of most other mammalian species, ours are remarkably unable to help themselves to the resources they need for survival. Yet they do not acquiesce passively to their profound dependence. With both acts and appearances, our newborns fulfill their needs by conveying vital messages to caregivers about their fundamental requirements for nourishment, warmth, and comfort.

Newborns' communicative expressions have two prominent attributes. First (to use descriptors suggested by Werner, 1957), they are best described within the matrix of global and diffuse *states of arousal,* not as a series of discrete and articulated acts. In other words, newborns often communicate using entire constellations of behavior that reflect their current psychobiological organization. Second, the newborn's communicative expressions succeed because adults readily share in their construction by lending meaning to these acts.

Newborns' Expressions within the Matrix of States

Researchers who describe newborns find it invaluable to place the infant within the framework of arousal states. As mentioned in Chapter 3, schemes for describing states of arousal typically include codes for crying, quiet sleep, REM (for *rapid eye movement*) sleep, quiet alertness, and drowsiness. Each of these states is characterized by a unique pattern of physiological and behavioral attributes (see, e.g., Wolff, 1987). Each moment of newborn activity can be placed within one of these states or within a transitional period between two states.

The newborn's capacity for states of arousal has profound significance for research on topics ranging from the organization of motor reflexes to the development of the central nervous system (Korner, 1972). In studies of early communication, an appreciation of neonatal states has led researchers to notice how newborns' expressiveness pervades the entire fabric of their behavior. For example, when newborns are in the state of crying, they signal their distress not only with a single, well-nuanced sound, but also with characteristic facial grimaces, breath patterns, skin coloration, limb movements (Wolff, 1987), and even clenched fists (Papoušek & Papoušek, 1977). When newborns indicate availability for shared alertness, they do so by entering into a quiet alert state marked by bright and shiny eyes, regular breathing, an attentive facial expression, and a still posture (Wolff, 1987).

Adults' Contributions to Newborns' Expressions

The second dominant attribute of newborns' communicative expressions is that they are fundamentally shared acts. Of course, the effectiveness of one person's expressions in some sense always depends on another person's reception. However, as the overlap in our organizing image suggests, this truism may be particularly apt during the newborn period.

In all likelihood, newborns produce incomplete communicative acts. Unlike acts produced by adults or even older infants, they lack inherent communicative intention. Before emitting a cry or a grimace, newborns have not plotted to produce a specific effect on their listeners, nor have they tailored their acts to fulfill a specific purpose. Rather, they unintentionally produce behaviors to which caregivers ascribe meaning. Thus, newborns' inchoate communicative acts (e.g., a lusty cry) are essentially completed by caregivers who generously infuse them with meanings and reasons ('Goodness, he must be hungry!').

Adults do not make whole cloth out of thin air. Newborns do actively produce expressions. Indeed, newborns seem well-equipped to compel caregivers to notice their appearance and acts and to weave them into a dialogue that makes human sense.

There is much evidence that adults readily assign meaning to newborns' expressions. For example, consider how adults typically react to the mere sight of a young infant. The ethologist Lorenz (1943; see Eibl-Eibesfeldt, 1989) once noted that human infants are biologically endowed with *babyishness* (a *Kindchenschema*) of chubby cheeks, a large forehead, and a small nose that most adults greet with adoring interest and interpretations about the immature bearer's needs. (This process has certainly not been missed by advertisers, pop artists, and cartoonists.) Thus, by supplying extra meaning that the infants cannot intend, adults transform a baby's appearance into a potent communicative signal.

Adults' reactions to a crying newborn provide another instructive example. Crying is universal and, especially in the first weeks of life, commonplace (Barr, 1990). Moreover, it is clearly the newborn, not the caregiver, who actively emits cries and who ceases crying (Rheingold, 1969). But it is an adult who seeks meaning in a newborn's cries; who hears them as a welcome signal of life and as a worrisome command for action. In addition, as we will see below when we consider studies of adult cry perception, caregivers actively try to understand what a cry may mean in terms of the infant's recent history ('When was he last fed?') and the culture's dictates ('She's spoiled by so much attention'), two sources of meaning that they, and not the infant, can access.

One final demonstration of how freely adults assign meaning to newborn acts comes from research using an odd procedure developed to examine how different adults interpret infant acts (Adamson, Bakeman, Smith, & Walters, 1987). In this study, adults were asked to watch a videotape of infants and to push a button every time they believed the baby did something that fit a specific instruction. For example, adults might have been asked to make a button press every time they thought the videotaped infant produced an *intentional* communication act. Alternately, they might have been asked to select acts they found *meaningful* (that is, acts that made sense to them, no matter whether or not they thought that the baby intended to convey a message).

The original study used videotapes of infants 9 to 21 months of age, and we will consider its details in Chapter 6. For present purposes, two of its findings are of particular note. First, parents (both fathers and mothers) readily selected, on average, almost 10 acts a minute when asked to note meaningful acts. Second, this rate was almost twice that produced by nonparents who had little experience with infants. A question thus arises: when do caregivers begin to interpret infant acts as meaningful? A recent thesis study by Wendy Phillips (1993) suggests that when prospective first-time mothers and fathers view videotapes of newborn infants, many of them are already willing ascribers of meaning.

Although the range was broad (one father-to-be hit the button only twice; one mother-to-be pushed it a record 103 times in 6 minutes), on average these soon-to-be caregivers noted that 6 times every minute, the babies they viewed were emitting acts that made sense to them.

In summary, when researchers study newborns' physical attributes and dynamic actions as expressive communicative acts, they notice global patterns of performance as well as specific behaviors. Newborns most likely do not intentionally attempt to use these patterns and behaviors to communicate with others. But to attentive adults, infants' displays seem rich with meaning.

This general view of newborns as expressive communicators has been elaborated in two different research literatures, one focusing on the newborn's cry, and the second on early alertness. We will consider each in turn in order to illustrate more fully how newborns are able to convey effectively both messages of distress and messages of availability.

Expressions of Distress

The research literature is now crowded with fascinating and varied information about newborn crying. Studies probe the physiology of crying, the spectral characteristics of different cry sounds, the relation between variations in cry sounds and infant health, adults' perception of cries, and the frequency of crying in different cultures. This expansive interest attests to the interdisciplinary nature of this research area as well as to the biobehavioral and social significance of a very young infant's cry. For example, an important recent book devoted exclusively to infant crying (Lester & Boukydis, 1985) includes European and North American contributors from departments of pediatrics, physiology, otolaryngology and communication science, neonatology, linguistics, and psychiatry as well as psychology.

This broad interest originated in naturalistic observations of crying newborns. Enormous patience is required to gather even the most basic information about the early occurrence of crying during infants' first days (and nights). For example, Peter Wolff (1966) devoted 24 hours over a 4-day period to each of 12 newborns, and then later went on to watch over 20 additional infants for 30 hours each week, for either one, three, or six months (Wolff, 1987). Sander and his colleagues (Sander, Chappell, & Snyder, 1982) even devised a precomputer-era monitoring crib to obtain around-the-clock recordings of newborn state activities.

Gradually, researchers also refined techniques to describe precisely the acoustic properties of cry sounds (Golub & Corwin, 1985). Researchers have long thought that variations in infants' cry sounds might contain important information about the overall integrity of infants' nervous systems and the continual fluctuations in their physiological processes. Their search for a diagnostic monitor fueled the development of increasingly precise techniques for characterizing cry sounds. These techniques range from diagnostic listening (which employs an attentive human ear) to time series analyses (which use devices which graph sound magnitude against time on a paper strip chart) to elaborate spectrographic analyses (which can produce a permanent visual record of both the frequency and timing of vocal energy as well as data related to dozens of acoustic features such as a cry's maximum pitch, its melody type, and the occurrence of voiced and continuous signals). Recently, computer-based procedures that use digital analysis have begun to ease the time-consuming and tedious task of generating such precise descriptions about the acoustic properties of a single sound.

Despite an arsenal of techniques, certain seemingly simple questions about crying as a communicative expression continue to challenge researchers. We will consider two of these questions: "How often do newborns cry?" and "What do adults think that a newborn's cries mean?" Although the explicit subject of the first question is the infant and that of the second is the caregiver, researchers are finding that the answers to both most likely reside in the interplay between the infants' and caregivers' contributions to early expressive acts.

How Often Do Newborns Cry?

Despite many attempts to keep track of newborns' cries, it is still difficult to pin down how often typical newborns cry. Some studies lead to estimates of 2 to 3 hours of cry state per 24 hours at the age of 6 weeks (or about 30 minutes of actual cry vocalizations; see Barr, 1990; Brazelton, 1962), while others in similar cultural settings suggest far lower amounts (e.g., Wolff, 1987, reports that when he eliminated data from days when the infants were clearly uncomfortable, he rarely observed more than 6 minutes of crying during a 4- to 5-hour-long daytime observational session in the first month, or 3 minutes in the subsequent months).

Different estimates of the amount of neonatal crying may reflect, in part, procedural differences (e.g., Barr and Brazelton relied on parental diaries; Wolff was in the room observing both the infants and mothers) and by marked individual differences between newborns. But the wide range of estimates probably also has a more intriguing source than mere methodological noise. One possibility is that, because crying is a communicative signal, its prevalence depends both on infants' propensity to cry *and* their caregivers' answers to these calls. This interactional explanation suggests that there may be many factors—some residing in the newborn, some located in the caregiver—that contribute to the amount of newborn crying.

Investigations of the newborn's contribution to the amount of crying have often focused on attributes of crying that may be considered species-wide. One candidate for a species-wide attribute is that cry sounds are part of an organized arousal state that all normally developing newborns enter. This tie lends predictability to the timing of crying. For example, newborns seem especially prone to emit cries as they wake from a period of sleep (Lester, 1985).

Another species-wide attribute of early crying is that it is modulated. Newborns can vary their cries from soft whimpers to piercing wails. The variability within the sounds that adults classify as cries provides an inherent source of nuance to the newborn's vocal expression of distress.

A further, and very intriguing, general attribute of crying may be its early development course. Ronald Barr (1990) has noted that this course typically follows a *normal cry curve*. This curve describes the relative (as opposed to absolute) frequency of crying episodes at different age points during early infancy. Data from several studies that track the amount of crying as a function of infant age reveal the same general pattern: first there is a rise in cry frequency, then there is a peak during the second month, and finally (to the relief of many a parent) a decline until it reaches a low level when the infant is about 4 months old.

Recently, Barr noted an important limitation to the claim that the normal cry curve is universal. All of the subjects in the studies used to generate the curve were from the industrialized West. The lack of cross-cultural data clearly rendered any claim of universality suspect. This realization has motivated efforts to gather evidence concerning how often infants cry in cultures other than our own.

An analysis of crying by infants from the !Kung San hunter-gathering society in northwestern Botswana (Barr, Konner, Bakeman, & Adamson, 1991) tested the universality claim of the normal cry curve. !Kung San adults care for their infants very differently than do Western adults (Konner, 1976, 1977). They hold and carry babies almost continuously (over 80% of the time), feed them frequently (averaging 4 times per *hour*), and respond always and almost immediately to infant signals of distress. Not surprisingly, !Kung San infants rarely cry for more than a few seconds and, overall, they are reported to be much quieter than Western infants.

Would the course of crying still follow the normal cry curve? The answer is yes. When Barr and his colleagues looked at how often !Kung San infants began to cry (using data from an archive of naturalistic observations carefully compiled by Konner in the 1970s), they found the familiar peak pattern for the frequency of crying and fussing over the first few months of infancy.

This study illustrates well the interactive nature of early crying. The presence of a cry curve in two very different cultural contexts indicates that crying may be an integral part of human newborns' regulatory system. The young infant is, in a sense, constitutionally equipped to emit frequently "a loud and clear sign of stress that internal or external requirements are not being met" (Lester, 1985, p. 8). But how long an infant stays in this state of arousal may be influenced by what caregivers do when infants enter this state. Among the !Kung San, who hold newborns closely, caregivers are positioned to pacify young infants almost as soon as they signal distress.

What Do Cries Mean?

Glimpses into another culture such as that provided by the study cited above invite a further consideration of how adults perceive infant cries. But even within our own culture, it is clear that adults react to crying with almost a boundless range of nurturing-organizing, ignoring, and, unfortunately, even harmful responses. As Wolff notes, "human cries are not a stable evolutionary guarantee of appropriate social interaction between infant and primary caretaker" (1985, p. 350).

A myriad of variables may help account for why adults respond differentially to infant cries. These include caregivers' culturally informed understanding of what causes and ceases cries, their level of experience with newborns in general and the specific crying infant in particular, their physiological response to cries, and their ability to perceive subtle acoustic variations inherent in different cry sounds.

This last variable has received considerable attention of late as several teams of researchers have made sustained attempts to document how different adults perceive different newborns' cries. This collective effort to understand adult cry perception provides a fine illustration of routine (or normal; see Kuhn, 1970) scientific investigation at its most productive. Together, researchers refined experimental procedures that carefully controlled (and narrowed) their view to the variables of main interest. Then, as research findings accumulated, they were integrated into a model of how newborns' cries gain meaning through adult interpretations.

One of the basic problems that first needed to be resolved by researchers interested in adult cry perception was how to characterize different infant cries. The sounds of crying are actually a varied lot. Cries produced by an individual infant vary over time. In addition, each infant produces cries that are different from his or her peers'.

The first strategy used by many researchers was to try to describe distinctive cry patterns or ideal types within an infant's cry repertoire. For example, Wolff (1969), in his path-breaking essay on "the natural history of crying and other vocalizations in early infancy," detailed the sound pattern of three basic cry types: *a basic or hungry cry* that is characterized by rhythmic and repetitive vocalizations; *a mad cry* that has the same temporal organization as the basic cry but differs in intensity and in the amount of turbulence in the auditory signal; and *a pain cry* that has a sudden onset, an initial long expiratory phase, and a prolonged silence of 3 to 7 seconds (which is long enough to leave many listeners anxiously waiting for the infant to resume breathing).

More recently, researchers have favored a second approach to the description of cries. They argue that cry types may be an artifact of the way in which adults perceive patterns, the very process that they wish to study. To avoid this confound, they suggest that rather than categorize cries, observers should characterize them along various dimensions defined in terms of gradations in several perceptually salient acoustic features. Such characterizations have proven to be useful both in the clinic, where they aid the diagnosis of neonatal medical problems, and in laboratories, where they allow researchers to present adults with carefully characterized stimuli.

The programmatic research of Philip Zeskind and his colleagues (see Zeskind, 1985, for a review) demonstrates the usefulness of describing cries in terms of gradations in acoustic features. During the past decade, they have targeted a group of cries which they think may act like a "biological siren" (Ostwald, 1972), alerting caregivers to an infant's extraordinary distress. Their search for this siren was prompted by the observation that some newborns emit cries which adults find unusually alarming, grating, and disturbing. They hypothesized that newborns who emit such cries may be experiencing biological problems and that these problems may place them at risk for future developmental difficulties.

To abstract this cry sound, Zeskind standardized procedures for eliciting cries (using a rubber band snap to the sole of the foot), and for the spectrographic analysis of audiorecordings of these cries. Because these procedures clearly evoke infants' discomfort, I hasten to add that cry studies, as all infant studies, are done only when an Institutional Review Board approves their procedures and then only when parents give their informed consent. (See Society for Research in Child Development, 1990, for ethical guidelines for research with children.)

Using cries of several newborns, Zeskind and his colleagues have been able to abstract a high-pitched, whistle-like sound from the cries of infants who have severe medical problems. Then, in several follow-up studies, they have learned more about the specific acoustic properties of this sound, who is most likely to emit such a sound, and how adults react to its presence. For example, Zeskind and Lester (1981) demonstrated that newborns who had difficult births that fortunately did not result in severe medical problems nevertheless tended to produce higher-pitched cries more than did healthy full-term newborns who had nonproblematic births. Zeskind and Marshall (1988) found that when mothers were asked to rate the qualities of different cries, they reported that higher-pitched cries were more urgent, distressing, arousing, and sickly than other cries.

The Zeskind and Marshall study is a good example of the sort of *analogue study* that dominates the literature on adult cry perception. In an analogue study, researchers ask adults to listen to and rate recordings of cries that have been selected to vary on a prespecified set of parameters. It is assumed that how adults respond during such *in vitro* experimental procedures approximates how they would respond during *in vivo* encounters with a crying infant. The primary benefit of an analogue study is that it allows researchers to sample across a range of values on certain parameters of interest (e.g., the pitch of cries) while minimizing the variability of other parameters (e.g., listeners' knowledge of the circumstances surrounding the cry) that are far harder to control in the world outside the laboratory.

Zeskind and Marshall focused on characteristics of the infants' signals. (See Murray, 1985, for a review of related work, and Gustafson & Green, 1989, for another fine example of this type of research.) Analogue studies may also focus primarily on variations in the characteristics of the adult listeners. For example, Ann Frodi and her colleagues (see Frodi, 1985, for a review) have performed a series of studies comparing how parents who vary on a specified characteristic (e.g., men versus women; mothers of premature infants versus mothers of full-term infants; mothers who have a history of reported child abuse versus nonabusive mothers) respond when they view videotapes of smiling and crying infants. Many of their findings provide intriguing material for discussion. For example, Frodi, Lamb, Leavitt, and Donovan (1978) found that although mothers and fathers did not differ in their overall pattern of physiological arousal to crying, their self-reported responses did differ, with mothers reporting both more positive and more negative mood changes in response to viewing the crying infant. Using the same procedure, Frodi and Lamb (1980) found that abusive mothers, as compared to nonabusive mothers, tended to perceive both crying and smiling as more annoying. Moreover, a comparison of their physiological responses suggested that abusive mothers may be blocking out both positive and negative emotional signals.

One of the main conclusions that has emerged from analogue studies of adult cry perception is that cries are most likely perceived as graded rather than as need-specific signals. In other words, cries convey information about the level of infant distress, not signals about the specific cause of the distress or even about whether the message is 'I am hungry' or 'ouch'. Note, for example, that in Zeskind and Marshall's study, mothers were able to report how a cry affected them (e.g., how aroused they felt) and what it revealed about the infants' general status (e.g., whether the baby was sick). However, they probably would not have been able to report accurately that the cries they heard were pain cries provoked by a rubber band snap as compared, for example, with hunger cries that occur just before a scheduled feed.

Gustafson and Harris (1990) provide strong support for this claim in a clever experiment that took the analogue procedure one step closer to reality. Using what they called a simulation method, they asked women (mothers and nonmothers) to babysit for a lifelike 1-month-old infant manikin in a nursery setting. Five minutes into the session, this artificial baby began to cry. The cries were recordings of real infants who were either waiting to be fed or who were being circumcised. The caregivers in this study all tried to quiet the baby, displaying a varied repertoire of caregiving acts including picking it up, talking to it, holding it to the shoulder, moving it rhythmically, providing tactile stimulation such as pats and kisses, checking its diaper, feeding it, giving it a pacifier, and even trying to interest it in a poster on the wall. However, they did not tailor their acts to the particular circumstances that caused the cries. In fact, manikins who ostensibly were crying from pain were fed sooner than manikins crying from hunger. Interestingly, on the level of cry perception, all of the adults in this study were able to discriminate the pain from the hunger cries in terms of overall level of distress when Gustafson and Harris asked them to rate the first moments of each of the four cries used in the simulation study. However, they were not able to accurately assign a cause to each cry.

Summary: The State and Sound of Crying

The Gustafson and Harris study provided adult perceivers with a much degraded version of infant crying. In reality, adults perceive infants' cries not only as a sound, but also, as the work on infant states suggests, as a fuller constellation of sights and tactile sensations. Moreover, adults perceive a cry within the context of their own history with this child ('When was she last fed?' 'Did I just pin a diaper on her?') and their cultural practices. (Consider, for example, what 9 minutes of crying might mean to a !Kung San woman who rarely hears a cry that lasts longer than 15 seconds.) Yet, despite its limited focus, the Gustafson and Harris study, in concert with other experimental investigations of adult cry perception, provides hard-won support for the notion that a newborn's expressions of distress are interpersonal events (Murray, 1979). Infants' cries vary in properties that signal to adults different levels of distress. Adults complete this signal by adding a wealth of human understanding to a species-typical plea.

Expressions of Availability

Except for their cries, newborns do not repeatedly produce distinctive expressions that routinely invite adult elaboration. At times, they may perform acts whose surface appearance can remind us of acts in our own repertoire. For example, with their mobile faces, newborns flash basic, universal expressions of happiness, sadness, surprise, interest, disgust, anger, and fear (Oster & Ekman, 1978). Sometimes these fleeting faces even seem to occur at appropriate moments as when they taste sweet, sour, and bitter solutions (Rosenstein & Oster, 1988).

More often than not, though, these first facial expressions appear to occur out of their expected communicative context. For example, newborns smile spontaneously during the state of REM sleep, not during the state of alertness. Because these grimaces occur without the usual social stimulation, several observers (e.g., Emde, Gaensbauer, & Harmon, 1976) call them *endogenous* (that is, coming from within) smiles, to contrast them with the social or *exogenous* (coming from outside) smiles produced by infants after the newborn period.

Other expressions, like the non-cry vocalizations that Lewis referred to as "sounds uttered in comfort" (1936, p. 24) in his classic study of early language, are rarely if ever produced by newborns. Newborns are able to make an assortment of vegetative noises such as burps and slurps that may invite a caregiver's interpretation, and they can produce small throaty sounds with the mouth closed or nearly closed (see Oller, 1980, who labels these *quasi-resonant nuclei* in his description of the first stage of infant speech production). But, as Kent (1981) convincingly argues, newborns are "anatomically ill-equipped to produce speech" (p. 162), a feat that in adults depends on the facile coordination of about 100 muscles. The essential anatomic structures to make oral (nonnasal) sounds are simply not in place until the infant is about 4 to 6 months of age.

Yet, despite the newborn's inability to produce an array of non-distress communicative behaviors, they still possess powerful ways of signaling their availability for periods of shared attentiveness. In a paradoxical way, infant crying appears to be one of these ways. The newborn's cry often draws a caregiver near and prompts the caregiver to act in ways that terminate it.

Moreover, many caregiving actions that succeed in terminating the infant's cry result in an attentive infant. In a series of studies,

Anneliese Korner and her colleagues demonstrated how caregivers, when they soothe newborns, often produce alertness as well. First, Korner and Grobstein (1966) observed that when crying infants were picked up and placed to the shoulder, they not only stopped crying, but in 88% of trials they also opened their eyes and became alert. In a follow-up experiment, Korner and Thoman (1970) compared the relative efficacy of body contact, vestibular stimulation, and the upright position in evoking visual alertness by monitoring each of 64 newborns' reactions to six common interventions that systematically varied the tactile, vestibular, and postural aspects of stimulation. Replicating their earlier work, they found that putting a crying baby to one's shoulder evoked alert scanning in over 75% of the infants.

A State for Social Availability

Newborns also seem to signal their availability for interaction by merely opening their eyes. Just as the sound of crying is the criterion act for the cry state that signals distress, the infant's open-eyed look exemplifies the arousal state of *quiet* or *inactive alertness*. In terms of early communication development, this state is crucially important, for only when infant and adult are both alert is the channel of communication fully open.

The state of inactive alertness is initially a "fragile and easily disrupted condition" (Wolff, 1987, p. 66). However, observational studies have repeatedly shown that infants in the first month of life enter this state frequently. Interestingly, the first period of inactive alertness typically occurs just after delivery, and it may last for well over an hour (Brazelton, 1979). Then, in the next few days, infants typically spend about 10% of their time in this state (see Berg, Adkinson, & Strock, 1973). Gradually, these periods become both more frequent and longer. By their third month, infants are often available for social interaction well over half of the daylight hours (see Wolff, 1987).

Even in the first week of life, the duration of a period of alertness depends in part on what other people do. For example, when Wolff presented infants in the first month with an interesting spectacle (a large red pencil moving rapidly in the visual field), the infants remained alert well beyond the time they would otherwise have fallen asleep. Another far more common spectacle that is apt to attract and prolong a newborn's attention is the caregiver's face, especially during and after feeding when newborns are most likely to be alert (see Sander, Stechler, Burns, & Lee, 1979).

The presence of a state of inactive alertness during the newborn period is consistent with our image of shared attentiveness. Although the newborn does not yet fill this state with specific communicative acts, this state provides a crucial frame for interpersonal contact. In addition, as we will see in the next section, a newborn's alert look appears to be a powerful social signal. Even during their first meeting, parents may react to eye opening with an elated greeting rich with human stimulation (see, e.g., the conversations of first meetings in Macfarlane, 1977).

Summary: The Newborn as an Expressive Communicator

Newborns' behavior is organized into discernible states of arousal that serve as a frame for their first communicative experiences. When they enter into a state of crying, their vocalizations and accompanying appearance convey distress to their caregivers, who typically try to terminate this compelling signal. When they open their eyes and appear alert, they provide a frame for moments of shared attentiveness.

Newborns as Receptive Communicators

Researchers who study newborns as receptive communicators face extreme methodological and philosophical challenges. As in any attempt to appreciate how one person understands the communicative acts of another, they must search overt behavior for clues about what goes on beneath the surface. Making such inferences is tricky (and some radical behaviorists might claim, inadmissible), even when the person can tell us what is on her mind. With newborns, the difficulties have long seemed almost insurmountable.

The central problem is that newborns have few ways to tell us about their experiences. Additionally, many of their possible clues can easily lead us astray if we confuse expressive and receptive capacities. The fact that newborns can produce smiles does not indicate that they perceive and appreciate their caregivers' smiles. Conversely, the fact that newborns cannot articulate the different phonemes of speech (such as the sound units [pa] and [ba]) does not imply that they are unable to hear the essential elements that compose human speech.

Given the challenge of gathering clear answers from newborns about their perception of others' communicative acts, it is understandable that scientists have long been wary of claims concerning newborns' subjective experiences. This caution has not, of course, stopped either speculation or debate; an understanding of the origins of subjective experience is simply too central to a developmentalist's interest. In recent years, this caution has fortunately not discouraged the invention of techniques that are, perhaps for the first time, coaxing relatively clear answers from young infants about their subjective experiences.

Any reading today of the literature on newborns as receptive communicators will surely need to be revised tomorrow. This area of research is filled with fresh empirical discoveries, often heralded in reports in journals like *Science* and then discussed at length in book chapters and convention symposia. Sometimes the empirical findings do not stand the test of replication (e.g., compare Condon and Sander's claim that newborns synchronize their movements to human speech as reported in their oft-cited 1974 *Science* article with the findings of Dowd and Tronick, 1986). At other times, the findings stand, but disputes still rage about whether available theories can handle them.

Nevertheless, four basic claims about newborns as receptive communicators can be abstracted from the fray. First, newborns are socially preadapted receptive communicators in that they seem to be selectively tuned to human communicative acts. Second, caregivers amplify newborns' reception of communicative acts by modifying their expressive acts in ways that harmonize well with their newborns' initial preadaptations. Third, as newborns actively attend to social stimulation, they are particularly attracted by events that they have experienced in the past. Finally, newborns experience others' communicative acts as global, amodal displays rather than as modality-specific, detail-filled expressions.

Social Preadaptation

Human newborns seem particularly receptive to human communicative acts. This bias seems to be built-in to their perceptual systems, which have been variously described as *selectively tuned* (Richards, 1974b) and *socially preadapted* (Schaffer, 1984) to human faces, voices, smells, touches, and tastes.

There is now ample support for this broad claim (see Schaffer, 1984, for a review). For example, it has been shown repeatedly that newborns seem predisposed to attend to human activities. Thus they will typically look at a person's animated face rather than at an inanimate object, and they often selectively listen to speech over non-speech sounds (see Sherrod, 1981, for a review). Moreover, there is mounting evidence, especially from studies of early speech perception, that preadaptation for the reception of human communicative acts may provide a firm foundation for later language development.

The first hint of just how well-equipped newborns may be for the daunting task of language comprehension was presented in 1971 by Peter Eimas and his colleagues, Einar Siqueland, Peter Jusczyk, and James Vigorito in a classic *Science* article. Their main finding was that both 1-and 4-month-old infants could tell the difference between two sounds, [ba] and [pa], that differ only by a single phonetic feature.

This finding fascinated developmentalists for two reasons. First, Eimas and his colleagues had formulated a truly elegant way to ascertain the perceptual experiences of very young infants. Second, the answer they received was, in the words of one recent commentator, both "startling" and "easily acceptable" (Aslin, 1987, p. 68).

The technique used in the Eimas study is called a *high-amplitude sucking paradigm.* In this paradigm, an infant sits wearing headphones, alertly sucking on a pacifier. The researcher makes the presentation of certain sounds contingent on how the infant sucks. Simplifying somewhat, first the researchers determine each infant's sucking base rate, taking into account both the pressure (i.e., amplitude) and the number of sucks per minute. Then, whenever infants exceed a criterion based on their base rate, they hear a particular speech sound on their headphones. Most infants react to what is presumably a novel stimulus by increasing their rate of sucking, typically from under 30 to over 50 sucks per minute. Over the course of the next few minutes, however, the rate of sucking decreases. Presumably the infants habituate to the speech sound they are hearing (recall the discussion of habituation in Chapter 3).

Once the rate of sucking shows a substantial decrease (20% or more) for two consecutive minutes, the procedure continues for an additional four minutes. During that time, half of the infants (the experimental group) hear a new and different speech sound in response to high-amplitude sucking, whereas the other half (the control group) hears the same old sound. If experimental but not control group infants dishabituate—that is, if they display renewed sucking vigor to listen to a new sound—presumably they hear the two sounds as different.

Eimas and his colleagues astutely selected the sound stimuli that babies would be asked to classify as old or as new. To appreciate the elegance of their choice, you need to know a bit about the complexities of human speech perception. In English (and many other languages) there are several pairs of consonants that are identical in every way except for their voice onset time (VOT), which is the time, relative to a discrete point, when the vocal folds begin to vibrate. For example, [b] has a VOT of about 10 msec and is called voiced, whereas [p] has a VOT of about 100 msec and is called unvoiced. Even though VOT can vary continuously (e.g., it could assume values of –20, 0, +20, +40, +60, and +80 msec), adult humans do not hear this variation. Instead, they perceive the sound categorically: synthetically produced sounds with a VOT below 25 msec are consistently identified as [b]; above as [p]. Thus, and this is important for the present discussion, otherwise identical sounds with VOTs of 20 and 40 msec are perceived as different, whereas sounds with VOTs of 40 and 60 (or even 40 and 80) are not.

Now back to the Eimas study. Using the six VOTs just listed, they created six synthetic sounds combined with the vowel [a]; adults hear the first three as [ba] and the second three as [pa]. For each infant, one of these sounds was chosen as their initial or old sound. Once they demonstrated habituation to the old sound by decreased sucking, a new sound was introduced. For some infants (selected randomly), the new sound was from the same adult phonetic group (e.g., VOTs of 0 and 20); for others, it was from a different group (e.g., 20 and 40). Generally, infants showed increased sucking (i.e., dishabituation) only when the new sound was from a different adult phonetic group.

This finding, coupled with the surge of studies on early speech perception that this first report inspired (see Kuhl, 1987, for an excellent overview of these studies and other, newer, lines of research on early speech perception), supports the conclusion that infants can hear phonemes before they can produce them. At a minimum, these findings reveal a newborn who is remarkably attuned to the subtle acoustic properties of human speech.

However, what are their maximum implications? Should we also conclude (as many have been tempted to do) that our newborns are preadapted to such an extent that they are preformed to be capable receptors of human communication? Here I urge extreme caution. First of all, we must not overgeneralize the findings. Recent studies of sensory systems other than audition have not revealed such subtle sensitivity to human features. For example, research on newborns' vision suggests that, although they detect movement and light/dark contrasts, their sight lacks sufficient acuity to perceive the details of facial features (Aslin, 1987). Indeed, studies of infants' perception of facedness consistently show that infants less than 6 weeks of age are not yet sensitive to the internal arrangement of features (Maurer, 1985) and that they do not discriminate between facial expressions (C. Nelson, 1985).

Secondly, we need to avoid filling the newborn with too specific an array of genetic instructions. For example, recent studies indicate that newborns are able to perceive a fuller complement of phonemes than we are. That is, they are set to hear all phonemes that might be used in any language, rather than instructions that confine them to a particular language. Gradually they attune the process of categorical perception so that they hear only those phonemes actually used in the language that they are acquiring (see Chapter 7).

In addition, newborns may end up acting in ways that are adaptive from the perspective of communication development because of their general endowment, rather than because of a specific genetic legacy. For example, they prefer to look at their caregiver's face because faces provide just the sort of moving, multimodal, filled with light/dark contrast, close-to-the-eyes stimulation that newborns can sense best, not because they are endowed with an innate detector for a generic human face. Stern calls this an example of "innateness once removed" (1977, p. 37) because the newborns' inherent design draws them toward the social world without having to specify its exact lines.

Finally, the classic chicken-and-egg dilemma of evolution demands interpretative caution. Are human newborns endowed with the ability to perceive speech sounds so that they might more readily acquire language? Or, as unlikely as it may seem initially, are human languages as they are because infants can learn them? In other words, does our species' unique linguistic competence capitalize on previously evolved perceptual predilections?

The appeal of this second possibility was bolstered by Kuhl and Miller's demonstration (reported in *Science,* 1975) that chinchillas (a squirrel-sized South American rodent) also perceive the voiced/voiceless distinction between [ba] and [pa] categorically. Thus, although human infants are indeed able to perceive acoustic differences relevant to language learning, we need not credit them with the innate knowledge that these different categories of sound are phonemes, the smallest gems of human languages.

In summary, my first claim about newborns as receptive communicators is that they are well-prepared to receive the sensory input that constitutes other people's actions. Given their sensory predilections, they are actively drawn into communicative events. Furthermore, when they pay attention to sounds that people make, they are receptive to acoustic nuances that are relevant to human language.

Infant-Modified Adult Expressions

My second claim is that adult partners alter their expressive acts in ways that markedly enhance newborns' receptive capacities. In other words, adults provide newborns with the sort of sensory stimulation that harmonizes well with their early perceptual sensitivities.

In part, adults cannot help but stimulate a young infant's senses as they provide care. For example, when a mother holds an infant to her breast, her face is positioned at just the distance (8 to 12 inches) where newborns' visual acuity is best (Stern, 1977). But adults' contributions include far more than such inadvertent adjustments.

Consider, for example, how adults tend to talk to newborn infants. First, it is noteworthy that adults often bathe newborns in rhythmic speech as they cater to newborns' many physical needs. Rheingold and Adams (1980) observed that both men and women on the hospital staff in an American nursery willingly "created the illusion of engaging the infants in a dialogue" (p. 401) by talking to them at length and acting as if the newborns understood them.

Also of note is that when adults address newborns, they adopt *prosodic patterns* (the intonational and temporal patterns of speech) that are distinctly different from patterns used during most adult-to-adult conversations. Fernald and Simon (1984) found that German mothers used higher pitch, wider pitch excursions, longer pauses, shorter utterances, and more repetition when talking to their 3- to 5-day-old infants than when speaking to adults. Extensive evidence (see Fernald, 1991, for a review) indicates that similar modifications in basic melodies of speech may occur in cultures around the world, from languages as different as Mandarin Chinese, a tone language, and American English, a stress language (Papoušek, Papoušek, & Symmes, 1991).

Although research is limited for sensory spheres other than sound, it is also likely that adults accompany their infant-modified speech with infant-modified visual and tactile displays. Stern argues cogently that caregivers present infants with a coherent "package" of stimulation that "to an observer, and perhaps the infant" is "experienced as a single communicative or expressive unit" (1977, p. 22). Thus, the temporal and intonational exaggeration of caregivers' speech is synchronized with a profusion of exaggerated facial expressions and rhythmic touches that adults would rarely direct toward an adult partner.

How do adults know how to provide an expressive complement to newborns' receptive capacities? Papoušek and Papoušek (1987) provide a deceptively simple but most appealing reply: they do so intuitively. As part of our species' evolutionary legacy, parents know how to complement and enhance their charges' competence in ways that support their entrance into and growing understanding of a new and complex environment.

No theorist has yet provided a fully adequate explanation of the process of intuitive parenting, and, as the Papoušeks acknowledge as a prelude in their fascinating discussion, their own analysis of parents' "fundamental didactic interventions" has taken them "across a dangerously soft terrain that could only be bridged by speculative arguments" (1987, p. 711). Here I will mention briefly only two points that need to be addressed by any adequate explanation.

The first point is that infants influence adults as adults modify their acts to suit infants. In other words, the richly responsive social world that adults present to newborns is, to a remarkable degree, controlled by the infant who may be perceptually predisposed to display preference for infant-modified acts.

Evidence for the complex interrelating of adult and newborn actions can be pieced together from several different studies. For example, Cooper and Aslin (1990) found that newborns prefer infant-directed over adult-directed speech. In a complementary study, Fernald and Simon (1984), in the research described above, provide a convincing demonstration that the mere presence of an infant may be an important stimulus for the adult's production of infant-modified expressive acts. In addition to describing what mothers did when they talked directly to their infants, Fernald and Simon described how mothers spoke when they were asked to make a 2-minute recording that they were told would be played to the baby at a later time. Although the mothers did make some prosodic modifications, they did not do so as markedly as when they spoke directly to the infant.

The second point is that adults' modifications, while in many aspects universal, are also profoundly cultural. Researchers are only beginning to consider how cultural factors influence adults' expressivity toward young infants. Preliminary findings persuasively suggest that developmental processes are systematically informed by culture. As Edward Tronick writes in his introductory comments to a collection of articles devoted to cross-cultural studies in the journal *Developmental Psychology,* phenomena are shaped by cultural processes that are "essentially social, communicative, and regulatory" even when "universal biological factors appear prominent" (1992, p. 566).

Consider the finding that mothers tend to actively attend to male newborns more than to female newborns (Bakeman & Brown, 1977; Korner, Brown, Reade, Stevenson, Fernbach, & Thom, 1988). This finding may be accounted for in part by biological factors. Perhaps mothers respond intuitively to subtle differences in newborn behavior that vary as a function of maturation, and male newborns tend to be less mature than female newborns. Even so, we would do well to consider also cultural-level factors that may be differentially informing intuitive parenting. How might culturally mediated attitudes about gender differences influence infant-modified parental acts? More generally, how do major cultural differences in how parents understand newborns and their needs for social engagement and disengagement (see, e.g., Stern, 1977) transfigure parental actions? Although researchers have yet to answer these questions, they have begun the important conceptual work needed to articulate them.

Preference for Familiar Social Events

So far, we have seen that newborns are interested in other people's communicative acts and that other people act in ways that may enhance this interest. Now, we turn to more specific claims about what newborns are most likely to appreciate as they attend to adults' infant-modified expressive acts. The first claim is that newborns are conservative receptive communicators; that is, they seem to detect and prefer expressions that they have experienced during their (albeit short) past.

Several of the studies that we have already considered exploit newborns' ability to recognize old versus new perceptual events. For example, the research paradigm Eimas and his colleagues used to examine newborns' categorical perception of speech sounds depended on their subjects' tendency to experience events in terms of their familiarity. Thus they could ask the subjects whether or not the sound they were currently hearing was one that they had recently (within the past several seconds) heard. In addition, they could manipulate experimentally which sounds (from a restricted domain of [ba]s or [pa]s) were old and which were new for different infants.

Several remarkable experimental studies have explored how stimulus familiarity influences newborns' reception of communicative acts. These studies indicate that history already infuses even the youngest infant's view of the social world. Infants seem to recognize, to prefer, and to actively seek stimulation that they have experienced previously. Also, given the typical course of events, this *perceptual conservatism* leads them to a rudimentary recognition of and preference for their own mothers' voices, faces, and smells.

Evidence for perceptual conservatism during the newborn period has been found for several sensory modalities. In the domain of smell, nursing newborns learn quickly to distinguish their mother's odor from that of other adults. Cernoch and Porter (1985) devised a choice procedure in which alert 2-week-old infants were placed in a bassinet so that a headturn left or right brought their noses within a half inch of a gauze pad that had been worn under an adult's arm for about 8 hours. By systematically varying who had worn the gauze pads, they were able to pit different characteristics against each other. The results suggest that breast-feeding (but not bottle-feeding) infants prefer their own mother's odor over that of other lactating mothers or women without children. However, regardless of how they were fed, infants did not yet reveal a preference for their fathers' odor.

In the domain of vision, there is mounting evidence that very young babies look preferentially toward their mothers as compared to other women. Field, Cohen, Garcia, and Greenberg (1984) found that 1- to 3-day-old infants looked longer at their mother's smiling face when it appeared before them than at a stranger's smiling face. Walton, Bower, and Bower (1992) reported that newborns less than 36 hours old sucked more to see a video image of their mother's face as opposed to a stranger's face.

In the domain of sound, the evidence for a familiarity effect is even more striking. As in the domains of sight and smell, infants discriminate and prefer previously experienced over novel auditory stimulation. In addition, they also appear to draw on specific auditory experiences that occurred prior to birth to inform similar judgments after birth.

The growing understanding of this astonishing experiential continuity across the divide of birth owes much to the remarkable scientific acumen of John DeCasper and his colleagues. In a short paper published in *Science* in 1980, DeCasper and Fifer reported two clever experiments that revealed the newborn's preference for the maternal voice. In both experiments, the way an infant sucked determined which of two audiotapes was played. In both cases, infants less than 3 days old quickly mastered complex rules regulating their sucking patterns in order to hear their mother's voice more often than the voice of another mother. For example, in the first study, infants rapidly shortened (or lengthened) the pause between sucking bursts when a shorter than usual (or longer than usual) pause produced their own mother's voice.

DeCasper hypothesized that newborns preferred their mothers' voices because of their extensive experience with them prior to birth. He supported this hypothesis with demonstrations that newborns prefer female voices to male voices and intrauterine heartbeat sounds to male voices, and that they did not seem to prefer their fathers' voices to those of other men. But it was not until he published (with Spence, 1986) the findings of a remarkable intervention study that the stunning implications of this claim were clear.

The study began 6 weeks before birth when, twice a day, the infants' mothers recited one of two passages (taken from Dr. Seuss' *The Cat in the Hat* and from Gurney and Gurney's *The King, the Mice, and the Cheese*) which differ markedly in terms both of the words used and prosodic qualities such as the pattern of syllabic beats. By birth, mothers had read their assigned passages an average of 67 times. Their babies were tested using the same differential reinforcement procedure used in DeCasper and Fifer's first study to determine if newborns preferred their mother's recitation of the story they were exposed to prenatally to a novel story, and if they preferred the familiar story over the novel one even if it were recited by another infant's mother. They found that newborns do prefer a familiar tale, and that this preference endures even if it means listening to a new person's voice.

Explaining the process by which newborns learn to recognize prior experiences regardless of sensory domain is no simple matter. As tempting as it might seem, the evidence does not warrant that we credit a newborn with knowledge of his or her mother as a person in any way comparable to the understanding of an adult or even a slightly older infant. Moreover, it remains unclear exactly what sensory cues newborns are using to inform their selection. In some cases, infants may be responding to cues other than the ones the experimenters intend. Thus, even though Cernoch and Porter conclude that the most parsimonious explanation of their findings is that breast-fed babies' more extensive exposure to their own mothers' odors may hasten their familiarization with "their mother's unique olfactory signature" (p. 1593), they entertain the possibility that lactating women produce qualitatively different and/or stronger underarm odors than other adults. Further, although Field and her colleagues contend that newborns can learn some distinctive features of their mothers' face, they have yet to satisfy skeptics who wonder whether their subjects might have been using extraneous information to regulate their visual scanning (see, e.g., Walker-Andrews, 1988).

Nevertheless, these many studies do converge on two amazing points concerning newborns' reception of social stimulation. First, newborns are far from naive observers for whom communicative acts are continually experienced as novel. Rather, they readily draw on prior experiences in order to color current ones. Second, newborns are neither neutral nor passive social partners. Rather, they display strong preferences for familiar stimulation, as long as the stimulation does not induce habituation by occurring continually without variation. As they express these preferences, they can act in ways that increase their exposure to the familiar social partners whom they are just beginning to know.

Amodal Perceptual Experiences

I have left the most controversial claim to last. Overall, there is strong consensus that newborns are receptive communicators who are prone to seek out their caregivers' familiar, infant-modified expressions. Most scholars agree that newborns experience these expressions differently than adults might. But exactly how best to characterize these differences is the subject of one of the liveliest debates in developmental psychology.

The characterization of newborns' receptive experience that I find most appealing paints a global view of first perceptual experiences. Initially, the world appears to be one of *perceptual unity* (Stern, 1985; see also Bower, 1989; Meltzoff & Kuhl, 1989; Rose & Ruff, 1987; Spelke, 1987). This unity is so profound that it appears to have only *amodal qualities*—those qualities such as duration, beat, rhythm, intensity, and shape that can be specified by every sense. Only with development will this unity be analyzed into separate sensory spheres such as sounds and sights, and only gradually will sensory-specific qualities such as timbre or hue be appreciated.

Although it is difficult for most adults to conjure up qualitatively different views of the world, it is useful to try to imagine how specific events might appear to an amodal perceiver for whom all perceptual modalities "speak the same language" (Meltzoff, 1985, p. 27). To such a perceiver, the auditory passage from *The Cat in the Hat* in DeCasper's studies might seem to be a pulsating, dynamic, undifferentiated flow of sensation defined by qualities such as duration, beat, and intensity, rather than a sound stream analyzed into meaningful words amid a poetic pattern. Moreover, the broadly smiling adult in the study by Field and her colleagues might be perceived as rhythmic movement and sharp contrasts rather than a silent face with dynamic features arrayed within a static space.

The mechanism responsible for amodal perception is still considered "mysterious" (Stern, 1985, p. 51), although many intriguing possibilities have been proposed. For example, Andrew Meltzoff (1985) proposed that newborns form supramodal representations as part of a process of active intermodal mapping (AIM). This suggestion has generated sparks because it directly contradicts Piaget's widely held view of sensorimotor development. As we discussed in Chapter 2, Piaget thought that the capacity for representation emerged at the end of infancy. Moreover, Piaget (1963/1936) proposed that the newborn's first perceptual experiences are more differentiated, not more unified, than an adult's experiences. He reasoned that because newborns do not yet routinely act in ways that link different sensory spheres together (e.g., touching something they see, or looking towards something they hear), they do not yet realize that the visual, auditory, and tactile sensations of an object all emanate from the same source.

Proponents of the amodal claim draw considerable support from studies that describe newborns behaving in a way that depends on the transfer of information between sensory modalities. Considering the high theoretical stakes, it is not surprising that such studies have often been greeted with extreme skepticism. Considering the dynamics of scientific investigations, it is not surprising that researchers have responded to such scrutiny with increasingly refined and clever experimental procedures.

To gain a fuller sense of the problems of interpretation, consider the now-common observation that newborns just after birth will turn their head and eyes toward a sound source (Brazelton, 1973; Muir & Field, 1979). This observation is an excellent example of a behavioral preadaptation that functions to foster social contacts since it tends to bring the newborn in visual contact with speaking caregivers. It is also an observation that can be (and too often is) loosely interpreted as evidence that newborns coordinate auditory and visual information to form the expectation that human voices emanate from human faces. But such an interpretation is readily open to challenge. It is at least plausible that the explanation for this observation is a far simpler reflex mechanism that operates without cognitive mediation.

To avoid such interpretative pitfalls, researchers interested in documenting early cross-modal transfer have devised several experimental paradigms that help them rule out rival hypotheses. One of the cleverest is the *perceptual paradox paradigm*. In this paradigm, the experimenter monitors a subject's reactions to stimulation that contains a crucial mismatch between two modalities. For example, an infant might be presented with a virtual object that looks normal, but when touched feels merely like thin air (Bower, Broughton, & Moore, 1970). Or, he might see his mother speaking directly in front of him, but due to an ingenious arrangement of speakers, hear her voice emanating from a location off to the side (Aronson & Rosenbloom, 1971). The empirical question is, do young infants act as if they experience such displays as paradoxical? If they do, we might then conclude that their experiences within the two sensory spheres are somehow linked.

How can we tell if they detect the paradox? In other words, how can we measure infant behavior in a way that allows us to be certain that they, like us, are experiencing an unexpected perceptual presentation? Finding a dependent variable has indeed proven to be a main sore point (see Broerse, Peltola, & Crassini, 1983). Typically, researchers have expected infants to act upset if they perceived the paradox. However, it is often difficult to quantify upset. For example, Aronson and Rosenbloom (1971) found that their 1-month-old subjects did not all express agitation and discomfort in the same, easily countable way. Therefore, they used as their dependent variable only one common and countable behavioral distress indicator, tongue protrusions, which they counted both before and after the displacement of a mother's voice away from her lips. They found that the number of tongue protrusions rose significantly soon after the displacement occurred, and interpreted this as evidence that 1-month-old infants perceived the face and voice as an integrated unit. However, other scientists soon questioned the validity of their measure. And, when they used different behaviors such as vocalizations as an indicator of distress or when they rated degree of upset on a scale ranging from contented to distressed, they often did not find support for the hypothesis that infants detected the paradox (e.g., Condry, Haltom, & Neisser, 1977; McGurk & Lewis, 1974).

Such disappointments spurred efforts to devise new paradigms that would demonstrate that newborns must indeed be amodal perceivers. Meltzoff and his colleagues have been particularly clever and persistent producers of what they call "existence proofs" (1985, p. 10). Their most distinctive research paradigm (Meltzoff & Moore, 1977) was designed to demonstrate systematically that newborns can copy an experimenter who repeatedly makes a facial gesture such as mouth opening or tongue protrusion. During such *neonatal imitation,* infants imitate acts that are invisible in the sense that they cannot see themselves performing the act that they observe their model making. To accomplish this feat, they must somehow translate visual into proprioceptive or tactile information.

Meltzoff and Moore (1977, 1983) claim to have demonstrated that infants less than 72 hours old will differentially imitate mouth opening or tongue protrusion. Field and her colleagues (Field, Woodson, Greenberg, & Cohen, 1982) have expanded this list to include pouting, lip widening, and mouth opening, which they contend occur in imitation of a model's happy, sad, and surprised facial expressions.

I find it most tempting to endorse Meltzoff's position. However, the scientific record is still incomplete. The literature is filled with a decade of reports by careful researchers who have failed to replicate Meltzoff and Moore's demonstration of neonatal imitation (see, e.g., Hayes & Watson, 1981; Koepke, Hamm, Legerstee, & Russell, 1983) as well as converging reports (e.g., Jacobson, 1979). Some thoughtful reviewers remain unconvinced that there is substantial evidence for neonatal imitation (e.g., Schaffer, 1984) while others (e.g., Stern, 1985) clearly find it convincing. At least one careful reviewer (Anisfeld, 1991) has recently deemed the record split, with robust evidence for the imitation of one gesture, tongue protrusion, which could plausibly occur without involving a process of amodal perception.

In summary, researchers have begun to devise clever ways to probe newborns' covert experience of their social partners' communicative acts. One intriguing but still not fully confirmed notion is that newborns are amodal perceivers. However, interest is high, and I expect that many studies to come will tackle the complex theoretical and methodological issues that prior research has helped to articulate.

Summary: The Newborn as a Receptive Communicator

Alert newborns are drawn toward the social acts of other people, especially communicative acts that caregivers modify to suit newborns' initial perceptual predilections. There is as yet no consensus concerning how newborns experience their social partners' acts. It is increasingly clear, though, that they perceive some stimulation, such as phonemes, that is crucial to communication development; that they recognize and actively seek maternal expressions; and that they may be particularly sensitive to perceptual qualities such as movement and tempo that are not specific to any one sensory modality.

The Communicative Channel between Newborns and Others

The expressive and receptive capacities of newborn communicators prepare them for social contact with their caregivers. As suggested by our organizing image of a moment of shared attentiveness (see Figure 2.5), early communication centers on this contact. The overlap of the newborn, the caregiver, and the open communicative channel figures prominently. In comparison, other aspects of communicative episodes—their referents, code, and even their message—are indistinct.

In this section, we will consider two main questions about the origin of communicative contact. First, when are caregivers and infants able to establish the communicative channel? Second, how do they do so? What are their respective contributions to this communal link?

Establishing the Communicative Channel

By definition, moments of shared attentiveness occur only when two individuals coordinate their periods of alertness. By the end of the first week, there are already signs that this interpersonal feat is being accomplished, although it took a particularly acute observer, Louis Sander, to understand its significance.

Sander (1977) argued that to understand early development, it is useful to view a newborn and her caregiver as parts of an "interactive regulative system" (p. 133). From this perspective, several early developmental tasks become evident that might otherwise remain obscured. Central among these tasks is the need to harmonize the flow of the caregiver's and infant's behavior. Only when they act in concert can a caregiver effectively fulfill a newborn's pressing needs and can a newborn begin to adapt to the complex temporal patterning of social life.

With this general view in mind, Sander (1962) began in the 1960s to chart the developmental course of newborn–caregiver interactions. For over a decade he and his colleagues executed several painstaking studies in which records were kept not only of what their subjects did but also exactly when their behaviors occurred. They adopted several time frames, including the circadian level (where cycles of events such as day and night take approximately 24 hours to complete) and the infradian level (where events such as moments of shared attentiveness transpire over minutes and seconds). Across their many studies, they sought an answer to one formidable question: How do infants and caregivers come to act together within an interpersonal system?

Two general conclusions from Sander's studies are directly relevant to our consideration of moments of shared attentiveness. First, soon after birth, both mothers and infants begin to alter their patterns of behavior so that the likelihood that they will be attentive simultaneously increases steadily. By the end of the first week, infants observed around-the-clock were already beginning to conform to the caregiver's preferred diurnal patterns of alertness and sleep (Sander et al., 1982). Moreover, on the infradian level, the overlap of infant alertness with maternal holding and verbalizations rose markedly over the first 8 days (Chappell & Sander, 1979). By the end of the third postnatal week, many caregivers and infants had arranged a predictable sequencing of events such as feeding, social interaction, and "open space" during awake periods (time when the alert infant is disengaged with the caregiver; Sander, 1977, p. 147).

Second, Sander concluded that, although each caregiver–infant pair constructed an interactive system that operated to serve universal tasks of providing the newborn with nurturing, their systems were nonetheless personalized. Through the specific way each participant timed and sequenced his or her behavior, each pair forged its own "unique and idiosyncratic characteristics of exchange" (Sander, 1977, p. 146).

The emergence of this interactive specificity was well demonstrated in an experimental cross-fostering study (Sander, Stechler, Burns, & Julia, 1970). During their first 10 days, each of nine newborns was cared for by one of two experienced foster caretakers. Then the caretakers were switched so that, for the 11th through 29th days, each infant experienced a new (but equally skilled) foster caretaker. Nine additional infants in the control group were each cared for by a single foster caregiver throughout the entire month-long study period. In both the cross-fostering and the control groups, a temporal fitting together or coordination of caregiver–infant sleep/awake patterns began to occur during the first 10 days of life. However, this pattern appeared disrupted during the next 2 weeks for the cross-fostered infants. Their pattern of crying and feeding changed (Sander, 1977), and they spent less time awake during the day than the control group infants.

Complementary Contributions to Communicative Contact

Sander and his colleagues interpreted their research findings, along with their many other studies, as an endorsement of his notion that newborns and caregivers join together to regulate exchanges within an interactive system (Sander, 1977). This conclusion is consistent with our claim that during the newborn period, infants and adults come together to forge a communicative channel.

Of course, a newborn and a caregiver must make strikingly different contributions to their common effort. I will now try to characterize their complementary contributions. As you will see, it is no simple matter to parcel up responsibility for a joint project. Not the least of my problems will be to find an appropriate vocabulary.

The Adult

In studies such as Sander's, it is often almost taken for granted that sensitive adults are able to adjust their own actions in order to facilitate the routine opening of a communicative channel. This assumption finds support in several well-executed microanalytic studies. For example, Bakeman and Brown (1977) systematically observed 45 African-American mothers as they fed their 3-day-old infants, taking note of when each person performed a communicative act. Recorded were such behaviors as "mother vocalizes to her infant" and "infant refuses the bottle." Then they determined, for each 5-second-long interval, who was acting: the mother, the infant, both, or neither. Their analyses of how these 4 codes were sequenced revealed that the mothers tended to time their activities so that periods of shared activity would result. This result led Bakeman and Brown to conclude that the mothers were "the guiding or controlling force" (p. 200) behind the lively communicative dialogues that ensued.

A main problem involved in characterizing the caregivers' contribution to very early social interactions is variability. It is clear from even the few available studies that skilled caretakers differ markedly in their sensitivity to infant cues and in their agenda. For example, Sander and his colleagues (1970) noted that the two experienced foster caretakers who took part in their cross-fostering study took to their tasks differently. One nurse seemed to follow a general method of caregiving (such as "demand" feeding) for all infants; the other was continually forming hypotheses about each individual infant and varying her actions according to these hypotheses. In light of such fundamental differences, even between two caregivers who share common cultural and professional commitments, it is imperative that researchers expand the range of their studies before finalizing a characterization of what adults bring to the formation of their first exchanges with infants.

The Newborn

Implicit in Sander's notion of an interactive system is the suggestion that, when newborns are participants in this system, they are both flexible and organized contributors to social interactions. We have already discussed studies that document how, over the first days of life, newborns act in ways that increase the likelihood of moments of shared attentiveness. The research record also suggests a newborn whose behavior is structured in ways that foster social contact.

Opportunities for social connection can be found interspersed throughout the stream of a newborn's behavior. Recall, for instance, the studies we reviewed earlier that demonstrate how newborns tend to stop crying and become alert when a caregiver picks them up. In addition, opportunities for an open communicative channel are liberally interlaced within the natural flow of routine events such as feeding.

Actually, feeding is a misnomer. Human beings do not just eat and drink; we dine. That is, we elaborate the intake of food with social nourishment. When a mother puts her newborn to breast, she also offers a view of her face and the sound of her voice, thus serving both the biological and the social functions of feeding.

Furthermore, human newborns' sucking seems to reserve periods for brief social interludes within feedings. We have already seen that newborns will readily modify the burst/pause pattern of sucking in accordance with the arbitrary rules of the high-amplitude sucking paradigm. Now it is instructive to speculate about what functions the burst/pause patterning might serve in more naturalistic settings. In this regard, Kenneth Kaye (1977, 1982a) has extended a particularly interesting proposal: the bursts clearly serve to transfer milk to the infant. Perhaps the pauses also serve a function: in this case, to provide a time for social exchange. In other words, by biological design, a place may be reserved during feedings for social connections.

Kaye (1982a) has amassed much data that are consistent with his proposal. First, he noted that the rhythmic interspersion of bursts within pauses seems to be uniquely human (J. Brown, 1973; Wolff, 1968). Second, he analyzed systematic naturalistic observations that show that mothers (be they nursing or bottle-feeding and inexperienced or experienced) tend to jiggle the baby or the bottle for several seconds when the baby pauses. Surprisingly, they tend to do this even though jiggles generally delay, rather than increase, the likelihood that the baby will resume sucking (Kaye & Wells, 1980), and even though, when asked, many mothers report that they jiggle in order to stimulate sucking.

At first reading, one might think that Kaye's findings lend important support to the notion proposed by Sander and others (e.g., Brazelton, 1982) that newborns rapidly enter into an interactive system. But Kaye (1977, 1982a) cautioned against such an interpretation; indeed, he marshaled these findings to argue in strong opposition.

Kaye's essential point was that the term *system* is being used too liberally. Granted, a newborn's behaviors affect social partners. But newborns do not intend to have certain effects or to anticipate certain outcomes. At birth, they are only organisms, and behavioral organization such as the burst/pause pattern of sucking is merely an endogenous cycle (Kaye, 1982b). Even if this cycle "evolved because of its utility in establishing social exchanges between mother and infant, this still does not mean it has the quality of a social exchange from the infant's point of view" (Kaye, 1979, p. 196). Thus, according to Kaye, instead of praising newborns, we should credit the caregivers who fit their own acts into natural rhythms of reflex behavior.

How should this disagreement be resolved? In part, further research which examines whether newborns make adjustments to fine-grained patterns in adults' activities may be enlightening. The empirical record contains convincing documentation that newborns' (see Sander et al., 1979, cited above) and perhaps even fetuses' (Sterman & Hoppenbrouwers, 1971) endogenous rhythms of arousal state can become synchronized with (or entrained to) environmental rhythms whose cycles occur over hours. But the case is still open concerning newborns' reactions to more micro-level regularities. Do newborns synchronize their movements to the rhythms of adult speech as Condon and Sander (1974) claim but which others (e.g., Dowd & Tronick, 1986) doubt? Does neonatal imitation of facial expressions depend upon rhythms of the model's repeated displays? If so, these phenomena may be manifestations of our newborns' inborn ability to synchronize their activity with the expressive acts of a partner (Sander, 1977, p. 138).

In part, the resolution of this dispute also depends on a terminological truce. The use of abstract words such as *system* and *dialogue* in reference to moments of shared attentiveness has had both benefits and costs. These words have inspired researchers to consider the temporal relation between a newborn's behavior and a caregiver's actions, and they have led to remarkable observations of the origins of patterned exchanges. For these reasons, I endorse their continued use. However, in the light of Kaye's challenging comments, it is crucial that these terms be applied with care so that we do not ascribe to freestanding newborns characteristics that derive from their overlap with supportive partners.

Summary: The Communicative Channel

The communicative channel opens with increasing regularity and frequency over the first month of life. Newborns as well as caregivers contribute to its opening, albeit in very different ways. The organization of newborns' activities includes predictable sites for social contact during routine caregiving.

Theme and Variation: Attention and Prematurity

One dominant theme has sounded throughout our discussion of the newborn as a communicator: newborn human beings are well-prepared by nature for social engagement. As expressive communicators, they appear and act in ways that draw partners near. As receptive communicators, they are naturally attuned to other people's behavior. Because of the endogenous flow of their activity, they participate with caregivers in a rudimentary interactive system.

In this concluding section, I will accent two strains in this theme. First, I will highlight the priority it accords to biological processes. This focus will prompt us to consider how shared attentiveness might vary as a function of the newborn's maturational and health status. Second, I will take particular note of the peculiar phrase, *well-prepared.* We will ponder how anticipations of a beginning point might be possible. Then, with an eye to the next chapter, we consider how moments of shared attentiveness might prepare aptly for the next phase of communication development.

The Priority of Biology

Mention of biological concepts is recurrent throughout discussions of the origins of communication. There are two related reasons for invoking terms such as adaptation and endogenous organization. First, as we discussed in Chapter 1, Piaget has inspired most contemporary developmentalists to view infants as sensorimotor organisms. From this perspective, issues related to the biological origins of psychological processes are paramount (see Piaget's seminal book, *Biology and Knowledge,* 1971/1967). Thus, even when studying a process as quintessentially social as communication, researchers have been primed by their theoretical perspective to ask how human newborns are readied by nature for this process.

Second, empirical studies clearly indicate that a newborn's biological status determines to a large degree how he or she may interact with other people. Neurology clearly delimits newborns' behavioral capacities, and physiology steers their ongoing activities. Thus the organization of arousal states, the burst/pause pattern of sucking, detection of phonemes, and attention to visual movement all realize potentials inherent in the newborn's nervous system. Communication with caregivers is mediated through these congenital capacities. Moreover, much of this engagement is directed toward regulating the newborn's appetite, sleep, and temperature (Als, 1979; Sander, 1977).

The importance of congenital capacities to early communication processes is illustrated by studies of newborns whose maturational status at birth is less than optimal. Research on the communicative behavior of healthy infants who are born 3 or more weeks sooner than the expected 40 weeks of gestation is of particular interest. Although some preterm infants experience additional medical problems, those for whom prematurity is the main concern allow researchers to document how variations in the maturity of the nervous system might affect early communication.

The preponderance of research suggests that less than optimal maturational status may compromise newborns' abilities to be expressive and receptive communicators. They may be less available for moments of shared attentiveness. For example, Lester, Emory, Hoffman, and Eitzman (1976) found that premature newborns were more difficult to arouse and oriented less responsively to sounds and sights than average weight full-term newborns during a standardized examination, the Brazelton Neonatal Behavioral Assessment (Brazelton, 1973).

Several experimental studies suggest that, even when preterm infants are responsive, the quality of their communicative behavior may be problematic. Adults in an analogue study of cry perception find their cries more aversive than a full-term infant's cry (Frodi, 1985; Frodi, Lamb, Leavitt, Donovan, Neff, & Sherry, 1978). In addition, McGehee and Eckerman (1983) concluded, based on descriptions of infants' behavior when an experimenter tried to engage them following a script of looking, touching, and talking, that preterm infants might be "responsive but unreadable" (p. 461) social partners. When they are just ready to leave the hospital (an event that for the preterms in their study occurred on average about a week before their expected due date and 8 weeks after their birth), preterms could alert to stimulation and engage in moments of mutual gaze. Compared to full-term infants, though, their organizational capacities seemed compromised in that they were less able to maintain their ongoing state of arousal and more likely to startle, make jerky motor movements, gasp, and grunt. McGehee and Eckerman speculate that such behavior may be difficult for a caregiver to interpret and respond to.

Observational studies that have compared mother–newborn interaction during feeding across full-term and preterm groups seem to confirm McGehee and Eckerman's suspicions. For example, Bakeman and Brown (1980; see also Field, 1977b) compared behavioral dialogues during feedings that took place just before hospital release and at 1 and 3 months after release. They concluded that mothers of preterms carried far more of the burden of maintaining the flow of the interactions than did mothers of full-terms.

It is important to emphasize (as did Bakeman and Brown, 1980) that organic problems do not translate directly into communication problems. Here it helps to view social interaction as a system. The partners must balance their relative contributions. When one partner's contribution is compromised, the other may compensate. The resulting interaction may appear atypical. But although such variations may augur subsequent difficulties, they may also be a source of crucial resilience at the beginning of development (see Goldberg & DiVitto, 1983, for more information about preterm infants' early development).

Preparation Past and Future

Moments of shared attentiveness during the days after birth provide a first context for communication. During these moments, an essential connection is stabilized between infant and adult.

Preparation for the context of communication extends far into our evolutionary past as social organisms. Although it is doubtful that human newborns possess specific genetic instructions to attend to specifically human stimulation (recall that chinchillas also probably categorize speech sounds along phonemic boundaries), they are preadapted to attend actively to caregivers. Furthermore, after several months of expectant anticipation, caregivers are clearly ready to engage with their newborn infants.

As a context for shared attentiveness is established, patterns that become central to the interpersonal engagements of the next developmental phase can be discerned. One nascent pattern is turn taking. In human discourse, partners take turns filling the communication channel, alternately speaking and listening. Precedents of this pattern are particularly evident during feeding when both newborns' sucking (Kaye, 1977) and adults' activity (Bakeman & Brown, 1977) tend to cycle on and off. By synchronizing these cycles—as when mothers fill sucking pauses with communicative jiggles (and, perhaps, when a newborn tongues during the pause between an adult's sequence of tonguing movements in a neonatal imitation paradigm)—a rudimentary form of turn taking is structured.

Furthermore, the focus on affective messages during the episodes of interpersonal engagement that characterize the next developmental phase is foreshadowed during moments of shared attentiveness. Compared to only slightly older infants, newborns possess relatively few ways to convey positive affective messages; indeed, the next developmental phase is heralded by the onset of social smiling. Nevertheless, the newborn's behavior gains meaning within the context of communication. When adults interpret their infants' inchoate expressions as human actions, they begin to fill the context of communication with content and to cultivate the human infant's potential for interpersonal engagement.

CHAPTER

5

Interpersonal Engagement

CHAPTER OUTLINE

Moments of shared attentiveness are the crowning communicative achievement of the newborn period. Newborns, endowed with expressions such as cries and open eyes and with a receptive bias toward familiar, dynamic social stimulation, are joined by caregivers who strive to cultivate the infant's first human connections.

During the second phase of development, the infant's initial fusion with other people is transformed into episodes of interpersonal engagement. Now caregivers and 2- to 6-month-old infants blend expressions of attention and affect to produce delight-filled dialogues-of-action (Newson & Newson, 1975), during which they appear to be dancing together in a split-second world (Stern, 1977).

Using the model introduced in Chapter 2, these episodes of interpersonal engagement can be depicted with an image that is dominated by a *communication channel* through which *messages* flow between two separate circles: one, the infant, and the other, the caregiver. The separateness of the two circles indicates that the infant is beginning to be able to participate as a distinct and independent agent within communicative events. The centrality of messages flowing within a channel serves to emphasize that now, unlike earlier, such events often focus on the varying content of messages, in addition to opening and maintaining contact. The presence of objects and the conventional communicative code in the background suggests that, as in the newborn period, these aspects of communication do not yet dominate the participants' interest.

In this chapter, this image organizes our review of research related to communication development from 2 to 6 months of age. In the first section, we concentrate on the infant circle to describe the dramatic developmental transformations that occur in expressive and receptive competence during the biobehavioral shift that occurs at about 2 months of age. In section two, we turn our attention briefly to the adult circle to describe more fully how caregivers tailor their communicative acts to suit emerging infant communicative skills.

We next turn to a series of microanalytic studies that document how young infants and adults act together to structure interpersonal coordinations and share emotional messages. Here we discuss how researchers have devised systematic ways to describe the organization of episodes of engagement, and how they have crafted data analytic and experimental procedures to test competing explanations of how infants and adults achieve such coordination. Finally, in our closing section, we consider variations on our central theme, taking as our specific concern the effect of maternal depression on early mother–child communication.

Changes in Infants' Communicative Competence

By the end of the 1970s, the research literature about young infants' astonishing perceptual, cognitive, and behavioral feats had reached enormous proportions. It was time not only to be awed by the surprising abilities of newborns, but also to sort through the data to see if consistent patterns emerged. In one particularly impressive effort, Emde and Robinson (1979) noted an interesting pattern that related to developmental timing. In research areas from neurology to learning, perception, and the expression of affect, infants undergo a dramatic biobehavioral shift at around 2 months of age.

This shift has two particularly striking qualities. First, it seems to occur with remarkable suddenness and clarity. Indeed, the change is so rapid and so distinct that many observers regard it as "almost as clear a boundary as birth itself" (Stern, 1985, p. 37) and argue that this marks the beginning of a new developmental stage. (In addition to Stern and Emde, see McCall, 1979; for a compatible but more fine-grained view of development levels around this time, see Fischer & Hogan, 1989.)

Second, although maturational factors are most likely the core cause of this shift, it is heralded by changes in expressive acts. Suddenly, communicative episodes take on a new flavor and texture as infants connect with their caregivers. Emde, Gaensbauer, and Harmon (1976) convey the enormity of these changes from the perspective of the parent who has, for weeks, been caring for a newborn who has as yet provided few clear-cut indications of interpersonal acknowledgment:

> There is little in life more quietly dramatic than a mother's moment of discovery that her baby is beaming at her with sparkling eyes. A week ago, or a month ago, he was less responsive, less human. Now, when he looks at her, he smiles, and they are seemingly joined in a new world of mutually pleasurable communications. (1976, p. 3)

Infants' New Communicative Expressions

The ingredients that transform infants' communicative presence in caregiver–infant interactions are spread throughout their behavioral repertoire. Here we will consider four that are especially pivotal: the arousal state of active alertness, gaze modulation, the social smile, and the coo.

The State of Active Alertness

It is a sure sign that the phenomenon one is studying has changed when a well-honed, reliable coding scheme no longer seems adequate to the task. This occurred to Wolff (1987) when he tried to use his scheme for neonatal arousal states to describe infants who were no longer truly newborns. He noted that a new category, alert activity, was required to describe infants during their second month. Further, by the third month of life, alert activity characterized almost 80% of infants' waking hours, whereas the occurrence of the common neonatal state of inactive alertness had undergone a noticeable decline.

To Wolff, the state of alert activity has several interesting characteristics. First, infants become capable of doing two things at the same time. Now, for example, babies can both rhythmically wave their arms *and* smile at another person. In addition, they can actively select events in the environment rather than being captured by specific stimuli in the environment. Finally, and most crucially, when in a state of alert activity, infants appear to initiate actions in addition to "simply reacting" (1987, p. 78).

Gaze Modulation

Visual gaze patterns usually provide the first indication that a 2-month-old infant is gaining greater control over his actions during periods of wakefulness. By then, oculomotor skills have developed to the extent that infants can move their eyes and heads to pursue moving targets smoothly (Aslin, 1987; Nelson & Horowitz, 1987), scan a human face for internal details as well as its outer contours (Haith, Bergman, & Moore, 1977; Maurer & Salapatek, 1976), and begin to focus both eyes on an object in mid-distance (see Aslin, 1987).

These new skills transform infants' expressive capacities within a social interaction, enabling them to routinely make and modulate visual contact with a partner. They can look directly at their partner's eyes and achieve moments of mutual gaze which serve as a most powerful organizer of nonverbal communication (Argyle & Cook, 1976). Moreover, they can modulate the direction of gaze in ways that vary, on a moment-by-moment basis, their reception of their partner's visible displays. They can, for example, look directly toward a partner, gaze a full 90° away, and even monitor a partner through peripheral vision. Further, as they become better able to view events clearly from a distance, they can begin to engage in communicative exchanges that occur at conversational distance, as well as interactions that transpire while they are being held (see Papoušek and Papoušek, 1977, who chart how interactive distance increases from the first to the fourth month of life).

The Social Smile

By the end of their second month, the endogenous smiles of the newborn have shifted to smiles with social meaning. Initially, infants seem to smile at most everything, although it is difficult to predict what will elicit smiling. These early *exogenous* (coming from outside) smiles often occur in close temporal proximity to other facial expressions such as frowns. Gradually, though, over the next month or two, social smiles become both more differentiated from other facial expressions and more specific. Thus, by 2½ to 3 months, infants are increasingly able to direct appealing openmouthed smiles at their caregivers' faces (Emde et al., 1976; see also Spitz & Wolf, 1946; Wolff, 1987).

In addition to a broad smile, the infant is now able to produce a rich variety of other facial expressions during communicative episodes. Many of these expressions can be reliably identified as emotional expressions. Of particular note are prolonged sequences of movements called *prespeech* (Trevarthen, 1979) during which the infant's lips and tongue move with or without accompanying vocalizations. Although these movements can be observed during the newborn period, they become much more distinct by the second and third month when, during a period of excited expressiveness, the infant may combine prespeech movements with expressive hand movements (Fogel & Hannan, 1985). An adult partner can often discern meaningful—and sometimes comical—messages within these displays of intent expression (see, e.g., pictures presented in Trevarthen, 1979, pp. 328–329).

The Coo

Beginning at about 2 months of age, infants greatly expand their repertoire of non-fussy sounds. To the vegetative sighs and smacks of the newborn period, they first add short vowel-like nasalized sounds that can be combined with a [g] or a [k] sound to produce coos and goos (Oller, 1980; Stark, 1978). Then, beginning at about 4 months of age, infants enter the expansion stage of vocal production (Oller, 1980), during which they add a wide variety of new sound types including laughs, raspberries (labial trills and vibrants), squeals, growls, yells, whispers, and whines.

Explaining New Expressions

The timing of the emergence of these new expressions is quite a puzzle. Why is their onset at 2 months of age, rather than at birth or several months later when the infant is able to locomote independently?

Researchers are far from articulating a reason for the timing of the biobehavioral shift and its concomitant burst of new expressions. However, their investigations do point to two contentions about the emergence of communicative acts. First, biological processes account for when these acts emerge and the basic form of these acts. Second, these acts are communicative because the infant's social partners readily harness them for social engagements.

There are several plausible reasons why one might think that 2-month-old infants learn to smile, coo, and make eye contact as they interact with their caregivers. To begin with, these acts have such obvious social significance, and newborns (as we saw in Chapter 4) are amazingly competent organisms who are able to share attentiveness with other human beings. However, these reasons have been repeatedly countered by evidence for a strong innate basis for the timing of the onset of these socially significant acts.

Take, for example, the case of social smiling. As we have already seen, newborns (and indeed, even prematurely born newborns) produce endogenous smiles, suggesting that the form of the act itself is mastered before social learning can occur. A maturational "push" (Emde et al., 1976, p. 76) seems to propel exogenous smiling when infants reach a particular state of organization, regardless of their chronological age (Crow & Gowers, 1979). Thus, prematurely born infants do not smile socially until they have spent the same amount of time maturing (approximately 46 to 48 weeks postconception, rather than postbirth) as a full-term infant. If an infant is born 8 weeks before her expected due date, she can be expected to smile socially 16 weeks after her birthday; 8 weeks will elapse before she matures to the status she would have typically reached in utero, and then 8 weeks more for the newborn period to elapse.

Observations of congenitally blind infants provide the most compelling evidence that human infants' social smiles are innate behavior patterns. In a carefully designed observational study, Selma Fraiberg (1971) found that blind babies smile. This is compelling evidence that young infants need not learn this facial expression through a process of visual imitation. Moreover, Fraiberg noted a developmental course that closely paralleled the one taken by sighted infants. Thus, during the second month of life, blind infants began to smile selectively to the sound of the mother's voice. However, no single powerful elicitor of smiling replaced the sight of a human face that readily prompts the smiles of a sighted infant during the third month of life. Fraiberg observed that the caregivers of blind infants often devoted an unusually large amount of play time in the ensuing months to games that involved bouncing, jiggling, tickling, and nuzzling because such tactile and kinesthetic stimulation, not vision, most reliably evoked a smile.

These converging observations suggest that the basic form and timing of the emergence of expressive communicative acts owes much to an infant's biological legacy. However, this legacy provides only the most general rules concerning the situations during which these acts are displayed. Young infants may therefore not need to learn how to smile, but they may need to learn display rules so that these acts function as communicative expressions.

Expressions such as smiling and cooing are not initially tied exclusively to social contexts. Indeed, observational studies suggest that during the first half year of life, they often occur in nonsocial situations. Piaget, for example, summarized his observations of his three children's smiling with the statement that "it is only very gradually that people monopolize the smile" (1963/1936, p. 72). He illustrated this claim with observations of his 2-month-old son Laurent smiling broadly when he saw his toys, his own left hand, and even when he gained a new perspective by arching his neck and looking backwards.

More recently, several psychologists have studied how infants react to different situations designed to vary their sensorimotor experiences systematically. Interestingly, young babies sometimes smile when they solve a sensorimotor problem or complete a task, even when no social partner is present (Sroufe & Waters, 1976; Wolff, 1987). Likewise, vocalizations do not necessarily seem to be tied to the presence of social partners. The rate of vocalization does appear to rise markedly when infants are with social partners who respond to their vocalizations (see, e.g., a classic study by Rheingold, Gewirtz, & Ross, 1959). However, as Schaffer (1984) noted, the few studies (e.g., Anderson, Vietze, & Dokecki, 1978) that document when young infants vocalize during a variety of conditions indicate that babies often produce non-cry vocalizations even when no social partner is in the room.

These observations suggest that infants' expressions may initially serve "multiple masters" (Wolff, 1987, p. 117); that is, they are not naturally tied to specific settings. Nevertheless, social settings are among the ones most likely to contain the stimulation requisite for evoking infants' expressive acts. As we will discuss later in this chapter, when infants produce these acts within view of caregivers, caregivers often perceive them as meaningful actions and act in ways that reflect this meaning to the infant. In short, when infants act within a social context, other human beings enrich their biological legacy.

Summary: New Expressive Capacities

Several weeks after birth, a dramatic shift occurs in infants' behavioral organization. As the overall quality of the expressive repertoire changes, milestones including the establishment of mutual gaze, the first social smile, and the production of coos and laughs are passed. Biological processes are largely responsible for transforming the newborn into an engaging human communicator who can readily and richly enter into finely tuned social interactions.

Infants' Emerging Receptive Competence

With their smiles and coos, 3-month-old infants are qualitatively different social partners from 3-week-old infants. However, from their perspective, has the experience of communication changed noticeably? Are their receptive capacities transformed during the biobehavioral shift?

This question cannot yet be answered with a single, simple statement. Clearly, change does occur, especially in infants' appreciation of their partners' visible expressions. But whether or not there is a generalized reorganization of infants' perception of communicative acts is still an open issue. We still know far too little about the subjective experiences of young infants. Moreover, we lack an adequate understanding of what constitutes receptive capacities for human beings before language dominates their communicative competence.

Nevertheless, the available research does provide support for three broad claims. First, from the second to sixth months of life, infants gain an ever-increasing appreciation of the nuances of other people's displays.

Second, they begin to be aware of the affective messages within some of their partners' displays. Third, they gain sensitivity to the split-second temporal characteristics of human communication.

A Growing Appreciation for Details

In the previous chapter, we noted that newborns excel as listeners who are already sensitive to sounds that are relevant to speech perception and are able to detect familiar auditory events. In contrast, we concluded that their initial experiences of visible displays are probably bereft of detail because of limitations in processes related to visual acuity and scanning. When 2- to 6-month-old infants are considered, this disparity between auditory and visual modes seems to lessen but not fade fully.

Recent investigations of early speech perception indicate that by 2 months of age, infants can make perceptual judgments about details of sounds that are crucially important to speech perception (Kuhl, 1987). For example, Marean, Werner, and Kuhl (1992) found that 2-, 3-, and 6-month-olds could hear the difference between two vowel sounds ([a] and [i]). More remarkably, infants of all three ages could make this categorization even when they heard [a]s and [i]s that varied in terms of speaker's voice (male versus female) and pitch contour (rising versus falling pitch). In short, they could recognize spectrally different sounds as perceptually equivalent very early in life, zeroing in on details that make a difference for speech perception.

This study leaves open the question of when infants begin to make such fine-grained auditory judgments. However, given the recent history of work in this area, I hazard the guess that this competence may exist before 2 months of age. Further, I suspect that the necessary evidence will soon be in place. Marean and his colleagues tout as one of the primary contributions of their study the power of their procedure (called OPP for *observer-based psychoacoustic procedure*) for asking very young babies such difficult questions. In this procedure, a young infant is trained to respond with a headturn when he hears a vowel change and not to respond when he does not hear a change; observers blind to what stimulus the infant is hearing judge whether the infant is participating in a vowel change or a no-change trial. As with many fine examples of systematic research, one result of their current study is a direct lead to the next one—in this case, an investigation of the newborn's competence.

Such a clear path of inquiry has not been laid out in the area of visual perception of communicative acts. In general, there is good reason to think that major changes in how infants perceive other people's faces may be occurring about 2 to 3 months after birth. The visual system matures rapidly during the first months of life. Several weeks after birth, infants begin to see details within a human face and to gain control over their scanning movements (although they probably cannot yet resolve details or sample arrays as well as a well-sighted adult; see Aslin, 1987).

Researchers have struggled long and hard to determine how the early flowering of the visual system influences the young infant's appreciation of other people. Over the past three decades, they have amassed considerable data related to infants' perception of faces (see Maurer, 1985; C. Nelson, 1985; Oster, 1981, for extensive reviews). They seem to be asking the right questions: Can infants perceive 'facedness'? When can they discriminate between their mothers' and others' faces? Unfortunately, young infants' answers have been quite baffling.

The source of the difficulty may lie in the varied ways in which the questions have been posed. Consider briefly how many ways exemplars of two facial expressions—for example, a smile and a fear face—might be presented to an infant. Do you present photographs, short film clips, live performers, or even holograms (Nelson & Horowitz, 1983)? Then, how do you determine if infants detect a difference? Do you monitor looking time using a habituation/dishabituation procedure or a visual choice paradigm? Or do you try to monitor more subtle signs of recognition, such as the infant's own facial expression?

Each methodological choice (and all possible combinations of the choices listed above can be found in the literature) may bring its own clouds over an infant's answer. For example, the expressions of live performers have more face validity than those of black and white still photographs, but they are also much more difficult to equate on dozens of potentially confounding variables, such as amount of movement and visual contrast. Moreover, although the infant's differential affective responses may be far more revealing than differential looking time, they are also far more difficult to code reliably and to interpret.

Methodological logjams such as this make it extremely hard to reach a clear consensus about when infants are first sensitive to the details of facial expressions that might be relevant to them as receptive communicators. Nevertheless, we can probably safely conclude that by their third month, infants perceive the difference between expressions such as smiles and frowns. Furthermore, they may also be able to discriminate within a category of facial expressions, so that they look longer toward an intense facial expression such as a beaming, broad smile than toward a weak smile where the mouth's corners turn up only slightly (Kuchuk, Vibbert, & Bornstein, 1986). However, we cannot yet be sure how infants make their judgments. Are they based on the analysis of features such as the eyes or the mouth, or are they somehow sensitive to the overall pattern of an expression?

One approach to these questions is through the study of the bimodal perception of speech. This phenomenon depends upon a perceiver's sensitivity to details within both the auditory and the visual domains. The results of an experiment by Kuhl and Meltzoff (1982; see also Legerstee, 1990) suggest that young infants may possess such sensitivity. In this experiment, 18- to 20-week-old infants were simultaneously shown two films of the same face. The woman was repeatedly saying the vowel [a] (as *pop*) in one film and the vowel [i] (as in *peep*) in the other. When the sound of one of the vowels emanated from a point midway between the two visual images, infants tended to look longer at the face that matched the sound, demonstrating their ability to detect precise correspondences between mouth movements and sounds.

Kuhl and Meltzoff (1982; see also MacKain, Studdert-Kennedy, Spieker, & Stern, 1983) suggest that the ability to detect the correspondence between audition and articulation (in other words, to lip-read) is but one instance of the young infant's predisposition to recognize intermodal equivalences (see Chapter 4). However, they wager that this particular manifestation of cross-modal perception may have especially important implications for communication development, because it may help to direct the infant's attention toward a specific speaker. In addition, they suggest that it may foster vocal imitation, a notion which they support with the observation that, during their experiment, several infants "seemed to be imitating the female talker, 'taking turns' by alternating their vocalizations with hers" (Kuhl & Meltzoff, 1982, p. 1140).

An Awareness of Affective Meaning

The reception of the details of others' displays is a necessary but not sufficient condition for the comprehension of partners' messages. Infants may distinguish between a smile and an angry grimace or selectively attend to speech rich with prosody over a monotonic drone, without being aware of the affective messages that we would perceive. Thus, to claim that infants are aware of the affective messages contained in their partners' expressions, we must go beyond documentation of discrimination and preference to the study of young infants' apprehension of meaning of emotional displays (see Oster, 1981, for a careful argument about the necessity of making this move).

Taking this step has led researchers onto complex theoretical terrain. Philosophers, linguists, and psychologists have continually debated the big question, "What is meaning," and they have often found that it eludes answer (see Katz, 1973, for a brief synopsis of some of the major issues involved). So that we do not lose our bearings on this terrain, I need to preface our consideration of the research with two orienting comments.

First, any communicative act has multiple meanings. This point is captured well in Jakobson's (1960) conception of the many facets of a communicative event and in the schematic images that it inspires (see Chapter 2, Figures 2.3 and 2.4). Depending on subtle—and potentially infinite—variations in how a person and partner mark different aspects of a communicative event, a single behavior may be transformed into any of a multitude of *acts of meaning* (Bruner, 1990; see also Adamson, 1992; Bruner, 1983a). For example, a person's smile may serve as a greeting when the channel of communication has just opened, an emotive expression of the person's tender feelings toward the partner, or a reassuring comment about a novel object. From this perspective, the development of the appreciation of meaning appears as a multifaceted process. Thus, inquiries into the beginnings of this process may be most fruitfully guided by several questions about how the infant comes to appreciate various aspects of this process, rather than by one overarching (and overwhelming) big question.

Second, during the early months of communication development, inquiries about the infant's appreciation of meaning usually involve questions about the emergence of emotive and conative meaning. As shown in Figure 2.6, the most prominent elements of episodes of interpersonal engagement are the speaker, the partner, and the message. This image prompts questions such as, "When do infants begin to appreciate their partners' messages about their current feelings?" and leaves other questions (e.g., "When do infants begin to understand messages about objects?") temporarily aside.

Even with a narrowed focus on affective meaning, researchers have found it difficult to gather unambiguous evidence that young infants apprehend the affective meaning of their partners' displays. There has been a plethora of studies and a prodigious mix of findings. The weight of the evidence supports Darwin's classic comment that his 5-month-old son "understood to a certain extent . . . the meaning or feelings of those who tend him, by the expression of their features" (1877, pp. 293–294). Even so, several scholars who have recently sifted through the evidence related to the recognition of emotion in the first months of life note that the interpretation of these data is often problematic (see Oster, 1981; Walker-Andrews, 1988).

Consider, for example, data that concern the young infant's imitation of emotional expressions. In addition to reports that newborns may imitate another person's facial expressions (Field et al., 1982; see Chapter 4), it has been noted repeatedly that newborns often cry when they hear another infant cry (Sagi & Hoffman, 1976; Simner, 1971). For example, Piaget began his analysis of the development of imitation with the observations that

> On the very night after his birth, T. was wakened by the babies in the nearby cots and began to cry in chorus with them. . . . At 0;0(4) [four days of age] and 0;0(6) he again began to whimper, and started to cry in earnest when I tried to imitate his interrupted whimpering. A mere whistle and other cries failed to produce any reaction. (1962/1945, p. 7)

Piaget then proceeded to puzzle about what such "vocal contagion" (1962/1945, p. 10) indicates about infants' understanding of emotional messages. Are they crying, as he ultimately concluded, because the voice of another person merely stimulates their own voices? Or, are they displaying affective attunement (Stern, 1985) or empathic distress (Sagi & Hoffman, 1976), two processes that depend on the capacity to resonate to a cry's emotional message?

Many commentators (e.g., Klinnert, Campos, Sorce, Emde, & Svejda, 1983; Stern, 1985) reserve discussion of the capacity for emotional resonance until the second half of the first year of life. But a recent study by Haviland and Lelwica (1987) indicates that even much younger infants may be able to appreciate information relevant to affective messages. In this study, 10-week-old infants watched their mothers express visually and vocally three emotional expressions: joy, anger, and sadness. Each expression was presented briefly four times in a row. Haviland and Lelwica contend that the infants not only discriminated between emotions and imitated (or matched) joy and anger, they also displayed "induced affect" (p. 103), during which they produced "meaningful patterns to specific emotional expressions" (p. 103). They became increasingly interested or excited when mothers presented the joy expression, upset and perhaps frozen and fearful during the anger presentations, and self-soothing (indicated by increased tonguing) in response to the maternal expressions of sadness.

Haviland and Lelwica argue that their findings support the claim that even young infants appreciate the affordances of emotional expressions. The term *affordance* is drawn from James Gibson's (1979) ecological theory of perception. This theory contains at its core the notion that people are active perceivers who pick up information about what their environment offers or provides; that is, we perceive directly the meaning or value of events in our environment. Gibson's examples usually referred to the inanimate environment. For example, human beings (but perhaps not fish) perceive that floors extend or afford support for locomotion and that cup handles extend or afford graspability.

Haviland and Lelwica (1987; see also Campos & Stenberg, 1981; Walker-Andrews, 1988) suggest that young infants perceive the affordances of emotional expressions. Before they appreciate the specific visual or auditory components of an expression and perhaps before they realize the relation between internal feeling and affective display, young infants may nonetheless resonate to an ecologically valid, whole emotional expression. If so, they would thereby have preliminary access to the emotional meanings that pervade the human social world.

Perception of Temporal Relations

By the third month of life (and perhaps, especially in the instance of audition, much earlier), infants' reception of temporal information is calibrated to the temporal scale of human conversation. Infants seem attuned to the rhythmic themes of speech, and they detect temporal contingencies between their own acts and those of their partners.

There is an intriguing relation between the young infant's appreciation of temporal patterns and the communication of affective meaning. In terms of reception, the apprehension of affective meaning is intrinsically bound to the perception of temporal qualities (Stern & Gibbon, 1979). Compare, for example, the connotations of a display composed of a staccato "hi," hasty glance, and brief lip curl, and one composed of a prolonged "h–i–i–i," a steady gaze, and a slowly expanding smile. Although we cannot be sure that young infants' appreciation of these two displays parallels ours, there is growing evidence (see Stern, 1985, for a review) that they are attentive not only to the static form of emotional expressions, but also to their dynamic form.

One crucial source of evidence of infants' sensitivity to the dynamics of emotional expressions is their own affective reactions to temporal qualities. Infants are far from a neutral audience of events. Moreover, and most crucial to our current discussion, they seem particularly aroused by events that contain stimuli arranged in certain temporal patterns or that stand in a particular temporal relation to their own acts.

Two examples will help to clarify the intertwining of young infants' temporal perception and emotional expression. The first example is the infant's gleeful reaction to a partner's run or rapid repetition of a behavior pattern (Fogel, 1977; Stern, Beebe, Jaffe, & Bennett, 1977). Early social interactions abound with runs of brief bursts of behavior (e.g., an adult's head nod and "hello, baby") separated by short pauses. An adult and infant may develop a few favorite runs, games such as "I'm going to get you" that appear to be fun for both participants.

From whence comes the pleasure? Conceivably a run might bore a baby. Recall the process of habituation (see Chapter 2). In studies that use the habituation/dishabituation paradigm, an infant's attention tends to wane when a display is repeated. Why do infants not habituate to a game? A plausible answer is that successful runs merge predictability with novelty. Although repetition dominates, variation also intrudes, often timed to the moment when habituation might otherwise begin. Thus, as Stern and his colleagues aptly note, from the point of view of the habituation paradigm, a run may be described as follows:

> an extraordinarily richly and subtly designed series of experimental stimuli consisting of many variable elements, each of which can be slightly varied at each successive presentation so as to re-correct the ongoing interaction. (1977, p. 190)

In terms of time, this view of runs is remarkable for two reasons. First, time itself may be the essence of a variation. In addition to changes in pitch, volume, or placement, a burst may be longer or shorter than its successor; it may occur slightly sooner or later than expected. Second, regardless of the element varied, to perceive and enjoy a run, an infant must be able to compare displays over time. Each of a partner's turns gains fuller meaning relative to prior presentations. The theme emerges over time. Further, the theme is dynamic. Over the course of an interaction, a run is varied in ways that are not preestablished at the onset (Walker, Messinger, Fogel, & Karns, 1992).

Our second example involves infants' perception of temporal contingency. Contingency awareness can be demonstrated experimentally during early infancy by setting up a situation in which a behavior that infants can readily and repeatedly perform is followed by an interesting spectacle. For example, reports abound of young infants who eagerly and gleefully learn to move their head, wave their arms, or kick their feet in order to move a mobile (Piaget, 1963/1936; Rovee-Collier, 1990; Watson, 1972).

There are two details of these reports that are particularly intriguing in terms of early communication development. First, at the same time infants are mastering whatever instrumental behaviors are required to bring about the interesting spectacle (e.g., kicking in order to make a mobile move), they also smile and coo vigorously. John S. Watson (1972) suggests that the smiles and coos occurring during contingency detection support what he calls *"The Game" hypothesis*. Adults often engage in gamelike interactions with infants that are rich in contingencies, and detection of such contingencies is accompanied by considerable smiling and cooing. Thus, Watson suggests, "The Game" is not important because people play it; instead, people "become important to the infant because they play 'The Game' " (1972, p. 338). Infants appear biologically disposed to seek out contingency experiences, be they produced by caregivers during everyday encounters or, far more rarely, by mobiles of a psychologist's design. Interestingly, when infants detect temporal contingencies, they display their pleasure by smiling and cooing. These accompaniments encourage people to continue to play "The Game" and, Watson argues, help to define these people as "social stimuli" (1972, p. 323).

The second intriguing detail of these studies is what Watson labels the "inferiority of perfection" (Watson, 1985, p. 175). He demonstrates in a series of well-executed studies that although 4-month-old infants are most readily able to detect perfect contingencies, they are most attentive to clear but moderate levels of *imperfect* contingency. That is, infants are most likely to be aroused when the contingency relation between their behavior and the subsequent stimulus is slightly imperfect (e.g., when a mobile does not turn every time a leg is kicked), rather than strictly conforming to a predictable pattern.

Watson argues that this surprising state of affairs may have considerable adaptive significance for human infants. For one, it helps infants to determine whether the behavior and the stimulus both come from themselves, or whether the stimulation comes from outside. Within infants' ecological niche, perfect contingencies are most likely to occur when their acts produce a self-sensation, as when an infant rubs her own hand against her leg. This act is guaranteed to be followed by a tactile sensation. In contrast, moderately imperfect contingencies are most likely to occur when an outside source provides the subsequent stimulation; try as they might, parents can never match an infant's behavior with perfectly consistent responses. In the process, caregivers may be providing the infant with information crucial for making the distinction between self and other.

Watson (1985) also suggests that each person an infant encounters may be imperfect in his or her own peculiar way. That is, each can be characterized by a unique pattern or signature of contingent responsiveness. If infants can recognize different signatures, they could also discriminate between familiar and unfamiliar ones. Thus, Watson speculates, infants' temporal perceptiveness may foster the crucial awareness that communicative episodes occur with different partners, some of whom are intimate familiars and others, relative strangers.

Summary: Emerging Receptive Competence

By their third month, infants perceive many of the details of a partner's vocal and visual expressions that may have escaped their notice just weeks earlier. When they focus on the details of displays, they appear receptive not only to the configuration of the displays, but also to the affective significance of certain stimulus patterns. Moreover, infants' appreciation of social partners may be enhanced by their sensitivity to when expressions occur.

Caregivers as Communicative Partners

The research on receptive capacities that we just reviewed indicates that 2- to 6-month-old infants are active perceivers, well-attuned to the affective and temporal qualities of human communicative acts. Now we consider how caregivers act to complement their infants' propensities. My major claim is that caregivers accentuate the affective and temporal qualities in their behavior that appeal to their young partners.

The Flowering of Infant-Modified Acts

Infant-modified acts are a special class of acts that people perform in the presence of infants. Adults' standard repertoire of communicative acts is often dramatically transfigured when they communicate with 3-month-old infants. Their faces may contort into exaggerated expressions of joy, surprise, or concern; their voices may cascade an octave or lilt a simple rhyme; their fingers may poke a beat to the infant's ribs or snap from his ear to eye. Should onlookers view only the adult side of such an exchange, they might well conclude that the adult's behavior is "deviant" (Schaffer, 1984, p. 52) or even "outright bizarre" (Stern, 1977, p. 10).

To gain a more exact characterization of infant-modified acts, researchers (e.g., Brazelton et al., 1974; Papoušek & Papoušek, 1977; Stern, 1977; Trevarthen, 1979; Tronick, Als, & Adamson, 1979) typically observe a mother (or, less frequently, a father or an unfamiliar adult; see Dixon, Yogman, Tronick, Adamson, Als, & Brazelton, 1981) who has been asked to play for a few minutes with an alert infant as researchers surreptitiously record the proceedings. Under such circumstances, almost all adults provide a steady stream of exaggerated, elongated, and redundant behavior. (See Trevarthen, 1979, for mention of rare exceptions.)

Stern's (1977) description of a mock-surprise expression, one of the infant-modified acts that occurs frequently, captures well the attributes of these peculiar behavior patterns. First, during these acts, the adult's face and voice tend to be exaggerated into a distinctive and almost stereotyped form. In the case of the mock-surprise, the adult's "eyes open very wide, the eyebrows go up, the mouth opens wide, and the head is raised and tilted up slightly," and the adult "says something like 'oooooh' or 'aaaaah' " (p. 11) in a manner that "looks like a caricature of an orienting or surprise response" (p. 12).

Second, these acts are often drawn out in time as well as in space. The mock surprise expression generally

> grows slowly almost as if the mother were performing in slow motion, gradually but dramatically building to the fullest degree of the display and then, once 'there,' holding the achieved position for an extremely long time. (Stern, 1977, p. 11)

Further, these acts tend to be repeated both within behavioral runs and at specific locations during an ongoing social interaction. The mock-surprise expression's particular place of privilege is the point when an infant opens the channel of communication with his or her partner.

According to Stern (1977), a mother may make a mock-surprise expression as often as several times a minute if her infant repeatedly turns attention toward and away from her.

This basic characterization of infant-modified acts has been elaborated in three interesting ways. First, researchers have gathered support for the contention that the adult's repetition of a limited number of specific expressions at specific moments may help introduce infants to *communicative intentions*. For example, Stern (1977) suggested that an adult's systematic placement of the mock-surprise expression at the beginning of periods of mutual gaze may serve to invite and to acknowledge the infant's interest in interpersonal contact. He also noted that adults tend to reserve specific places within an interaction for other expressions that express communicative intentions such as 'I want your attention' or 'Let's delight together'.

For example, Stern, Spieker, and MacKain (1982) documented that when a mother speaks to an infant who is not looking at her, she is likely to use phrases with a rising intonational contour, such as "Watcha looking at, huh?" and "Heh?" When her infant is gazing at her happily, she tends to produce phrases with a sinusoidal-bell contour such as "You're the cutest little thing in the whole world." and "Way to go." Stern and his colleagues suggest that, as mothers restrict their use of specific forms to certain places within an interaction, they may be helping infants realize that different acts can express different communicative intentions.

Second, researchers like Trevarthen (1979, 1988) have observed that adults subtly vary a small stock of expressions. For example, although a mother may usually enact a mock-surprise expression by slowly opening her mouth wide and arching her eyebrows, in one playful instance she might suddenly purse her lips and flash her brows. Thus, even though the basic vocabulary of acts may be limited, adults enliven their enactment. Such animation may prevent habituation while it introduces the infant to the continual vagary of human conversation.

Third, researchers are beginning to appreciate more fully how culture qualifies infant-modified actions. Several extensive cross-cultural investigations have recently provided descriptions of local versions of infant-modified behavior that illustrate the cultural distinctiveness with which parents make generic modifications. When Marc Bornstein of the United States and his colleagues from Argentina, France, and Japan compared how mothers from urban settings in each of these four cultures spoke to 5-month-old infants during free play in their homes, they found that "mothers everywhere intend to share feelings and contribute to emotional exchanges via their affect-salient speech to babies" (Bornstein et al., 1992, p. 598). But mothers from different cultures enacted this common agenda somewhat differently. Japanese mothers were most likely to use affect-salient speech comprised of ungrammatical, incomplete phrases, songs, and nonsensical, onomatopoeic utterances (see also Fogel, Toda, & Kawai, 1988). Argentine mothers made the most direct statements, and American mothers asked the most questions. In each instance, the researchers argued that cultural forces influence parental beliefs that in turn shape maternal speech in ways that may help to socialize infants into a specific cultural community.

Cultural differences may even be evident when adults and infants are viewed using a standard observational procedure. For example, naturalistic observations indicate that although both Gusii mothers from rural Kenya and American mothers from Boston are responsive to their 4-month-old infants, they differ in culturally significant ways. Overall, Gusii mothers seem most intent on soothing their infants and minimizing their arousal, a goal that differs markedly from the goal of visual and vocal stimulation and positive emotional arousal often ascribed to Boston mothers (LeVine, 1990; Richman, Miller, & LeVine, 1992). These different aims were evident even during a standardized play session in which mothers sat face-to-face with their young infants. Unlike Boston mothers, who looked at their infants continually while they tried to elicit a reciprocal exchange of smiles and coos, Gusii mothers tended to avert their gaze whenever their infants became excited (Dixon, Tronick, Keefer, & Brazelton, 1981).

These interesting glimpses into mother–infant interactions in cultures other than our own suggest that adults can orchestrate interpersonal engagement with an infant around diverse themes and with a variety of acts. Such observations are only a beginning; there is clearly a pressing need to broaden our lens even further to view how mothers (and in some cultures such as the Efé foragers of Zaire, fathers, other adults, and children; see Tronick, Morelli, & Ivey, 1992) enact cultural scripts as they respond to young infants.

As researchers continue to venture from their starting place in Western culture to describe a fuller range of adult behavior, they will certainly raise new challenges. At minimum, they will surely press us to place our own infants' acculturation experiences along a broader continuum. For example, compared to either !Kung or Efé caregivers, even very responsive American caregivers appear to tolerate astonishingly prolonged expressions of distress. More radically, cross-cultural researchers may fuel important questions about whether forms of social interaction such as mutual gaze that appear so central to early adult–infant communication in our culture—and to our theories of early communication development—may be scarce or even absent within another culture (see, e.g., Ochs, 1988; Schieffelin & Ochs, 1986).

Explaining Adult Modifications

Why, as adults engage in the necessary provision of care, do they modify their repertoire of communicative actions? It is certainly conceivable that they might well go about their business without producing infant-modified expressions. Yet, even compared to caregivers interacting with newborn infants, the partners of 2- to 6-month-old infants appear extraordinarily willing to express affectivity.

A full explanation contains several layers. For example, one might argue that to understand why adults modify their communicative acts, we need to appreciate more fully the general psychobiological processes that support human capacity for intuitive parenting (Papoušek & Bornstein, 1992; Papoušek & Papoušek, 1987). Further, one might seek an explanation within caregivers' own developing notions of their infant or even within their own experiences of having been parented themselves.

Clearly, caregivers respond not only to the moment-to-moment fluctuations of an infant's behavior but also to their more enduring interpretation of an infant's rapidly changing persona. In particular, many theorists have speculated that the timing of the dramatic change in an infant's communicative competence holds very positive significance for parents. The newborn period is often experienced as one of emotional challenge (Shereshefsky & Yarrow, 1973). As Robson (1967) once provocatively remarked, nature may well have been wise in reserving infants' eye-to-eye contact and social smiles until several weeks into infancy. Coming when they do, they may be experienced by parents both as confirmation that the infant is a "more human" being (Emde et al., 1976, p. 150) and as "payment for services rendered" (Robson, 1967, p. 15).

Further, one might also try to account for caregivers' affective responsiveness in terms of specific processes that occur during social exchanges. For example, "The Game" hypothesis proposed by Watson (1972; see above) to account for infants' smiling and cooing might be extended to explain caregivers' affective responsiveness as well. Recall Watson's suggestion that infants experience as positive the detection of a contingent relation between their own activities and environmental events, including their caregiver's communicative acts. From an adult's point of view, an infant's glee may provoke delight as well as serve as a stimulus for the repetition of the extraordinary displays that facilitate the infant's expressions of interest and pleasure. Thus, adults may be more prone to exaggerate the prosody of their speech to a 3-month-old than to either a newborn or a toddler (Stern, Spieker, Barnett, & MacKain, 1983) because the 3-month-old may be the most likely of the three to be amused by such affectively rich vocalizations.

Summary: Infant-Modified Communicative Acts

When young infants interact with their caregivers, they encounter responsive partners who produce appealingly exaggerated communicative acts. These infant-modified actions may help to introduce infants to a variety of communicative intentions and to culturally specific ways of displaying affective messages.

Within Episodes of Interpersonal Engagement

Periods of interpersonal engagement with caregivers gradually consolidate from an infant's second to her sixth month. The first tentative exchanges of emotional expressions are transformed into smooth, albeit still wordless, dialogues, during which partners alternate turns and convey nuanced affective messages. It now seems appropriate to talk in terms of a genuine partnership in which both people contribute to the *mutual* regulation of attention and affectivity. In other words, their interactions conform to a single structure, co-constructed through bidirectional influences, rather than imposed by either the infant's endogenous cycles or the adult's current agenda.

In this section, we first consider how this interactional structure is typically framed by the infant's cycles of visual attention. Then we focus on the process of mutual regulation that is thought to transpire within this frame. During this discussion, both observational and experimental studies concerning the dynamics of interpersonal events are considered.

Infants' Attention Modulation

Almost every recent issue of the major journals in developmental psychology contains at least one article about early infant–adult social interactions. The methodological uniformity of these articles is almost as striking as their frequency. Most researchers observe mothers and infants as they sit opposite one another in a face-to-face position. Most observe only when the infant is alert and at least in a moderately pleasant mood. Most instruct the mother to act as she typically does. Most videotape the proceedings and then repeatedly review the evidence to compile a detailed description of each participant's behavior.

The many decisions that underlie these methodological commonalities were first delineated in edited volumes published in the mid-1970s (e.g., Lewis & Rosenblum, 1974; Schaffer, 1977). Among the most influential contributions were chapters written by Brazelton, Stern, and their respective colleagues (Brazelton et al., 1974, 1975; Stern, 1974; Stern et al., 1977; see also Trevarthen, 1977). Several aspects of their innovative arrangements for the observation of adult–infant social interactions have been incorporated into the well-worn script of current research. However, along with their precedent-setting procedures, these pioneering studies also sowed the seeds for interpretive disputes that continue to thrive within the field.

Perhaps one of the most far-reaching decisions was to give priority to the infant's modulation of visual attention toward and away from the caregiver. This choice was informed by the realization that even when infants and adults both contribute to the structure of an ongoing interaction, they do not donate the same assets. Infants' primary contribution is their moment-by-moment modulation of attention; adults make a matching donation of responsive, attention-maintaining auditory, visual, and tactile actions.

This line of reasoning led Brazelton and his colleagues to conclude that an infant's "cycle of looking and nonlooking, or attention and nonattention" was "the unit of choice" for detailed descriptions of how very young infants interact with their mothers (1974, p. 49). Similarly, it prompted Stern to decide to "focus almost exclusively on the continuously operating 'on' and 'off' of infant visual attention" that "provides the regulatory background in which other expressive behaviors are largely prepared for, occur, and terminate" (1974, p. 195).

The emphasis on infants' attention—and more particularly, on infants' visual attention—has considerable intuitive appeal. As we noted earlier, the ability to initiate and maintain eye contact is one of 2-month-old infants' most striking social achievements. Moreover, the regulation of gaze is one of young infants' few means of modulating the effect of external stimulation on their internal state (Brazelton et al., 1974, 1975; Stern, 1974). If infants are becoming overaroused, they can look away; they cannot tone down the volume of a voice or walk away.

In addition, close tracking of young infants' visual attention during social interactions led to an intriguing result. Both Stern and Brazelton found that even though there is considerable variability in the relative amount of infants' gazing at and gazing away from mothers during periods of face-to-face interaction, the distribution of gaze-to-gaze intervals remains quite constant. Brazelton (et al., 1974) reported an average of 4.4 cycles of attention/nonattention per minute, and Stern (1974) reported a median gaze-to-gaze interval of 6.8 seconds. These comparable findings support the suggestion that infants' pattern of gaze alternation toward and away from a social partner may be controlled by intrinsic biological processes, as well as by current interactive events.

In the Brazelton and Stern studies, the mothers almost always maintained a steady gaze on their partner. That is, at least overtly, mothers did not cycle their attention. Even more interestingly, they modulated their other communicative activities in seeming synchrony with the infants' cycles of attention. Thus, Brazelton and his colleagues noted that

> The most important rule for maintaining an interaction seemed to be that a mother develop a sensitivity to her infant's capacity for attention and his need for withdrawal—partial or complete—after a period of attention to her. (1974, p. 59)

Stern expressed a similar conclusion when he summarized his observations with the statement that

> the goal of play activity is the mutual regulation of stimulation so as to maintain an optimal level of arousal which is affectively positive. The mother contributes to the regulation by almost constantly altering her behavior, using as cues changes in the infant's visual attention and state. (1974, p. 210)

To track fluctuations in infants' visual attention and concomitant changes in maternal behavior, both Brazelton and Stern made three additional methodological decisions, all of which continue to shape current research. First, they both decided that they could best study crucial processes if they confined their observations to periods when the adult and infant were both available for social play. Brazelton actively orchestrated this situation in the laboratory by asking each mother to play with her infant as he or she sat in a custom-built, adjustable, reclining seat (designed by Trevarthen; for pictures, see Trevarthen, 1977, pp. 242–245). In contrast, Stern (1974) observed mothers and infants at home for an entire morning, selecting out brief segments of spontaneous social play. These two procedures still plot the range of observational strategies found in recent work. They also illustrate researchers' rather narrow concentration on samples of mother–infant interaction "while it was going well" (Brazelton et al., 1974, p. 51).

The second methodological decision was to preserve observations using film and, as soon as it became available, videotape. The value of being able to view a segment repeatedly, particularly in slow motion and from the various angles that more than one camera can afford, cannot be overstated (see Bullowa, 1979). The suspicion always lingers, however, that what adults do in front of a researcher's camera may be only a pale reflection of their activities beyond its reach.

Thirdly, both studies paid particular attention to the flow of actions as they occurred second-by-second (or in Stern's case, .6 sec by .6 sec). This approach reflects a commitment to the more general notion that microanalytic data techniques might help to reveal the intricate patterns between actions over time, and that in turn, such patterns might help us to understand how caregivers and young infants can construct together finely synchronized interactions.

Thus, as with any central methodological choice, the initial decision to organize observations of communicative behavior within the frame of infants' gaze influenced subsequent decisions, from how to position subjects to the length of the temporal interval used for coding observations. Therefore, it is important to review the rationale behind this decision whenever a new study is being planned, to consider its merits for each new case.

Such a review is particularly crucial when a researcher sets out to investigate infant–adult communication within a new cultural or clinical context. In some contexts, the visual channel may not be the primary location of infants' attention modulation. In some cultures, mothers are hesitant to look continually toward their infants (see above; LeVine, 1990). And, in some parent–infant dyads, blindness of either partner cuts the visual channel. Crucial adaptations might be missed in such instances if researchers focus primarily on the infant's gaze patterns.

For example, Adamson, Als, Tronick, and Brazelton (1977) reported how a sighted infant differentially altered her gaze patterns during periods of interpersonal engagement when she interacted with her blind parents. Her gaze patterns framed social interactions when she interacted with sighted familiar adults and with her father, who retained many of the mannerisms of a sighted person after he lost his sight late in childhood. In particular, he modulated his facial expressions, timing them relative to his daughter's gaze, which he reported that he could monitor by locating the sound of her breath. In contrast, the infant actively and continually averted her gaze from her congenitally blind mother's immobile face, resisting all efforts to entice face-to-face orientation. Nevertheless, this mother and daughter did sustain mutually regulated periods of interpersonal engagement. By the end of the first month, the mother often sat the baby on her lap, facing outward. From this vantage point, the mother was able to monitor the infant's state of attention through her body movements and sounds, and the infant was able to attend to her mother's responsive vocalizations and touches.

Reciprocity and Synchrony

Despite their common insights and methods, the Brazelton and Stern studies did not converge completely. Although both noted regularities in the alternation of infants' gaze, their results were interpreted in a subtly but, from the perspective of current research, importantly different manner. Brazelton and his colleagues (1974, 1975) stressed patterns in the flow of infants' attention, suggesting that they might be conforming to underlying biological cycles or rhythms. They noted that these cycles might exist on several levels. For example, they noted that attention during a typical period of interaction can be broken into segments of *initiation, orientation, state of attention, acceleration, peak of excitement, deceleration,* and *withdrawal or turning away.* Within each segment, an infant's attention would alternately build up and wane.

Stern, in contrast, spoke only in terms of distributions of mothers' and infants' gazes toward and away from each other. Indeed, he explicitly cautioned that if the biological underpinnings of gaze alteration were organized rhythmically, "the constraint in social gazing would be immense, and the flexibility required for the social task would not be available" (1974, p. 202). Further, while Stern carefully stuck close to the data and shied away from terms that he could not operationalize (but see his more recent discussion of infants' subjective experience in Stern, 1985), Brazelton and his colleagues wrote provocatively about *reciprocity* and *synchrony* without providing precise empirical definitions.

The stage was set for follow-up studies that might better explicate these compelling concepts. Several research teams took on this challenge. Using the general methodological approach laid out in the early studies, they have been investigating two complex issues. The first concerns how best to characterize the temporal structure of periods of interpersonal engagement. For example, do adults and infants routinely alternate their bursts of action so that they conform to a turn-taking structure? The second issue involves the source of these structures. Are they imposed by the mother or by the infant's endogenous rhythms of attention? Or do the partners negotiate the structure as interactions unfold?

For two decades now, researchers have pursued these two issues. Although they do not yet agree on the reasons why infant–adult face-to-face interactions are intricately structured, they have evolved a series of strategies that have revealed some of the fascinating nuances of these interpersonal events. These strategies can be divided into two complementary categories (see Chapter 3): the application of microanalytic procedures that generate fine-grained descriptions of interactions and the use of experimental paradigms that help to untangle infants' from adults' contributions to these interactions.

Engagement Observed: Microanalytic Approaches

In order to study the temporal structure of adult–infant interactions, investigators usually adopt procedures that allow them to note fine details related to *what* acts occurred *when* within a stream of behavior. These procedures are often called *microanalytic* (in contrast with narrative reports or global ratings) because they generate detailed information about the occurrence of prespecified codes that can then be analyzed using quantitative data analytic procedures.

Investigators have tended to represent adult–infant interactions in one of two ways. The first tactic entails the precise coding of successive behavioral events or time intervals. Researchers might note, for example, every time an infant smiles or an adult vocalizes. Alternatively, they might observe for a prespecified time interval (for example, 1 second or 15 seconds) and note whether it contained an infant's smile or an adult's vocalization. Either way, this *categorical sequence* (or discrete behavior) approach results in sequences of categorical or nominal data. That is, the interaction can be represented as a series of codes that specifies (within the limits of the coding scheme and the coder's accuracy) what transpired during an interaction. (For a general introduction to this popular approach, see Bakeman & Gottman, 1986; for well-executed examples of its use in the study of mother–infant interaction, see Fogel, 1988, and Kaye & Fogel, 1980.)

The second tactic—the *phase scaling* approach—stems from Brazelton's (et al., 1974) description of the various segments of a period of interaction. Tronick and his colleagues (Gianino & Tronick, 1988; Tronick et al., 1979; Tronick, Als, & Brazelton, 1980; see also Beebe & Gerstman, 1980) have developed a particularly interesting version of this approach which elaborates on the suggestion by Brazelton and his colleagues that there is a certain amount of "affective attention available to each member of the dyad" (1974, p. 55). Essentially, they scale participants' level of involvement over the course of an interaction. This is done by first describing each participant's behavior (using the categorical sequence approach). Then these codes are weighted and summed. Based on the score that is derived, each second of an interaction is then assigned to one of several phases which are arranged in terms of the amount and affective quality of attention displayed. This approach generates a description of each partner's level of affectivity and attention in terms of a series of *monadic* phases that vary along a dimension ranging from *avoid* through *monitor* and up to *play* and *talk*.

These two approaches can provide complementary views of the same interaction. The categorical approach clearly involves less manipulation of data codes. However, the phase scaling approach may help to capture nuances in the fluctuation of attention better than codes that are tied more closely to specific behaviors. Several published exchanges have debated the relative merits of sticking close to observables. For example, even though Fogel (1988) faults the monadic phase scaling procedure for lacking the conceptual and empirical validity of discrete codes (a charge that Cohn and Tronick, 1988a, attempt to counter), he acknowledges that it permits the application of elegant statistical procedures, such as spectral analysis, that the categorical sequence approach alone does not.

Happily, these two tactics are currently yielding converging findings about how infants' attentional behavior is organized during periods of interpersonal engagement. For example, Kaye and Fogel (1980) videotaped 1½-, 3-, and 6-month-old infants as they interacted with their mothers. They then used the categorical sequence approach to describe when infants' attention was *on* and *off,* when mothers' facial expressiveness was *on* and *off,* and the relation between infants' attention and maternal facial activity. One of their central findings was that, in disagreement with the conclusions of Brazelton and his colleagues (1974; see also Lester, Hoffman, & Brazelton, 1985), neither the infants' nor the mothers' activities appeared rhythmic in any periodic sense. Instead, mutual regulation appeared to be achieved by *short-term bidirectional responsiveness.* That is, both the mother and infant seemed to be reacting to what their partner just did; neither seemed to be continually synchronizing acts to the partner's periodic cycles. Cohn and Tronick (1988b), in an elegantly and tightly argued study that used a monadic phase scaling approach, provide converging evidence for this claim.

Analyses of both discrete behavioral and scaled monadic phase codes have also begun to produce interesting suggestions about how adults and infants influence each other's activities during periods of interpersonal engagement. For example, there is growing evidence that the relative influence of the adult and the infant changes developmentally, although there is as yet no consensus about the pattern of change. Cohn and Tronick (1988b) report that mothers and 3- and 9-month-old infants are equally influential in directing the flow of the interaction while at 6 months, infants are more likely to take the lead. In contrast, Kaye and Fogel report that the exchange becomes steadily more balanced as infants shift from "mere responsiveness to spontaneous, reciprocal communication" (1980, p. 463).

In addition, researchers have begun to notice patterns other than the reciprocal pattern of conversational turn taking within mother–infant interactions. For example, Kaye (1982a) found that there were periods when maternal and infant actions clearly overlapped, as well as periods when their actions alternated. For instance, a mother might nod her head and smile as her infant vocalizes (an example of *backchanneling*), or she might mirror the vocalization in an attempt to prolong it (an example of *chorusing*). In either case, smooth communication involves the co-occurrence or synchrony of behavior rather than turn-taking alternations.

Furthermore, there has been a growing appreciation of the developmental significance of moments when the interaction does *not* appear to be running smoothly. For example, Stifter and Moyer (1991) recently suggested that infants may take momentary breaks from an interaction to regulate their arousal level, a maneuver that allows them to remain within the interaction. In support of this notion, they report that during a pleasurable game of peekaboo, 5-month-old infants are more likely to avert their gaze when they have just smiled intensely than when they have reacted with less glee.

An emphasis on the positive function of seemingly rougher moments during infant–adult interactions can also be found in several recent discussions of the phenomenon of *miscoordination*. Researchers have had to switch perspectives in order to attend to miscoordination. At first, they were most impressed by how well infants and adults could match and synchronize their respective actions and attention during periods of face-to-face interaction. Then they began to notice that these processes were far from perfect. For example, Tronick and Cohn (1989; see also Messer & Vietze, 1988) observed that the phenomena of mismatching monadic phases (for example, the infant is in *avert*; the mother in *talk*) and dissynchrony (e.g., an infant moves to a phase higher on the scale, while his mother moves lower) occur considerably more often than matching and synchrony, although these important phenomena did occur.

These observations suggest that during early social interactions, partners must often repair interactive missteps. Tronick and Cohn speculated that this process of reparation may serve to foster the development of infants' interactive skills (see also Tronick, Ricks, & Cohn, 1982). Golinkoff and Gordon raised a similar point during a discussion of the language-filled conversations that occur much later in infancy. They urged researchers to pay particular attention to how infants and adults repair a misunderstanding, because it may be during these negotiations that "the infant is gaining much insight into what does and does not work for creating joint attention and a shared focus" (1988, p. 122).

In summary, several recent studies indicate that probably by an infant's third month and certainly by the middle of her first year, the organization of episodes of shared interpersonal attention is actively negotiated by two influential partners, not simply assured by the infant's endogenous, rhythmic processes or by the adult's continual adjustments. These episodes may thus provide the arena for such critical processes as the mutual regulation of affect (Gianino & Tronick, 1988) and the production of specific communicative acts such as vocalizations (see, e.g., Stevenson, Ver Hoeve, Roach, & Leavitt, 1986) and facial expressions (e.g., Trevarthen, 1979). Moreover, as young infants and their caregivers communicate, mutual regulation may lead both to streams of smooth synchrony and alteration and to moments of mismatch and disengagement. Engagement in such episodes may therefore provide infants with their first experiences of interpersonal negotiation based on ongoing behavioral and emotional adjustment.

Engagement Manipulated: Experimental Paradigms

Analyses of ongoing social interactions reveal the responsiveness of both infant and adult during episodes of shared attention. However, they do not allow us to ascribe with confidence certain capacities to young infants. Is Trevarthen (1988) correct that 2-month-old infants can express *awareness*? Do young infants appreciate the affective meaning of an adult's display? Or are caregivers so prone to interpret even unintended acts as meaningful (Adamson et al., 1987) and so skilled in modulating their own expressive actions (Kaye, 1982a) that they orchestrate early social interactions so that their infants merely appear to be, but are not really, active participants?

One strategy for addressing such questions entails manipulating adults' activity so that their contribution to the interaction is constrained. Through experimental controls, researchers hope to view the infant's capacities separately from the adult's supportive actions. In general, these studies provide convincing evidence that young infants are capable contributors to periods of interpersonal engagement. They demonstrate not only that young infants notice changes in their partners' activities, but also that they can act adaptively when faced with unexpected communicative displays.

Typically, experimenters ask mothers to alter their behavior, although some clever researchers have developed ways to use video technology to alter it only from the infant's perspective (e.g., Gusella, Muir, & Tronick, 1988; Murray & Trevarthen, 1985). Although acting atypically in front of one's infant takes considerable effort, adults are often able to comply with a researcher's request for a few minutes. In some instances, their task is made relatively easy because the manipulation, such as asking mothers to imitate their infants' behavior, does not dramatically disrupt the infant's positive attention and affect (Field, 1977a, b; Symons & Moran, 1987). However, in most experimental studies the manipulation disturbs the natural flow of an interaction.

One particularly popular procedure requires that the adult stare at the infant with a neutral, unchanging expression. This *still-face* paradigm (Tronick et al., 1978; see also Chapter 3) has been used in numerous studies (see Cohn & Elmore, 1988; Ellsworth, Muir, & Hains, 1993; Field, Vega-Lahr, Scafidi, & Goldstein, 1986; Fogel, Diamond, Langhorst, & Demos, 1982; Gusella et al., 1988; Legerstee, Pomerleau, Malcuit, & Feider, 1987; Stack & Muir, 1992).

Infants as young as 2 months of age detect and react rapidly to their mothers' still-face displays, often by dampening their displays of positive affect and decreasing their attentiveness. This effect has been documented repeatedly by systematically comparing infants' behavior in the still-face condition with their behavior during periods of normal face-to-face interaction (Tronick et al., 1978) or even periods when they are left alone (Field et al., 1986). However, the qualitative character of their reaction is best captured by narrative reports (or better yet, videotaped records) that provide a fuller picture of an infant's dramatic appraisal of the unexpected display. For example, Tronick and his colleagues reported as a typical response the following reaction to the entrance of a mother who remained still-faced:

> As the mother enters, [the infant's] hand movements stop. He looks up at her, makes eye-to-eye contact and smiles. Her masklike face does not change. He looks away quickly to one side and remains quiet, his facial expression serious. He remains this way for 20 seconds. Then he looks back at her face, his eyebrows and lids raised, his hands and arms startling slightly out toward her. He quickly looks down at his hands, stills for 8 seconds, and then checks her face once more. This look is cut short by a yawn, with his eyes and face turning upward. His fingers pull at the fingers of his other hand, the rest of his body is motionless. The yawn and neck stretches last 5 seconds. He throws out one arm in a slight startle and looks briefly at her face. Arm movements are jerky, his mouth curves downward, his eyes narrow and partially lid. He turns his face to the side, but he keeps his mother in peripheral vision. He fingers his hand again, his legs stretch toward her and rapidly jerk back again. He arches forward, slumps over, tucks his chin down on one shoulder, but he looks up at her face from under his lowered eyebrows. This position lasts for over a minute, with brief checking looks at the mother occurring almost every 10 seconds. . . . (1978, pp. 7–8)

This narrative illustrates two important aspects of the infant's typical reaction to a still-faced mother's violation of the expected rules of interpersonal engagement. First, infants rapidly regulate their affectivity in response to a partner's displays. When an adult enters, infants orient and smile. If this greeting is not reciprocated, though, infants quickly sober and look wary.

Second, infants are typically able to modulate their attention so that they do not have to fully sever the communicative channel. They do not completely shut off their own availability to their partner by crying or falling asleep. Rather, they restrict the channel by taking short glances, peripheral peeks, or yawn-interrupted looks.

It is too early to present a consensus view of the processes that underlie infants' attentional and affective responses during experimentally distorted interactions; indeed, important data are still being collected. However, there are now some intriguing threads of evidence that may ultimately be woven together.

One thread involves developmental changes with respect to which aspects of their partners' behavior most affect infants. Clearly the still-face paradigm alters the quality of the adults' expressions across several modalities. By systematically varying the still-face procedure, it may be possible to discern the relative importance of tactile, facial, and vocal stimulation during ongoing social interactions. In particular, we may gain a fuller understanding of the communicative functions of touching during early social interactions.

Recent studies suggest that young infants may be particularly sensitive to disruptions of interactive touching. For example, Gusella (et al., 1988) compared the way in which 3- and 6-month-old infants reacted in the still-face condition during two studies that used different contrast conditions. In the first study, mothers were asked to interact normally, using as they wished their faces, voices, and hands. In the second study, mothers were asked to interact normally but to refrain from touching the infant. Six-month-old infants were sensitive to changes in their mothers' face and voice, regardless of whether or not maternal touch was allowed during the contrast condition. However, the younger infants displayed a significant difference between the contrast and still-face conditions only when touch was permitted during the normal interaction.

Moreover, in a series of studies using carefully crafted modifications of the still-face paradigm, Stack and Muir (1990, 1992) found that an infant may react positively to an adult's active touching even when the adult is not modulating her facial expression and her voice. For example, they have found that 5-month-old infants' negative reaction to an adult's still face is often mitigated when the adult actively touches the infant, even when the infant cannot see the adult's hands. In contrast, passive touching did not reduce the still-face effect that occurs when no touching is permitted.

These findings raise several interesting possibilities that need to be explored further. Perhaps the deletion of touch during social interactions with young infants may itself present the infant with a partner who is acting unexpectedly. Perhaps touch is a particularly potent (but so far underappreciated) attention-getting procedure that adults contribute to the regulation of the first periods of interpersonal engagement (see Kaye & Fogel, 1980).

A second thread involves the relation between periods of normal and experimentally distorted interaction. In their initial study, Tronick and his colleagues suggested that there may be a brief carryover from the still-face condition to an immediately subsequent period of social interaction. When a still-faced mother returned to normal, an infant usually monitored her warily for a moment. Occasionally an infant would arch away "as if he had not forgiven her the previous insult" (1978, p. 10) before reengaging with her. More extensive study of the carryover across conditions suggests that even brief experiences with distorted interpersonal engagement may be cumulative. For example, infants tend to display less optimal affect and attention even after their temporarily still-faced mothers resume their normal activity (e.g., Fogel et al., 1982; Gusella et al., 1988).

This line of research is beginning to reveal young infants' remarkable sensitivity to partners' activities as well as their persistence in seeking renewed engagement with a partner who is at least momentarily nonresponsive. These two qualities were highlighted by Cohn and Elmore (1988), who modified the still-face paradigm so that mothers became still-faced briefly whenever the babies expressed positive affect. They were especially troubled by the infants' willingness to repeatedly engage in interactions with their oddly acting mother because they think it may indicate that "the potential to learn maladaptive patterns of interaction during infancy appears to be high" (1988, p. 502).

Yet a third thread adds new data which further elaborate the young infants' social–perceptual competence. Researchers have long hypothesized that even young infants discriminate the social from the nonsocial (e.g., Brazelton et al., 1974; Trevarthen, 1977), but designing adequate studies to test this hypothesis has proved extremely difficult (e.g., compare the findings of Frye, Rawling, Moore, & Myers, 1983, and Legerstee et al., 1987). Recently, Ellsworth and her colleagues (1993; see also Legerstee, Corter, & Kienapple, 1990) expanded the still-face paradigm to allow comparisons between 3-month-old infants' reaction to people (both mothers and strangers) during interactive and still-faced conditions, and an assortment of still and interactive objects which varied in their degree of facedness. Infants seemed to possess a rudimentary ability to categorize events into people and objects by reserving their communicative behavior such as smiling and vocalizing for adults, regardless of their current level of responsiveness.

Summary: Studies of Interpersonal Engagement

A large and diverse group of researchers has focused on describing the interplay between adults' and infants' actions during periods of interpersonal engagement. Together they have refined observational and experimental procedures that allow the precise description of communicative behavior. Overall, their investigations leave little doubt that 2- to 6-month-old infants and their caregivers can fill the communicative channel with modulated affective messages.

Theme and Variation: Affect and Maternal Depression

One of this chapter's central themes is that communication between young infants and their caregivers involves a mutuality of their attention and affect. Nuanced expressions reflecting each participant's current engagement are blended to compose an ongoing dialogue.

In this section, this theme is elaborated in two ways. First, we consider some implications of the contention that communication during this developmental period involves the sharing of affect. During this discussion, the distinction between interpersonal and intrapersonal processes is emphasized. Then we consider how disturbances of an individual's affective expressiveness such as those that are concomitant to maternal depression may alter the process of interpersonal engagement. Second, we view episodes of interpersonal engagement within a developmental perspective relative to previous periods of shared attentiveness and future periods of joint object involvement.

The Sharing of Affect

During periods of interpersonal engagement, infants as young as 2 months of age often appear to be fairly adept communicative partners. During an ongoing social interaction, they can express themselves with clarity and modulate their level of receptivity to their partners' actions.

It is tempting to consider these stunning performances as affirmation that young infants as individuals can be accomplished communicators, as long as the topic remains focused on the immediate relation between themselves and their partners. However, such a conclusion may be unwarranted. H. R. Schaffer captured its shortcomings well when he lamented that

> conclusions about *interactions* are different from conclusions about *interactants;* yet, on the basis of the former, some authors have been tempted into ascribing considerable competence to individual infants, describing their behavior in terms of "primitive intentions," "expectations," "communicative skills," "readiness to share," and so forth. Such terms are highly interpretative. . . . (1984, p. 77)

An issue involving the *unit of analysis* lies at the core of Schaffer's concern. He is charging that it is unwise to generate conclusions about *intra*personal processes (intentions, skills, and such) when the unit of analysis is really *inter*personal. In term of Werner and Kaplan's (1963) image of the primordial sharing situation (see Figure 2.1), we must not be misled to think that processes occurring in the area of overlap between the mother and infant necessarily also occur outside of this area. In terms of Vygotsky's (1978; see Chapter 2) image of the zone of proximal development, we must try to determine whether an infant is able to perform an activity without the active guidance of a more sophisticated partner.

Several psychologists have recently tried to embrace this issue rather than to despair about its implications. For example, Tronick has urged researchers to shift their unit of analysis from the individual infant who "is isolated, independent, and without context" to "the infant in contact with an adult" (1982, p. 2). Further, he has suggested that during early infancy, it may be most fruitful to conceptualize the infant and caregiver as an *affective regulatory unit* (p. 3). In other words, during episodes of interpersonal engagement, the actions of an infant and a caregiver are interrelated within an exchange that has the regulation of affectivity as its primary aim.

This perspective has focused attention on the quality of ongoing regulations during infant–caregiver interactions, as well as on the relation between current communicative episodes and later relationships. It highlights the inevitability of moments of friction as each participant actively adjusts his or her behavior. For example, Tronick and Cohn (1989; see above) were inspired by this view to notice that ongoing interactions inevitably contain moments of miscoordination. Moreover, it has prompted concern about the long-term effects that might arise if an infant joins an affective regulatory unit that persistently malfunctions (Stern, 1977, 1985).

It is important to note that there is often remarkable resiliency within parent-infant dyads. Particularly impressive are reports of how affect sharing can be achieved despite congenital blindness of either the parent (Adamson et al., 1977, summarized above) or the infant (Als, 1982).

Case reports also document how difficult it often is to predict whether current interactive difficulties are the beginning of a permanently maladaptive pattern. For example, when Stern cataloged various ways that mothers and young infants can fail to establish a satisfactory pattern of regulating attention and positive affectivity, he repeatedly cautioned against viewing current "missteps in the dance" (1977, p. 109) as enduring arrangements. He illustrated his concern by noting how many dyads spontaneously resolve formidable interactional difficulties. One of his case reports contains a painful description of a mother who continually intruded and overstimulated her 3-month-old daughter who reacted with active gaze aversion and negative affect. In his narration of this report, Stern expresses both his alarm at witnessing the emergence of an unrelenting chase/dodge pattern and his relief that somehow this mother and infant were able to break out of this disturbing pattern.

Nevertheless, there is growing concern that some mothers who are experiencing significant psychological problems may repeatedly disrupt rather than support affective regulation in ways that negatively impact future communication development. Researchers have been especially interested in the effect of maternal postpartum depression, both because it is a prevalent disorder and because it seems to strike to the core of the mother's crucial contribution to early development.

To study the effect of maternal depression on early episodes of interpersonal engagement, researchers have skillfully combined systematic observational methods and experimental manipulations of maternal behavior. They are finding indications that maternal depression may have an immediate effect on affect sharing.

Monadic phase analyses of social interactions between mothers with depressed mood and their 3-month-old infants suggest that their interactions tend to be less synchronous and more negative than those between nondepressed mothers and infants (Field, Healy, Goldstein, & Guthertz, 1990; see also Cohn, Matias, Tronick, Lyons-Ruth, & Connell, 1986). Experimental manipulations revealed a similar phenomenon. When nondepressed mothers simulated depression by speaking in a monotone, remaining relatively expressionless, and minimizing body movements, their young infants tended to greet only briefly and then avert their gaze and express negative affect (Cohn & Tronick, 1983).

Evidence is also accumulating that suggests that infants may initially actively attempt to adjust to their depressed mothers' relatively unresponsive behavior, but that over time, they too may become unresponsive. Cohn, Campbell, Matias, and Hopkins (1990) report that, although the interactions of depressed mothers and their 2-month-old infants are far less positive than those of nondepressed pairs, the degree to which infants and mothers influenced each other's behavior did not seem related to the mothers' diagnostic status. By infants' fourth month, however, the interactions of depressed mothers and their infants increasingly lack contingent responsiveness (see Cohn et al., 1986; Field et al., 1990). Tiffany Field and her colleagues (Field et al., 1988) have suggested that the infant too has developed a depressive style. In a study that compared how infants of depressed and nondepressed mothers interacted face-to-face with their own mother and with a nondepressed stranger, the researchers found that infants of depressed mothers may not only generalize to interactions with other adults, but also seem to elicit depressive behavior from a nondepressed partner.

These studies support the notion that infants regulate interaction in ways that affect their developing engagement with others (Gianino & Tronick, 1988). Thus, depressed mothers' flat affect, inattentiveness, and irritability may be abstracted as the initial and as a continuing cause of disturbed interpersonal engagement. However, as Field and her colleagues suggest, their infants may begin "to turn to self-regulatory behavior such as head and gaze aversion in an attempt to reduce the negative affect engendered by unresponsive maternal behavior" (1988, p. 1575). Thus they too may contribute to a less than optimal developmental process as they actively modulate their attention and affect in response to their mothers' less than optimal regulatory activities.

Turning Outward toward Objects

Compared to periods of shared attentiveness, episodes of interpersonal engagement have a coherent texture as each partner directs undivided attention toward the other and displays distinct expressions of affect.

These episodes also have an extraordinarily intimate quality. Two partners with vastly dissimilar skills join together as two confidants who share emotional presence.

As depicted in Figure 2.6, not all aspects of communication are brought to the forc during episodes of interpersonal engagement. Objects and events in the immediate surrounding are not explicitly referenced. The symbolic code is not yet used intentionally to convey messages about the past or future. Nevertheless, the forthright focus on each other and on the communicative channel prepares for the appearance of objects and symbols. When patterns of interpersonal regulation become familiar by the sixth month of life, infants suddenly become fascinated with objects and events that lie beyond the current connection between themselves and their partners. Their new curiosity unsettles established interactional patterns.

As the scope of communication expands to accommodate new interests, new developmental challenges arise. A new arrangement of triadic attention between infant, partner, and objects must be formed; new modes of communicative action, such as gestures and words, are soon to be acquired. It is noteworthy that infants approach these challenges only after months of immersion within episodes of interpersonal engagement. Already able to face partners who can guide their new explorations, infants turn outward to objects.

CHAPTER

6

Joint Object Involvement

CHAPTER OUTLINE

By their fifth month, infants share intricately textured episodes of interpersonal engagement with their caregivers. Both partners actively contribute to these episodes, and both seem to find them amusing. But then these episodes suddenly fade from view. Infants who just weeks before delighted in face-to-face conversation begin to turn their attention away from their partners and toward objects.

Observers have long been struck by both the suddenness and the promise of this turn toward objects. For example, in his account of the origins of intelligence, Piaget (1963/1936; see Chapter 1) focused his observations during the middle of the first year on the emergence of acts on objects. Almost a century ago, Milicent W. Shinn began the chapter entitled "The Era of Handling Things" in her *The Biography of a Baby* with the observation that her 5-month-old niece "sprang into this era suddenly, within four days . . . unlocking a dozen other doors of mental life" (1900, p. 141).

In the domain of communication, the advent of object interest places the infant at the entry to referential communication. During the next several months infants and their partners negotiate the process of importing objects and events into the interpersonal sphere. By the end of this third developmental phase, they are able to share object-focused topics and elaborate upon their common interests in their surroundings. They can request objects from each other, and they can refer each other to interesting events. Moreover, they can begin to comment on these events, conveying messages about their details and their affective significance. Thus, as long as the topic remains present, infants near the end of the first year and their social partners can enter episodes of joint object involvement that serve a range of fundamental communicative functions.

The developmental path leading to object-focused communication is filled with many challenges. Some of these arise because infants must master new communicative acts that pertain primarily to objects rather than to the communicators themselves. They must, for example, come to look where an extended index finger points rather than at the digit itself. They also must realize that a gleeful laugh might relate information about the desirability of a toy as well as a statement about the vocalizer's pleasure.

An additional challenge stems from the inherent complexity of the attentional demands of joint object involvement. This complexity is depicted in the model of a communicative episode introduced in Chapter 2. Notice that in the image for the third phase of communication development (Figure 2.7), the *message* is depicted as a triangle that joins the two *participants* and *objects*. This new triadic arrangement supports referential messages such as "Look at this" and requests such as "Give me that." To convey such seemingly simple messages, communicators achieve a complex coordination of attention between each other and an object. A singular focus would result in either interpersonal engagement as the infant attends to the partner, or it would sever the communicative channel as the infant attends exclusively to objects.

In this chapter's first section, we consider the emergence of infants' capacity to convey and comprehend object-focused messages, paying specific attention to how they begin to coordinate their attention to both people and objects, and to master the communicative functions of requesting and referring. In its second section, we switch our focus to caregivers to describe their contribution to joint object involvement. Here we note how adults often enhance infants' object interest with interpretations, scaffolds, and cultural props and plans.

In the third section, we examine how infants and caregivers structure episodes of joint object involvement. Here we consider how they manage their communication, and we weight their relative contributions to orchestrating communicative routines. In addition, we discuss various explanations for why and when object-focused communication emerges. In the closing section, we abstract one of this period's dominant themes, the interplay between infants' object interest and adults' developmentally attuned support. Then we consider the striking variations on this theme that occur when an infant has a developmental disorder such as autism which may hinder his or her capacity to attend to certain aspects of the environment.

Infants' Object-Focused Messages

Piaget's (1963/1936) observations of his three children provide a useful sketch of two phases in the movement from body-focused (or *primary*) action schemes to object-focused (or *secondary*) ones. Beginning at about 4 to 6 months of age, infants repeatedly perform a single action on an object so that they can "make interesting spectacles last" (p. 196). For example, Piaget (1963/1936, Observation 111, pp. 198–199) recorded how, during her sixth and seventh months, his daughter Lucienne tried to use her favorite scheme of pedaling to move objects as diverse as an eraser in her hand, a hanging puppet, and a watch held near her face. Unlike previous episodes of leg movements, here Lucienne was focusing attention on her action's effect on objects rather than on the activity in and of itself. Then, after developing a repertoire of secondary schemes, Piaget's offspring began to coordinate these schemes into a series of two or more acts, all related to a single topic. For example, Piaget reported how at 9 months of age, his other daughter, Jacqueline, pulled on a string in order to grab hold of the attached toy duck (Observation 121, p. 215).

Piaget touted the significance of a 6-month-old's use of secondary schemes because now "the child really begins to act upon things" (1963/1936, p. 209) to preserve the interesting effects of her acts on objects. But he saved his greatest praise for the 9-month-old's first efforts at coordinating secondary schemes, proclaiming them to be the infant's "first actually intelligent behavior patterns"

(1963/1936, p. 210). Now, he thought, the infant's actions were undoubtedly *intentional* because she performed one scheme as a *means* in order that a specific *end* brought about by the performance of the second scheme could occur.

For our purposes, it is interesting that Piaget recorded several incidents during which the object of an infant's secondary scheme was a person rather than an inanimate thing. For example, he noted that Lucienne often pedaled her legs to get him to resume moving his hands, wagging his head, or opening and closing his mouth (Observation 116, p. 204). In his discussion of the emergence of the coordination of secondary schemes, he reported examples (Observations 127 and 128, pp. 223–224) in which the infant produced an action directed toward a person (e.g., gently moving Piaget's hand) as an intermediate step in producing a coveted result (e.g., having Piaget tap his cheek and drum on his eyeglasses). In short, as his children began to organize their actions on objects, they used their actions in interpersonal as well as in solitary contexts.

Piaget did not use these observations to discuss communication between people about objects. However, his work set the stage and, to a large measure, the agenda for such studies. First, during the 1960s, it inspired several psychologists to notice the nuances of the development of object manipulation skills. For example, Bruner (1969; see also White, 1971) discussed developmental changes in attention and intentionality in "Eye, Hand, and Mind," an essay he wrote in Piaget's honor. Then, in the 1970s, when several scholars began to ask how preverbal infants communicate about objects, they drew heavily on Piaget's work for guiding themes.

Two quite different groups of psychologists met over the issue of the emergence of object-focused communication (Adamson & Bakeman, 1982). One group became intrigued after its members studied social interactions during the early months of life (see Chapter 5). Their curiosity was piqued when they noticed that, unlike slightly younger infants, 6-month-olds who visited their laboratories for studies of early communication development often actively avoided their mothers' pleas for face-to-face play (Kaye & Fogel, 1980; Trevarthen & Hubley, 1978). This unexpected shift away from episodes of interpersonal engagement toward object absorption was later systematically verified in several longitudinal studies. For example, Lamb, Morrison, and Malkin (1987; see also Messer & Vietze, 1984) found that positive engagement during face-to-face social interaction steadily surged to a peak between 3 and 5 months and then declined.

A second group of researchers came to the study of early object-focused communication from the study of early language development (see Chapter 7). Almost simultaneously, many careful observers (e.g., Bates,

Camaioni, & Volterra, 1975; Dore, Franklin, Miller, & Ramer, 1976; Greenfield & Smith, 1976; Halliday, 1975, 1979) ventured back to infancy to see what infants are doing just before they begin using words. They were richly rewarded with observations of vocalizations and gestures that appeared to be important precursors to language. For example, Halliday announced the discovery of what he called a *proto-language,* a child tongue that "comes into being considerably earlier [than the mother tongue], at a time that is likely to be nearer the middle of the first year of life than the middle of the second" (1979, p. 172).

Each group of researchers brought different questions to the study of joint object involvement. The former sought to trace the transformation of earlier structures of interpersonal engagement; the latter to untangle roots of later-developing symbolic communication. Yet many from both groups recognized the need to observe infants closely as they developed nonverbal ways to use voices, gaze, and hands to convey messages to a partner about objects. Moreover, all were deeply influenced by Piaget's suggestion that this developmental period is characterized by two interrelated themes: the coordination of different acts and the emergence of intentionality.

These two themes permeate the voluminous literature about the emergence of object-focused communication that has accumulated over the past 20 years. In the following review, we first attend selectively to the theme of coordination of acts. We will find it central to how psychologists conceptualize the beginnings of infants' communication with partners about objects and the integration of already-developed communicative acts such as smiles and cries into object-focused dialogues. Then, we consider the emergence of communicative acts that serve the two fundamental intentions of requesting objects from a partner and referring a partner to an object.

Coordinating Attention between People and Objects

When two adults communicate, their coordination of attention between people and objects is usually so smooth that it is transparent. Yet upon reflection, it is clear that each person is modulating attention skillfully between different foci while maintaining an overarching state of engagement with both his partner and their joint topic. During the second half of their first year, infants typically master the rudiments of this complex coordination.

This important achievement builds upon the accomplishments of earlier periods, including the interpersonal engagement of the 3-month-old and the object-fascination of the 6-month-old. Its effect on communication is enormous. As Stern argued cogently, there is a "leap to intersubjective relatedness" (1985, p. 133). Now infants are positioned to share their own subjective experiences of objects with other people. Trevarthen and Hubley (1978) label intersubjectivity that encompasses both object-related and interpersonal topics *secondary intersubjectivity,* marking its crucial difference from earlier (or primary) intersubjectivity (see Chapter 5) using Piagetian-inspired terminology. Others (e.g., Bakeman & Adamson, 1984) have used the term *coordinated joint engagement* to focus specifically on infants' emerging capacity to attend simultaneously with a person and a shared object.

The developmental time line for the emergence of coordinated joint engagement spans several months. Its earliest manifestations occur around 6 months of age when a baby may switch her gaze back and forth between a caregiver and an object that lie in the same visual field (Newson & Newson, 1975). It is not until about 13 months of age, though, that most infants maintain periods of sustained attention to both a partner and objects (Bakeman & Adamson, 1984; Bates, Benigni, Bretherton, Camaioni, & Volterra, 1979; Harding & Golinkoff, 1979; Sugarman-Bell, 1978).

In order to chart the emergence of coordinated joint attention, Bakeman and I (Adamson & Bakeman, 1982; Bakeman & Adamson, 1984) did a longitudinal study in which we videotaped infants from 6- to 18-months of age as they played with their mothers. Inspired by studies of younger infants' arousal states (e.g., Wolff, 1987; see Chapter 4), we characterized how the infants deployed their attention to people and to objects in terms of engagement states. Our coders were trained to use a scheme that included codes for attention to both a person and a shared object (called *joint engagement*) as well as for attention only to the partner (*person engagement*) and attention only to objects (*object engagement*). They were also asked to differentiate two forms of joint engagement. During periods of *coordinated joint engagement,* the infant actively attends to both another person and the object that they share. For example, an infant might repeatedly look up from a book and smile towards his mother as she points to and names pictures. In contrast, during periods of *supported joint engagement,* the infant attends to the same object that the partner is actively involved with, but the baby does not appear to be aware of her involvement. For example, an infant might be intently absorbed in holding a toy truck still as her mother fills it with blocks. While this mother and infant are sharing an object, the infant has not opened a communicative channel, much less explicitly acknowledged her partner's role in elaborating the object world.

As expected, even at 6 months of age, the infants we observed devoted far more attention to objects than to people. Their high rate of object interest remained constant throughout the next year. In contrast, their attention to people changed significantly over the same time period. Person engagement, already rare at 6 months of age, steadily declined. Coordinated joint engagement began to appear at 12 months of age, although its rise was not marked until we observed again at 15 months. By then, almost all infants entered this state at least once while they played with their mothers.

This developmental time line contains a curious gap. Person engagement seems to fade before infants routinely integrate their involvement with objects with interpersonal engagement. However, this gap was not necessarily a period of communicative silence. Rather, all of the mothers that we observed worked deliberately and successfully to entice and maintain periods of supported joint engagement (Adamson & Bakeman, 1984). They encouraged shared object exploration, for example, by making an object come alive with sound and movement or by demonstrating how to operate a toy that the infant was inspecting.

In summary, coordinated joint engagement is the likely developmental heir of person engagement. However, the inheritance is not passed on without the contribution of more sophisticated communicative partners. Mothers (and in theory, any competent and willing adult) seem to induce a state of joint engagement before infants are capable of such performances on their own. In this way, partners may lend their support as the infant develops schemes for handling objects and then ways of coordinating these schemes. Moreover, with this support, interesting objects can be transported into communicative episodes months before infants can accomplish this movement on their own.

Coordinating Affective Expressions and Object Involvement

As infants turn their attention from person engagement to joint engagement, their repertoire of communicative acts expands to include gestures such as pointing that serve to direct attention toward objects. However, before we consider these new acts, it is important to ask about the fate of earlier-developing communicative acts such as smiles and cries.

The answer is twofold. First, within the moments of person engagement that remain, affective expressions retain their earlier-developed functions of regulating and filling the communicative channel. Second, the infant's affective expressions gradually become integrated into episodes of object involvement. They may mark the beginning of episodes of coordinated joint engagement, serving as a greeting or phatic acknowledgment that the communicative channel is open. In addition, infants may begin to use affective expressions as comments about shared object-focused experiences, and to seek out their partner's affective opinions about objects.

Affect as a Marker of the Communicative Channel

Even after objects become the favorite topic of shared focus, infants use affective expressions to acknowledge the beginning of interpersonal contact. For example, Bakeman and I found that 6- to 18-month-old infants tend to cluster their smiles and positively valanced vocalizations at the beginning of person and joint engagement episodes. In contrast, the beginning of periods of supported joint engagement, as well as periods of solitary object engagement, tend to be more sober affairs (Adamson & Bakeman, 1985).

Over time affective greetings combine with conventionalized acts (Bakeman & Adamson, 1986; see also Chapter 7). Many 12-month-old infants can punctuate the opening and closing of the communicative channel with a cheerful vocal "Hi" and an exuberant wave 'bye-bye'. Moreover, the message itself may become the focus of a routine exchange. For example, infants nearing their first birthday typically delight in the universal hello-and-goodbye game of peekaboo (Sroufe & Waters, 1976). Moreover, many 1-year-olds have perfected fake cries and shrill shrieks that are sure to open up the communicative channel with their caregivers (especially in public settings such as supermarkets; see Reddy, 1991, for examples).

Producing Affective Comments about Objects

During the last half of their first year and sometimes even earlier, infants begin to giggle at a partner's joke with an object (Sroufe & Waters, 1976) and to "muck about" as they engage in joint object–person play (Reddy, 1991; Trevarthen, 1988). For example, an infant may grin after an adult turns a doll on its head, or she may squeal with pleasure while teasingly retracting an object that she has just offered a partner.

The smooth incorporation of affective comments into such interchanges takes many months to perfect. In our longitudinal study, Bakeman and I found that positive affective comments were initially confined primarily to periods of supported joint engagement when a caregiver made objects move with a burst/pause temporal pattern reminiscent of earlier face-to-face interactions (Adamson & Bakeman, 1985). A 9-month-old infant might, for example, respond with a broad smile, gleeful squeal, and full-body shimmy of delight each time his mother scooted a doll toward him during a repetitive game of "I'm going to get you." Then infants progressively shortened their positive affective expressions and relied increasingly on vocalizations alone. Moreover, they started to use them in contexts that were less dependent on repetitive adult structuring. By 12 months of age, they often produced positive affective expressions during activities such as book reading and pretend telephoning, and by 18 months of age, their smiles and laughs punctuated periods of coordinated joint engagement.

The function of negatively toned expressions also seems to undergo a similar expansion during the end of the first year. As an infant turns attention outward, new reasons for crying emerge, including fear of new people, uncertainty about unfamiliar events, and frustration during play with objects (Lester, 1985). Gustafson and Green (1991) documented the developmental course infants follow as they begin to produce cries to comment to caregivers about objects. They found that cries, like positive affective expressions, became briefer by the end of the first year. Moreover, although *simple cries* (those occurring without looks or gestures) occurred throughout the first year, by 6 months infants were also coupling some of their cries with looks to the caregiver. By 12 months, a substantial proportion of the infants whom they observed were also producing *elaborated cries* that co-occurred with object-focused gestures such as pointing or with caregiver-directed reaches and tugs.

In summary, infants gradually harness an earlier-developing communicative form, affective expressions, to serve communicative functions during object-focused exchanges. As these acts are incorporated into the attentional frame of joint object involvement, infants begin to share their subjective experiences of objects with their social partners.

Seeking Affective Comments about Objects

By the end of the first year, infants not only produce affective comments about objects, they also actively seek others' emotional opinions. This tendency to consult others is strikingly evident when a 1-year-old infant is suddenly confronted with a novel event like a noisy new toy or a nosy stranger. Rather than react immediately, he may temporarily reserve judgment while engaging in a form of active emotional communication called *affective social referencing* (Campos & Stenberg, 1981). Here the infant looks warily at his caregiver, listens to her comment, and only then behaves relative to the event. If the caregiver expresses fear, the infant may fret and retreat; if she smiles encouragingly, he may happily advance toward the object. In short, the partner's message has helped the infant resolve his uncertainty about an ambiguous event.

Dozens of articles and essays (see, e.g., Feinman, 1992) have been devoted to detailing the emergence of affective social referencing. There are several reasons for this interest. Conceptually, affective social referencing appears as a prime milestone in the development of intersubjectivity and in the transmission of culture. Methodologically, affective social referencing has proven to be particularly amenable to controlled investigation.

With regard to intersubjectivity, it is interesting to consider what knowledge of other people infants reveal when they seek their opinions about objects. Many observers (see, e.g., Bretherton, 1992; Stern, 1985) suggest that infants' intentional pleas for another person's emotional reactions indicate that they possess a rudimentary *theory of mind.* That is, they seem to understand (without, of course, being able to expound on their theory) that other people have minds that contain a private or subjective store of intentions and information. Furthermore, they seem to assume that there is enough overlap between their own mind and other people's minds for the two to "interface" (Bretherton, 1992), so that communication about objects can transpire. Over the past decade, research on the emergence of children's theory of mind has been one of the most active areas in developmental research as investigators debate whether and how such theories are formulated (see, e.g., the edited volumes by Astington, Harris, & Olson, 1988; Frye & Moore, 1991; and Whiten, 1991; for an interesting account of social understanding at the end of the first year, see Moore & Corkum, in press).

The asymmetry of knowledge during early affective social referencing is also conceptually interesting. Given infants' social context, it is almost inevitable that when they are uncertain about the meaning of an object, they end up consulting with caregivers who are far more experienced than they are in the ways of the world. Thus infants' search for information allows them access to their caregivers' vast store of experience with and knowledge of objects (Kaye, 1982b; Rogoff, 1990).

Given the theoretical significance of infants' affective social referencing, it is fortunate that this process has been rather easy to transport into the laboratory. In particular, our understanding of affective social referencing has been enhanced by the repeated use of a carefully controlled *ASR paradigm* introduced by Mary Klinnert (1984; Klinnert et al., 1983).

The essential elements of the ASR paradigm parallel the phases that occur naturally. First, the infant is confronted with an event that is likely to induce uncertainty. Researchers have used novel objects such as large robots (Walden & Ogan, 1988) or small mechanical toys (Rosen, Adamson, & Bakeman, 1992), a stranger (Feinman & Lewis, 1983), a live animal (Gunnar & Stone, 1984; Hornik & Gunnar, 1988), and even a moderate visual cliff (that is, an apparent drop-off in the floor's surface that might be too steep for the infant to negotiate; Sorce, Emde, Campos, & Klinnert, 1985).

Second, the researchers wait for the infant to look toward the communicative partner. When this occurs, the partner complements the infant's request with a clear message about the affective significance of the uncertainty-provoking event. Partners are usually trained to provide a specific emotional message, such as happiness or fear, using a standardized facial expression either alone (Klinnert, 1984; Sorce et al., 1985; Zarbatany & Lamb, 1985) or in combination with verbal script (Hirshberg & Svejda, 1990; Walden & Ogan, 1988). One of the advantages of the ASR paradigm is that the match between message and object can be systematically manipulated. For example, partners in one group may be instructed to smile broadly when their infants are faced with a mooing cow toy, while those in a second group may be asked to make a fearful face.

Finally, the researchers assess the infant's actions after he or she observes the adult's emotional message. They may code infants' movements relative to the object and to the partner, as well as their emotional reactions. This information allows them to determine if infants act in accordance with the partner's message.

Studies using the ASR paradigm have provided convincing demonstrations that 1-year-old infants pursue affective appraisal about objects and events from their mothers (Dickstein & Parke, 1988; Klinnert, 1984; Rosen et al., 1992), their fathers (Hirshberg & Svejda, 1990), and friendly strangers (Klinnert, Emde, Butterfield, & Campos, 1986) in different settings (Walden & Baxter, 1989). Moreover, they demonstrate that infants' behavior toward ambiguous events is often regulated by adults' affective messages (Gunnar & Stone, 1984; Hornik, Risenhoover, & Gunnar, 1987). Broadly, positive expressions are followed by approach to the object, and negative expressions by avoidance (Klinnert, 1984; Sorce et al., 1985; Walden & Ogan, 1988; Zarbatany & Lamb, 1985).

However, extensive use of the ASR paradigm has also given rise to some unresolved issues. First, some 1-year-olds appear to seek and use adults' appraisal of objects not only when they are uncertain, but also when they have already begun to form an opinion (Hornik & Gunnar, 1988; Rosen et al., 1992). This finding suggests that as early as the second year of life, affective social referencing is becoming incorporated into ongoing negotiations between infants and their partners about objects' emotional meaning (Emde, 1992).

Second, intriguing group differences have been documented in the process of affective social referencing. For example, Rosen, Adamson, and Bakeman (1992) found that gender affected the way in which fear was conveyed to and received by 12-month-old infants. Mothers tended to produce less intense fearful messages when they were communicating with daughters than with sons. Yet only the girls'—and not the boys'—distance from a novel, noisy toy was modulated by maternal messages. This pattern of findings converges with other demonstrations that, by 1 year of age, girls may be more wary in novel situations than boys (e.g., Gunnar & Stone, 1984; Jacklin, Maccoby, & Doering, 1983; cf. Gunnar, 1980). Moreover, it is consistent with the contention that, at least in our culture, mothers may communicate different emotional messages to daughters and to sons about new events (Block, 1984; Deaux & Major, 1987).

In summary, research using the ASR paradigm demonstrates that, by the end of their first year, infants often seek an adult's affective appraisal when they are faced with uncertainty. It also suggests that affective social referencing may be integrated into ongoing dialogues about the meaning of objects.

From Acts on Objects to Gestures about Objects

Because there is almost total overlap between what 6-month-old infants handle and the topic of their actions, they often unwittingly communicate about objects. However, 6-month-olds do not yet intentionally formulate object-focused messages for their partners. Nor have they yet mastered the means to convey specific messages about an event, especially if it is distant in space or time.

Over the next many months, infants begin to gesture to convey object-focused messages, and they become increasingly able to do so with flexibility and precision. These gestures are a varied lot. They combine hand, head, and body movements, visual regard, and vocalization. Although these new communicative forms may contain elements as universal as the extension of an index finger or the nod of a head, they often also contain idiosyncratic ones that make sense only when one shares a common history with the infant. For example, one infant may utter a breathy "ha" and another "didi" while pointing toward an interesting object (Bates et al., 1975; Dore et al., 1976).

Yet, regardless of modality and personal history, all gestures are, by definition, used as a means of *intentional* communication (Clark, 1978). Further, they are *nonliteral* acts in that they *convey* a message to another person about an object rather than operate directly on the object.

Infants seem to take a common developmental path as they move from actions on objects to gestures about them. Their movement along this path has four interesting characteristics. The first involves a predictable change in attention deployment during object-focused communicative acts. At first, an infant usually looks directly at the target object while the partner completes the communication by opening the communicative channel and inferring the infant's aim. For example, the partner might comment on the object that the infant is inspecting, or he might hand the infant an object when she reaches for it imploringly. Then, beginning around 9 months of age (Bates et al., 1975), infants begin to look back and forth between the object and the partner. They might, for example, glance up at the adult while straining toward an object, acting as if they expect the adult to be a social tool who will help to achieve a desired goal. In such episodes, the infant's object-focused gestures have become explicitly triadic, with the infant positioned as the pivot between objects and partner (see Figure 2.7).

The second characteristic involves the changing relation between the infant's gesture and the immediate communicative context. Initially, gestures are rendered obvious by their context. For example, a young infant's first intentional requests may be directed toward an object so close at hand that the meaning of his open-palmed gesture, straining body, and pleading "mmmm" is almost a repetition of the meaning provided by the physical arrangement of self and object. Gradually, though, the act becomes distanced from its object, as the path between the gesture and its focus lengthens (Werner & Kaplan, 1963). This movement allows the infant to communicate about topics that stand well beyond a literal tracing of the triangle between the infant, partner, and object, eventually including topics that are not in the immediate field (see Chapter 7).

Third, infants' first gestures are often formed from old material. In terms of form alone, many 1-year-old infants' gestures are already within the behavioral repertoire of far younger infants. For example, 4-month-olds can cry, shift their gaze toward an object, reach for and grasp objects, and extend their index fingers. But these acts are not used as intentional gestures toward objects. Gradually, however, these forms are harnessed to serve object-focused communication. In the process, they gradually are transformed into ritualized (Bates et al., 1975) or conventionalized (Bruner, Roy, & Ratner, 1982) signals, rather than instrumental or natural acts. An abbreviated fuss coupled with an open-and-shut hand movement intentionally proclaims a desire; a pointing finger toward an object signals a site for joint attention.

Fourth, the time frame for the initial movement from act to gesture is surprisingly uniform. During the last quarter of the first year, a sweeping transformation occurs in gaze alternation, in distancing of act and object, and in forms of the signals used. At the core of this transformation is the emergence of *intentionality*. In brief, the infant begins to communicate in ways that appear *planned*. For example, Bretherton notes that an infant now seems to have a "prior awareness of the effect that a message will have on the addressee" (1992, p. 54), and Bates, O'Connell, and Shore write that the 9-month-old now "understands something about how communication works and intends to use those behaviors to communicate" (1987, p. 161).

Studying intentions is so notoriously difficult that American psychologists have sometimes urged their colleagues to disregard them as a research topic (see, e.g., Watson, 1913; Baum & Heath, 1992). At issue in part is how a researcher can access an actor's private or subjective experiences. This task is rendered especially tricky during infancy. Infants cannot, of course, step outside their own performance and report their motives. Moreover, adult partners are often so eager to lend their own interpretations to their infants that they are apt to treat infants as if they had intentions even in circumstances when they most likely have no rationale in mind.

Fortunately, most investigators are acutely aware of the grave dangers that can plague inferences about intentions. This awareness has fueled some superb science. First, considerable attention has been paid to explicit criteria for deciding whether or not a gesture is intentional. For example, Bates and her colleagues (1975; see also, Harding, 1984) operationalized intentionality by insisting that three behavioral criteria be met. The infant must alternate gaze between the object and partner. She must use a ritualized gesture rather than a purely instrumental act. Finally, if her first attempt fails, she must persist towards her goal by repeating, augmenting, and perhaps even substituting signals.

In addition to operationalizing intent, researchers have tried to approach the problem from a number of complementary directions. The result is a large and diverse body of work that ranges from richly textured naturalistic case studies of two or three infants to elaborately controlled laboratory-based experiments.

The emergence of two communicative intentions, requesting and referring, have been studied intensely. Gestures that develop to serve these two intentions all entail a triadic arrangement between the infant, the partner, and an object, but their predominant emphases differ. Requesting gestures focus more on the partner than on their shared topic. They serve the conative function of telling the partner what to do with an object. In contrast, referring gestures focus more on a specific event than on the partner. They serve to declare or indicate a topic for joint contemplation. Moreover, although both requesting and referring are first accomplished primarily through gestures of the hand (with vocalizations gaining ascendency only months after they first occur; see Chapter 7), they stem from separate behavioral roots.

Requesting

By about 9 to 10 months of age, infants begin to issue clear orders to other people to help them meet their nonsocial goals (Bates et al., 1975, 1979). They may request an object from a partner, invite the partner to engage in a joint activity, or ask for help while manipulating an object (Bruner et al., 1982).

Until recently, researchers (e.g., Bates et al., 1975; Bruner et al., 1982; Clark, 1978; Trevarthen & Hubley, 1978) have usually studied the emergence of such imperatives by observing infant–adult pairs over several weeks and even months as they work out ways to understand each other's desires. In the hands of masterful narrators, this case study approach can be exceptionally illuminating. It can be used to draw out overarching patterns without losing sight of informative particulars.

The essay by Bruner and his colleagues (1982), "The Beginnings of Request," is an excellent example of this genre. They videotaped two English boys, Jonathan and Richard, in their homes from the ages of 8 months to 18 and 24 months, respectively, as each played with his mother and, occasionally, his father or the observer. The researchers then selected from their archive all communicative episodes that included requests initiated by the infant. For an act to be considered a request, the infant had to signal clearly both that he wanted something and what he wanted, to persist if need be, and to acknowledge, if only briefly, his partner.

The 200 or so episodes that were selected were carefully reviewed in order to characterize changes over time in the objectives and the procedures of requesting. In terms of objectives, both infants initially asked for objects that were close at hand. Until 13 months of age, all of Richard's and the majority of Jonathan's requests targeted nearby objects. Then these requests for nearby objects progressively vanished as requests for distant and absent objects, for joint enactment, and finally, for supportive actions began to occur. In terms of procedures, requests were first executed by reaching toward an object with an outstretched arm and open hand. Before 11 months, accompanying vocalizations were rare and limited to "effort grunts." Then, at about 14 months of age, each infant started to produce his own version ("hummh" and "heeah") of an insistent demand call.

The researchers' familiarity with each infant and their close attention to each episode's details helped them to clarify developmental patterns. For example, they could explain away the unexpected finding that from 8 to 10 months Jonathan, in addition to requesting nearby objects, also made some requests for supportive actions, a request form that otherwise was not observed until well into the second year. Inspection of each episode revealed that these unexpected requests were probably not really intentional requests after all, since each involved a grab for his mother's nearby hand while Jonathan was attempting to stand. Moreover, their curious disappearance could readily be explained by Jonathan's increasing steadiness on his feet.

Another example illustrates well how attention to a nuance can capture an important developmental moment. Bruner, Roy, and Ratner noted that, at first, both boys only requested objects held by another person when the object was within grabbing distance. Yet neither boy grabbed the object (except in one instance when one of them made an outright snatch of a desired object that was being held by another infant). This astute observation provides convincing fuel for the argument "that the child in this early period already recognizes request as a means of altering possession by indirect means" (Bruner et al., 1982, p. 98).

As insight-filled as case studies such as this may be, they cannot provide all the data needed to chart requesting's early developmental course. The details of naturally occurring episodes are prone to misinterpretation for several reasons. First, we cannot be sure that the researcher's selectivity has not distorted the phenomenon under study, perhaps by highlighting the intriguing rather than the typical episode. Second, without imposing some control over the partners' activity, it is difficult to untangle the infants' intentions from the partners' wise guesses and generous interpretations.

Two strategies are currently being used to supplement naturalistic observations and narrative descriptions. The first strategy entails systematic coding of relatively constrained naturalistic observations. Roberta Golinkoff's (1986) study of the preverbal negotiation of failed messages is a fine exemplar. She reasoned that it might be informative to select for precise analysis infants' communicative attempts that adults do not understand immediately. She purposely picked a situation—lunchtime in a high chair—that operates as "a naturally occurring infant-constructed 'test' of communicative capability" (p. 472) because infants so confined are often forced to seek assistance. She then videotaped three infants three times each, early during their second year, and had coders locate and characterize episodes when an infant was not readily understood.

Golinkoff found that mothers were far from omniscient. Indeed, they failed at first to understand their infants' goal in half of the episodes infants initiated. Three characteristics of preverbal communication were apparent during these failures. First, not all preverbal signals were equally effective. For example, infants' manual gestures directed toward objects seemed much easier to understand than their nonverbal vocalizations. Second, infants were remarkably persistent as they negotiated the meaning of their messages with their mothers. Negotiations contained, on average, over 7 turns per episode. Third, infants reacted to their mother's comprehension failures with considerable creativity. They were able to repair their first signal by repeating themselves, by augmenting their signal (for example, exaggerating the previously unsuccessful act) and, especially during the last observational period, by substituting an alternative signal.

Other recent observational studies have replicated and extended Bruner and his colleagues' and Golinkoff's work. For example, Rogoff,

Mistry, Radziszewska, and Germond (1992) observed two infants as they played in their high chairs. By the last quarter of the first year, both infants emitted clear, intentional requests for adult assistance (or what Bruner et al., 1982, would probably have called requests for supportive action). Aspects of these instrumental acts such as stylized gestures and attempts to establish eye contact could be observed before then. However, only as the infants neared 1 year of age did they communicate with sufficient clarity so that two independent observers could agree reliably about when they were intentionally seeking assistance.

Researchers' second strategy for investigating the nuances of requesting entails experimental manipulation of a partner's responses to the infants' communications. For example, Marcos and Chanu (1992) observed 14- and 18-month-old infants in three staged situations. In all three situations, the mother placed five toys and a box of cookies out of reach, a procedure that promoted much requesting. Each time the infant produced a request for one of the objects, the mother reacted in one of three predesignated ways: she seemed willing to comply, but she acted as if she did not understand the request and asked for clarification; she seemed willing to comply but she responded with the wrong object; or she refused to satisfy the request.

The results revealed an intriguing developmental pattern. Even the 14-month-old infants intensified their behavior more (by, for example, fussing) when their mothers refused their requests than when their mothers merely misunderstood. Thus, they seemed to realize that different types of maternal misunderstandings demanded different responses. However, only the 18-month-old infants tailored their reactions to suit the specific type of misunderstanding. For example, when the mother asked for clarification, particularly when she selected the wrong object, 18-month-olds relied more on vocalizations than on gestures. Presumably they were attempting to specify the object they desired.

Taken together, these studies indicate that, by the end of the first year, infants intentionally issue imperatives. Using these requests, the infant can regulate the partner's actions on specific objects and events in the immediate context. These demands are conveyed by a variety of nonverbal gestures and, somewhat later, nonverbal vocalizations. Moreover, infants' requests become increasingly adapted to the specifics of a particular dialogue.

Referring

Infants must solve two related problems before they can communicate using acts that point out or allude to specific objects and events. First, they must understand that these acts draw attention outward *toward* an object ('Look over there at that!') and *away* from one's partner. A person's gaze at an object directs attention away from her face; a pointing finger indicates a location other than the hand. Second, they must appreciate the *nonliteral* meaning of most attention-drawing (or *deictic*) acts. Except in rare instances (as when a person attracts attention to an object by tapping it so that it makes a loud sound), the person addressed must essentially overlook the "face value" of the act to look away from the commanding face or finger, often despite its compelling quality.

It has been difficult to find an entry into the study of infants' use of deictic acts. During ongoing interactions, caregivers often maintain communication with an object-absorbed infant by monitoring and then following an infant's gaze and hand movements (see below as well as Adamson & Bakeman, 1991, and Schaffer, 1984). Their actions may so entwine those of their infants that it is often hard to determine when an infant can first comprehend adults' deictic acts or produce his own well-formed deictic acts.

In 1975, Scaife and Bruner reported the surprising results of an experiment that allowed a relatively unimpeded view of infants' comprehension of object-directed gaze. In this study, an experimenter first made eye-to-eye contact with an infant. Then he or she silently turned head and eyes 90° and stared off in that direction for 7 seconds before turning back to the interaction. For each infant, this simple procedure was repeated twice, once with a turn to the left and once with a turn to the right. Even as early as 2 to 4 months of age, some infants followed the adult's line of regard on some trials; by 8 to 10 months of age, a majority did so.

This study was greeted as an important challenge to prevailing claims that young infants were so egocentric that they could not even appreciate another person's visual perspective (Butterworth, 1987). It also prompted several experimental elaborations. For example, George Butterworth and his colleagues (Butterworth & Cochran, 1980; Butterworth & Grover, 1990) have conducted a series of studies in which mothers were instructed to interrupt social interaction with their infants to glance at target objects positioned at various locations in an otherwise barren room. They found that from 6 to 18 months, infants responded in three different ways to their mothers' looks toward objects.

Initially, infants' comprehension seemed subject to serious limitations. Six-month-old infants were most likely to follow their mothers' gaze toward an object that was already in their own visual field, especially if the object's movement attracted attention. However, infants would not continue to follow mothers' gaze if it shifted to additional targets, nor were they able to follow a gaze that was directed toward an object behind their backs. Butterworth and Grover (1990) suggest that this pattern of findings is consistent with the operation of an *ecological* mechanism. The infant follows the mother's gaze; in most natural settings, this directs the infant's attention toward an interesting object and leads, secondarily, to a " 'meeting of minds' in the self-same object" (p. 611).

Limitations in the infant's comprehension of deictic gaze seemed to be gradually surmounted. By 12 months, infants monitored the specific direction of a deictic gaze so that they could select which one of several targets their partner was eyeing. Butterworth and Grover (1990) suggest that infants do this by using a *geometric* process that allows them to plot a line between mother and the referent of her gaze and then to relate this line to their own position.

By 18 months, infants had made yet another advance as they began to follow their mothers' gaze to seek objects that were initially outside their own field of vision. For example, they often turned around to view an object located behind their own backs when their partners gazed toward this location. According to Butterworth and Grover (1990), these infants are now able to use an emerging *representational* mechanism to extend joint reference to space beyond the immediate here and now.

Essentially the same experimental paradigm has been applied to the related problem of when infants comprehend the point of a partner's extended index finger. During ongoing interactions, it is difficult to abstract the effective signal; adults almost inevitably look and talk about where they point (Murphy & Messer, 1977). Even in an experimental study, it has not been possible to dissociate manual points from visual ones, so at best we can talk about how infants comprehend the combination of manual and visual deictic acts. Interestingly, Grover (in his doctoral dissertation, summarized in Butterworth & Grover, 1990) found that the addition of a manual point did not hasten the advent of comprehension of deictic gazes. At both 6 and 9 months of age, infants were as likely to look at the pointer's hand as at the targeted object. Only at 12 months of age, when infants were able to use a geometric mechanism to follow a gaze, did they follow a partner's manual points swiftly and smoothly toward the target's exact location.

In summary, infants and adults may join focus on an object when infants follow an adult's gaze with or without a manual point toward an object. There are several mechanisms that may underlie an infant's nascent comprehension of deictic acts. A younger infant may mirror the adult's head turn and end up intrigued by the object that then appears in center stage; a 1-year-old may use the adult's line of gaze or finger as a pointer toward an object; an older toddler may understand this pointer relative not only to the current lay of the land but also to an emerging cognitive map that includes places that they are not currently perceiving. In all cases, however, infants can end up orienting towards an object that the adult was the first to view.

So far, we have considered how infants come to comprehend others' deictic acts. Now we turn to the issue of when infants begin to intentionally shift their own gaze and point their own index finger to refer others to objects. Here we must once again try to disentangle adults' supportive actions from infants' accomplishments. At issue is not whether adults follow infants' gazes and hands, which they clearly do. Rather, it is whether infants realize that their own behaviors, such as a gaze toward an object, can have signal value as an attention-directing act.

This issue is difficult to address, in part because infants' gazes toward objects and extended finger movements are woven into social interactions well before they are recruited to serve a referential function. Nevertheless, researchers have long been fascinated with the origins of the production of deictic acts, especially manual pointing.

In part, their inquisitiveness has been fueled by the perennial claim that pointing is a uniquely human act (Werner & Kaplan, 1963). According to this claim (which may well be false, at least with regard to the Bonobo or pygmy chimpanzee; see Savage-Rumbaugh, McDonald, Sevcik, Hopkins, & Rupert, 1986), only human beings extend their index finger when they are attending to an object. Moreover, only human beings develop an understanding of the point of a point. Extend an index finger in front of your dog and she will focus on your finger; extend your finger in front of a toddler and he will seek beyond it for an interesting sight.

The study of manual pointing's origin is also energized by the enduring debate over the initial function of human communication. Two broad alternatives have been articulated. The first proposition is that we initially communicate because we want and need others to do our bidding. Evidence that pointing emerges from acts such as grasping and reaching, which bring desired objects to the infant, would be in line with this proposition. The second proposition is that, in addition to pleas for assistance, infants are motivated to communicate by an inherent desire for intersubjective experiences. Evidence that pointing arises from exploratory and attention-directing manual acts such as finger-poking at a new toy would support this proposition.

Given the high theoretical stakes, it is not surprising that evidence has been gathered in favor of both propositions. As early as 1912, the venerable Wilhelm Wundt noted in his massive *Völkerpsychologie* that a point was "nothing but an abbreviated grasp movement" (cited in Werner & Kaplan, 1963, p. 78; see also Lock, 1980). Other developmentalists, however, countered this view with reports that the precursors of pointing are rudimentary acts of contemplation that direct attention outward toward an object and thus, in essence, "push it away" rather than draw it near (Bates et al., 1987, p. 161; see also Bruner, 1983b). For example, Shinn (1900; for additional citations, see Werner & Kaplan, 1963) described her niece's first manual points in terms of attention direction:

> First the baby began to use her forefinger tip for specially close investigations; at the same time she had a habit of stretching out her hand towards any object that interested her. Combining these two habits, she began to hold her forefinger separate from the other (outstretched) fingers when she thus threw out her hand towards an interesting object; then, in the second week of the [ninth] month, she directed this finger alone towards what interested her; and by the third week, the gesture of pointing was fairly in use. She pointed to the woodshed door, with her mewing cry, when she wished to see the kittens; to the garden door, with pleading sounds, when she wished to be taken thither; . . . She pointed in answer, instead of merely looking, when we asked, "Where is grandpa?" (p. 220)

This infant's first points seemed motivated by interest in objects. Even when they were not fully differentiated from a request, the plea itself was not for help possessing a specific object, but for assistance obtaining a new orientation so that an object might be more readily contemplated.

As suggestive as Shinn's account is, its scope is too narrow (and its observer perhaps too subjective) to weigh in as decisive data. Nevertheless, the bulk of a century's accumulation of data is consistent with her account and with the proposition that referential pointing is rooted in the complex of acts related to orienting rather than pleading (Lock, Young, Service, & Chandler, 1990). From a developmental perspective, pointing emerges from actions that are related to attention directing, not from actions that are related to gaining contact with objects through grasping. In addition, the existing data suggest that pointing-for-self precedes pointing-for-others (Schaffer, 1984; Werner & Kaplan, 1963; although, interestingly, pointing-to-the-self as an act of self-reference is considerably later still, Bates et al., 1987).

The behavior of index finger extension has been traced back to 2 months of age (Trevarthen, 1977), and even then, its production seems to be related to alertness. For example, Fogel and Hannan (1985) found that index finger extensions occurred quite frequently by the third month and especially when an infant is in an affectively neutral, attentive state. By about 6 months of age, infants begin to point as if to direct their own attention when they are exploring an object that interests them. By 11 months, they may even augment the point with an arm extension and direct it intentionally toward an object or location (Fogel & Thelen, 1987). For example, a newly walking infant may steer through space by first pointing straight ahead with finger and arm and then marching in that direction.

Only at about 12 months, after nearly a year of preparation, do infants produce manual points as intentionally communicative acts. At this time, they regularly call their partner's attention to an object by pointing with the index finger, and they routinely check to see if the message is conveyed (Bates et al., 1975; Leung & Rheingold, 1981). Yet even then, infants have not fully mastered the complexity of a simple point. It may be several weeks more before infants regularly look at their partners while simultaneously pointing to an object, an indication that pointing is not only intentional but also produced as a *dual directional signal* between partner and object (Masur, 1983; see also Murphy & Messer, 1977).

Also by 12 months of age, infants routinely add sounds to their deictic gazes and gestures (Butterworth & Grover, 1990; Leung & Rheingold, 1981; Masur, 1983). These "positive vocalizations" (Leung & Rheingold, 1981, p. 219) differ from the vocal demands that often accompany requests. But like their first vocal pleas, each infant develops his or her own idiosyncratic vocalizations such as *um* or *da,* for "singling out the noteworthy" (Bruner, 1983b, p. 77). In the next chapter, we consider how such unconventional demonstratives are transformed into *this* or *that* (Werner & Kaplan, 1963).

The relatively late emergence of communicative pointing speaks to the difficulty inherent in displacing attention toward the object and away from the partner. In this regard, it is noteworthy that infants produce the gestures of object showing and offering weeks before they produce communicative points toward objects (Bakeman & Adamson, 1986; Bates et al., 1979). Show/offers incorporate the referred-to object within a grasp, minimizing the distance between the gesture and the target object. This overlap may allow young infants to "stumble from the hand to the relevant object" (Murphy & Messer, 1977, p. 352). However, they still must work out the problem of how to use directive signals to refer to distant objects.

Summary: Developing Ways to Communicate about Objects

Both observational and experimental investigations suggest that during the last quarter of the first year, infants begin to understand and produce acts that allow them to communicate with partners about objects. As objects are drawn into communicative episodes, infants and their partners use earlier-developing communicative acts such as smiles and cries to comment about them. In addition, they begin to use gestures that are composed of vocalizations, manual movements, and gaze patterns to serve communicative intentions such as object requesting and referring.

Adults' Contributions to Joint Object Involvement

As infants master the rudiments of object-focused communication, they almost always do so in the company of more sophisticated adults. This asymmetrical arrangement of communicative partners allows caregivers to surround infants with mature ways of communication, cognition, and culture. In this section, we discuss how researchers have described these vital contributions to joint object involvement. Then we consider some important challenges to current accounts of the adult's repertoire.

Aspects of Adults' Assistance

At least in front of an observer's camera, many Western mothers (and the few fathers who have been observed) display enormous energy and resourcefulness during episodes of joint object involvement. Researchers have abstracted several ingredients from this impressive activity that they think may be essential to infants' communication development. Their lists often include interpretations about the meaning of infants' behavior, supportive actions that scaffold infants' incipient attempts at new skills, and culture-specific props and plans.

Interpretations

Kaye (1979) once aptly remarked that caregivers "thicken thin data" by making informed guesses about what an act might mean whenever they interact with a young infant. In an important sense, caregivers act as skilled interpreters who translate a poorly formed production into their own native language.

Acting as an interpreter for a year-old infant is both a difficult and multifaceted process. Even the initial step—the selection of acts from the stream of infant behavior—may present problems (Ryan, 1974). Young infants tend to produce inarticulate and unconventional communicative acts, and their inventory of acts changes rapidly.

Nonetheless, these difficulties do not appear to stop parents from construing infants' acts as meaningful signals (Bruner, 1983c). Caregivers, for example, often provide an almost continuous stream of verbal interpretations or "background chatter" during play periods with their 6- to 18-month-old infants (Adamson & Bakeman, 1984). They have also been remarkably willing to find meaning in infants' actions in studies that use the interpretation paradigm described in Chapter 4. In one such study (Adamson et al., 1987), adults were asked to watch videotapes of 9- to 21-month-old infants who were playing with their mothers and toys and to press a button each time they thought that the infant performed a communicatively meaningful act. Other adults performed the identical task except that they were instructed to press the button whenever they thought the infant was intentionally communicating. Mothers and fathers (but not nonparents) indicated that they saw meaningful acts 10 times per minute on average, even when the infant was only 9 months old and even when, according to subjects who were asked to note intentional communication, the infant was not producing a communicative act on purpose.

This experiment suggests that adults may ascribe meaning without requiring that the infant intend to produce a meaningful act. For decades, the distinction between meaning and intention has tantalized researchers who would like to determine whether or not adults attribute intention to infants' acts before infants can actually perform intentional acts. That is, they want to know if adults embrace an *'as if' pretense* (Vedeler, 1987) by allowing infants' intentions to reside initially "in the eye of the beholder" (Scoville, 1984). Some theorists (e.g., Newson, 1978; Shotter, 1974; see also Bruner, 1983c; Harding, 1984; Kaye, 1982a) argue that when adults mark certain acts as intentional, even when they are not explicitly so, they ease infants' development toward intentionality by lending infants a more developmentally advanced rationale for their actions.

Despite its appeal, this hypothesis eludes testing. The primary difficulty is definitional (Vedeler, 1987). Whether or not the ascription of intention to an act involves pretense depends on one's minimal criterion for accepting that an act is intentional. What may seem like a pretense to an observer who equates intentionality with planfulness may not be as fanciful to another observer with a less stringent criterion. For example, Trevarthen (1979; see also Vedeler, 1987) contends that even 2-month-olds may act intentionally whenever they direct their actions towards objects, no matter how unskillfully. According to this analysis, caregivers who ascribe communicative meaning in young infants' actions may be *clarifying* rather than *creating* intentions.

Such assertions are not easy to test. Still, the "as if" hypothesis is important in that it alerts us to the *co-constructive* nature of adults' interpretations. It leads us to consider both adults' understanding of what constitutes a certain type of act and what sort of cues an infant is providing. There is considerable variability in both adults' and infants' contributions. Some adults may be more liberal translators; some infants may provide more legible behavioral texts.

Susan Goldberg (1977) has proposed a particularly interesting account of how variation in this process might influence subsequent development. She suggests that infants may vary in the *readability* of their communicative acts, and that variability in readability may critically affect caregivers' feelings of being effective parents, which in turn may affect how they respond to the infants' nascent communicative acts.

There have been several attempts to elaborate Goldberg's notion of readability, especially as it relates to the acts of infants at risk for communicative problems such as infants with Down syndrome. For example, Hyche, Bakeman, and Adamson (1992; see also Sorce & Emde, 1982) found that during a button-pressing task similar to the one described above, mothers were more likely to attribute meaningfulness and intentionality when they were watching normally developing 7-month-old infants than when they saw slightly older infants with Down syndrome who were behaving at the same developmental level. This result held regardless of whether or not the mother had herself reared a child with Down syndrome. However, no differences were found when the normally developing infants and the infants with Down syndrome were compared at 10- and at 16-month developmental levels. These findings suggest that the acts which announce the emergence of object-focused attention may initially be muted when an infant has Down syndrome.

Adults also differ among themselves concerning criteria for readability. Experience with infants may affect an adult's reading of infants' acts. In the Hyche (et al., 1992) study, mothers who had reared infants with Down syndrome noted more acts overall than mothers who had not, suggesting that their experience may have sensitized them to respond to less salient behaviors, regardless of an infant's status. You may also recall that Adamson (et al., 1987) found that nonparents were significantly less likely than parents to select meaningful acts as they watched videotapes of infants. Perhaps they were less sensitive to subtleties of infants' nonverbal behavior. Or perhaps they noticed nuances but shifted more of the burden of proof onto the infants, demanding that they make their meaning clear.

Scaffolds

When adults communicate with infants about objects, they can maintain the triadic arrangement of infant, partner, and object. Indeed, during episodes of supported joint engagement, adults' actions may be so crucial that without them, object-focused communication would not transpire. In other words, their actions act as *scaffolds* that hold an emerging communicative structure erect (Bruner, 1975; Wood, Bruner, & Ross, 1976).

The research literature now contains detailed accounts of maternal scaffolds, including narrative reports (e.g., Bruner, 1983c; Trevarthen & Hubley, 1978) and systematic microanalytic studies (e.g., Adamson & Bakeman, 1984; Hodapp, Goldfield, & Boyatzis, 1984). These investigations reveal how smooth and seamless adults' efforts to sustain an on-going dialogue can be. Often their scaffolds so skillfully support the current flow of a social interaction that they seem to blend into its natural contours. For example, a mother might readily focus on the object her 7-month-old infant is looking at and elaborate the object with gestures and verbal comments, all the while never requiring that the infant coordinate attention between her and the object (Collis, 1977). She might draw an object into a patterned run that was first formulated during periods of interpersonal engagement (Tronick et al., 1979). Or, she might display affective expressions that reflect her infant's emotional experiences as he attempts to manipulate an object (Stern, 1985).

Studies of caregivers' scaffolds indicate that they develop in tandem with their young infants. For example, in our longitudinal study, Bakeman and I found that mothers paralleled their 6- to 18-month-old infants' developmental advances (Adamson & Bakeman, 1984). When mothers interacted with their 6-month-old infants, they presented their infants with an animate, literal world. Their acts tended to highlight themselves and the communicative channel, and if they extended to include objects, they often made the objects come alive with sound and movement. When mothers produced acts such as gestures or words that gain meaning through social convention, they almost always augmented them with movements of self and objects that clarified the acts' message. In contrast, mothers of older infants seemed less like stars in a relationship and more like narrators of the world surrounding them and their infants. They primarily marked objects rather than themselves. Nevertheless, their actions remained fundamentally social in quality as their messages relied increasingly on conventional acts that were often patterned by shared routines such as bookreading and give-and-take. Thus, as infants gradually widen their communicative sphere to include objects and eventually codes, adults alter their actions so that they are well aligned with their partner's developing skills.

Given the changing nature of adult scaffolds, it may be more fruitful to characterize the qualities of their components than to catalog each of their bricks and planks. One intriguing quality of many adults' scaffolding actions is their close resemblance to the infants' current activities. Infants (perhaps like most of us) seem to enjoy being imitated, and adults often seem to oblige (Hay, Stimson, & Castle, 1991; Kaye, 1982a). Yet, when adults imitate infants, they rarely provide perfect duplicates. Rather, their copies expand the original, elaborating it in ways that are developmentally more advanced than what the infant might produce on her own.

As the example of imitation suggests, adults often bring "something more" to infants' encounters with objects. Their capacity to elaborate on infants' actions has intrigued many researchers (e.g., Hodapp et al., 1984; Turkheimer, Bakeman, & Adamson, 1989; Vandell & Wilson, 1987), especially those influenced by Vygotsky's theoretical notion of the zone of proximal development (1978; see Chapter 2). In many investigations of joint object involvement, an underlying premise is that it contains not only momentary supports, but also crucial plans for future development. In terms of communication development, these plans inevitably include a specific culture's ways of using conventional codes.

Cultural Props and Plans

An extended consideration of conventionalized communicative acts is reserved for Chapter 7. However, it is important to underscore here the general theme that infants from birth on are immersed within a culturally specific sphere which "stores an extraordinarily rich file of concepts, techniques, and other prosthetic devices" (Bruner, 1985, p. 32) crucial to human development. These devices include such mundane objects as high chairs and spoons (Valsiner, 1987) and such momentous human achievements as language and other symbolic tools (Vygotsky, 1978).

Caregivers provide access to these props, work actively to modulate infants' selective interest in various aspects of the human world, and offer affective interpretations. They also demonstrate how to use objects and how to communicate about them in culturally appropriate ways. Moreover, even when caregivers are not deliberately showing infants what to do, they cannot help but model mature communication.

As Vygotsky argued, "the very essence of cultural development is in the collision of mature cultural forms of behavior with the primitive forms that characterize the child's behavior" (1981, p. 151). An important part of this collision is the melding of the child's means of communicating desires and ideas with the adult's culturally mediated plans for the child. Adults reveal these plans in their interpretations of the young infant's actions and in the limits they set on the child's behavior. Furthermore, increasingly over the course of infancy, infants become aware of and attempt to conform to these adult norms, be they strictures for appropriate action (see Kagan & Lamb, 1987) or means for conventional communication (see Chapter 7).

Compared to interpretations and scaffolds, cultural props and plans have tended to elude researchers who have observed object-focused communication emerge. They surround each communicative event (as in Figure 2.7), making them difficult to notice unless communicative episodes are sampled far more broadly than they have been in most studies of joint object involvement.

A Broader View of Adults' Contributions

Understandably, researchers began characterizing adults' contributions under conditions that optimized their chances of observing communicative episodes. Thus, they have typically asked mothers from their own subculture to show them how they play with their infants for relatively brief periods of time. Yet there is mounting concern that such observations have let us catch only a small glimpse of what adults routinely contribute.

The broader one casts an observational net, the more varied adults' contributions appear. First, one notices that playful periods of shared object exploration probably occur relatively infrequently during the course of an infant's typical day (Clarke-Stewart, 1973). Further, one realizes how, by focusing on object-focused play, one may miss some of adults' less supportive acts. Catherine Urwin (1986), taking a psychoanalytic perspective, argued this point forcefully when she chided developmental psychologists for their "idealized but also grossly impoverished view of mother–child relationships . . . in which adults' readings scaffold the child's intentions within an increasingly familiar world." To her eyes, this world contains far too "little room for pleasure and distress, or for conflict and aggression" (pp. 264–265). This criticism highlights how little is currently known about adults' contributions to naturally occurring communicative episodes when their aim is to soothe infants' unease or to channel infants' attention away from certain events.

Second, one begins to notice adult partners who may not act like Western mothers. Even within the same society, there are important subcultural differences in how adults engage in object-focused communication with infants. For instance, when Carlile and Holstrum (1989) compared how Western parents and indigenous Chamorro parents in Guam interacted with 5- to 10-month-old infants, using a standard procedure which included videotaping and the availability of toys, they found that Western mothers were more likely than either Western fathers or Chamorro mothers and fathers to adjust their activities to match the infants' interests and developmental level.

Third, one notices that there are marked cultural differences in social arrangements that influence which adults are available to contribute to joint object involvement. This important point has received considerable attention of late as a general theoretical organizer for the study of early socialization (see, e.g., Whiting & Edwards, 1988). There are now several cross-cultural studies that indicate that many infants communicate with many partners in addition to their mothers. For example, in her comparative study of infants in four social environments in Israel, Rivka Landau (1976) found that although mothers provided the most social stimulation regardless of environment, they were far more dominant in middle- and lower-class home environments than in either kibbutz or bedouin environments, where infants were likely to interact daily with several familiar people. Observations of multiple caretaking among the Efé in the Ituri Forest of Zaire (Tronick, Winn, & Morelli, 1985) and the Fais Islanders in Micronesia (Sostek et al., 1981) also suggest that infants may be placed in situations in which several individuals engage together in communicative episodes.

It is not yet clear how best to characterize the range of adults' communicative actions with 1-year-old infants. As Western researchers go far afield to observe infants of a non-Western culture (or, increasingly, vice versa; e.g., Rogoff, Mistry, Göncü, & Mosier, 1993), observations of early object-focused communication will almost surely challenge our current images of infants' education for object-focused communication. It is already apparent that cross-cultural variations cannot be neatly placed on a scale of the quality of adults' interactive skills or sensitive responsiveness (Schaffer, 1989). Further, it is evident that when Western parents behave as if an infant is an intentional being or act as if the infant can understand what they say, they may well be adopting an attitude towards infants that is bound by culture and history rather than broadly held by all parents (Ninio, 1979; Vedeler, 1987; see also Sigel, 1985).

Summary: Supporting Shared Interest in Objects

Adults make many contributions to episodes of joint object involvement with infants. They can make finely tuned adjustments that scaffold their infant's current communicative skills. Further, as they engage with infants in object-focused exchanges, they bring to the infant important cultural messages about objects.

Structuring Object-Focused Communication

By the end of the first year and increasingly during the first half of the second, infants and their partners are able to communicate with each other about a broad array of topics drawn from their immediate environment. Underlying the diversity of topics is the stable triadic organization of infant, partner, and object depicted in Figure 2.7. This structure presupposes rules for regulating the beginning and ending of joint involvement, as well as procedures for alternating speakers and for selecting and shifting topics. In Bruner's words, infants and their partners must agree upon a *format,* "a rule-bound microcosm in which the adult and child *do* things to and with each other" (1982, p. 8).

In this section, we consider how infants and their partners manage episodes of object-focused communication. Of central interest is how they parcel up responsibility for regulating attention so that they can both sustain joint object involvement and communicate specific messages about the objects that have captured their common interest. Then we discuss some recent explanations for why the structure of object-focused communication does not emerge until late into an infant's first year.

Managing Communication about Objects

The negotiation of formats for communicating about objects begins when an infant first displays interest in objects, and continues well into early childhood (see Kaye, 1982a, and Schaffer, 1984, for reviews). Initially, the adult assumes primary responsibility for their patterning, following the infant's attentional lead, controlling the sequencing of turns, and allowing the infant to vocalize—and hence, to interrupt—at will (Schaffer, 1984). But as infants become increasingly aware of their partners' contribution to what is happening to objects, they start to actively supplement their explicit concern for objects with attempts to manage their partners' actions (Rogoff, 1990).

As infants take a more active role in the management of object-focused communication, they begin to display mastery of some fundamental rules of conversational management. These rules include culturally specific strictures about the coordination of vocalization and gaze. For example, an English adult will typically look at a partner when the partner is speaking, a rule that their infants begin to follow with some regularity by the beginning of their second year (Schaffer, Collis, & Parsons, 1977). Toward the end of this year, infants even become skilled in subtleties such as the *terminal look,* a signal that speakers use when they are about to offer the floor to their partner (Rutter & Durkin, 1987).

Infants also become increasingly skilled at relating the content of their turns to the content of their partner's turns. One particularly interesting relation between turns involves the matching or imitation of what one's partner has just done. Imitation may help to acquaint infants with adults' conventionalized ways of communicating about objects (see above). Moreover, it may foster conversational management skills. For example, 1-year-old infants can go over to the object that another person is manipulating and imitate the partner's actions on the object, thereby initiating an episode of joint object involvement and confirming the other's message (Eckerman, Whatley, & McGehee, 1979; Užgiris & Kruper, 1992). Note also that when infants duplicate their partner's object-related actions, they succeed in completing a round of communication, thereby sustaining a conversational topic (Užgiris, Benson, Kruper, & Vasek, 1989).

Although there is broad agreement that infants gradually develop skills for managing object-focused communication, researchers are still not sure when they first are able to employ specific skills. Much of this uncertainty arises from a methodological dilemma. It seems reasonable to monitor infants' new skills in communicative contexts, such as mother–infant play, that support their use. However, these contexts are also likely to contain adult scaffolds that may make it appear that an infant possesses skills that are actually joint constructions. Paradoxically, scaffolds may also conceal an infant's current communicative capacities if they lighten interpersonal demands in order to facilitate object manipulation.

Researchers have used two strategies to view infants' skills without the interference of adults' scaffolds. The first strategy involves the experimental manipulation of adults' contributions to routine adult–infant play sequences. The second involves observing infants with same-aged peers who presumably scaffold far less often and less skillfully than more sophisticated partners.

The predictable structure of many social games during infancy makes them particularly amenable to experimental manipulation. Perennial favorites such as peekaboo, stack-and-topple, and point-and-name all entail mutual involvement, repetition, and alternate turn taking (Gustafson, Green, & West, 1979) that are often enhanced by adults' scaffolds (Hodapp et al., 1984). In a well-designed experiment, Ross and Lollis (1987) asked how infants would react if adults temporarily suspended their supportive actions by inexplicably failing to take a turn during an ongoing game.

Ross and Lollis found that infants were surprisingly cognizant of the structure of a disrupted object-focused game. When a game was proceeding without a hitch, infants focused far more on its focal event, such as toppling blocks or beating a drum, than on communication with their partners. However, when the adult forced a pause in its progress, infants often showed that they were aware of the adult's participation and that they appreciated the game's basic turn-taking structure. Moreover, they were able to request adults' renewed involvement. Even 9-month-olds filled the unexpected pause with vocalizations and other communicative signals. And by 15 months, infants were able to tell the adult in no uncertain terms that they wanted her to continue the game. Thus, when necessary, infants seemed able to rise to the occasion, taking a more active role than they usually do in managing communication.

Ross and Lollis's study suggests that when infants are embedded in ongoing patterned exchanges, they can detect and try to mend a momentary breach in the interaction. However, their experiment does not address questions about the limits of infants' nascent understanding of how to manage object-focused dialogue. Do they know how to manage interactions which are not tightly patterned like the social games? Are they able to compensate for variations in their partner's responsiveness to their communicative signals?

To study the limits of infants' communication skills, it is helpful to observe infants playing with same-aged friends. Peer interactions during infancy have been studied in many ways for many reasons (Mueller & Vandell, 1979). Before we consider specific studies of joint object involvement among peers, two general points need to be acknowledged. First, there are probably no purely peer–peer interactions during infancy. Adults set the stage in a myriad of ways. They provide infants with the opportunity to engage with each other, and even when adults refrain from actively managing their interaction, they typically stand ready to spring to action should a disturbance occur. In addition, adults influence the structure of peer play through their control of important variables such as the familiarity of the partners and the number and type of objects (Eckerman & Whatley, 1977). In short, peer-peer communication necessarily occurs within the confines of a social world arranged by adults.

Second, infants can communicate with each other. When they do so, they draw from a repertoire similar to the one they used with adult partners at a somewhat earlier age (Mueller & Vandell, 1979). For example, at 6 months of age, infants may smile and touch each other, especially when no toys are present (Eckerman & Whatley, 1977; Jacobson, 1981; Vandell, Wilson, & Buchanan, 1980). By 18 months of age, they are beginning to incorporate affective comments into periods of coordinated joint engagement with a same-aged peer (Adamson & Bakeman, 1985) and to produce conventionalized communicative acts such as words that were initially directed only toward adults (Bakeman & Adamson, 1986).

With these two points in mind, we can now concentrate on how two infants orchestrate object-focused communication. The general conclusion is that they initially have considerable difficulty. When Bakeman and I (1984) compared mother-infant and infant-infant communication during our longitudinal study, we were struck by how rarely two infants shared attention to the same object. One-year-old infants did greet their friends, but they seemed unable to sustain shared interest in an object or even to convey a brief affective comment about it (Adamson & Bakeman, 1985).

The initial dearth of object-focused communication between peers is in stark contrast to the object-filled interactions between mothers and infants. Motivational differences may account, in part, for this contrast; most mothers are surely more willing than most infants to share an interesting toy. But there are additional reasons that are related more directly to the structural demands of coordinating attention between one's partner and objects. Adults, compared to peers, may be better able to foster supported engagement because they maintain a shared memory system with the infant (Kaye, 1982a), which may free the infant from the need to attend simultaneously to both partner and object. Further, adults are better able to regulate an object's actions so that it moves in predictable ways. Even a familiar peer is a remarkably unpredictable partner, prone to sudden movements of self and toys. Not surprisingly, sharing objects with such a partner typically awaits the ability 'to keep an eye on' the partner.

By 18 months of age, infants do begin to enter and maintain periods of coordinated joint engagement with peers (Bakeman & Adamson, 1984). At this time, peer interaction gains a new complexity as infants begin to exchange objects, contact the same toy, and imitate each other's actions (Eckerman, Whatley, & Kutz, 1975). However, the structure of object-focused communication is still so fragile that it is easily disrupted if one of the infants fails to take his or her turn (Ross & Goldman, 1977). Clearly, many issues involved in coordinating actions with a peer are not routinely resolved until well after infancy's end (Gunnar, Senior, & Hartup, 1984).

Explaining the Onset of Joint Object Involvement

A puzzling pattern can be abstracted from studies of the emergence of object-focused communication. There is a breach in the developmental time line. Infants are interested in objects well before they can intentionally draw them into communicative episodes. This gap may be filled by the caregivers who embed an object-absorbed infant in communicative episodes during periods of supported joint engagement. However, it is still months before infants can master the new triadic arrangement of infant–partner–object communication. This long delay is enigmatic, especially in light of the very young infant's evident glee during communicative episodes and the slightly older infant's ability to perform object-directed actions.

In this section, we consider three provocative explanations of this seeming delay. Although they provide different reasons for why the structure of object-focused communication emerges when it does, it is important to note that the first two share an inclination to locate the primary source of change within the infant. The third explanation does not so much disagree with this propensity as it expands upon it, placing the developing infant within a wider system of influences.

A Cognitive Factor

Many Piaget-inspired researchers have argued that the emergence of a triadic arrangement for communication must await an overarching cognitive reorganization. As a general notion, this position has many adherents (Adamson, Bakeman, & Smith, 1990; Nelson, 1979). It has, however, been difficult to settle its specifics. At issue has been how broad a reorganization to seek.

Traditional Piagetians have tended to search for an overarching new structure of actions (e.g., the coordination of secondary circular reactions) that might promote new accomplishments in all cognitive domains (see Demetriou, 1988, especially the chapter by Fischer & Farrar, for a discussion of this approach). Others have looked instead for *local homologies* (Bates et al., 1979), constellations of specific domains that undergo change simultaneously, presumably because they depend on the development of a common structure. This second approach has led to the recognition of some particular relations between intentional communication and certain aspects of cognition.

More specifically, the emergence of intentional object-focused communication has been found to most closely parallel changes in an infant's appreciation of causality. For example, Harding and Golinkoff (1979) found that infants who intentionally vocalized to their mothers during a frustrating encounter with an inoperative toy were more likely to pass two Piagetian tasks designed to probe their understanding that effects (e.g., the sudden movement of their chair) have causes (an examiner who shifted the chair) than infants who did not call upon their mothers for help. Elizabeth Bates and her colleagues (Bates et al., 1979) also found that changes in gestural communication between 9 and 13 months correlated with changes in intentional tool use (as well as changes in imitation), but not with changes in other cognitive domains such as object permanence and spatial relations. This pattern of findings suggests that as infants develop an appreciation of means–ends relations, they may begin to realize that they can act both to influence people and to manipulate objects in pursuit of specific outcomes.

An Innate Impetus

As satisfying as these demonstrations of local homologies are, they answer our question on only one level. They speak to the issue of what 'software' the child has in the form of cognitive structures. But, as Bates and her colleagues cogently note, they make "no claims whatsoever about the role of environmental versus genetic factors in bringing about the set of relationships observed" (1979, p. 131).

In his theory of *innate cognition,* Trevarthen (1988) has argued that a genetic factor underlies the emergence of intentional object-focused communication. He does not dispute neo-Piagetian findings related to regularities in development between, for example, causal understanding and intentional communication. Yet he does contend that such results should not blur the distinction between causal knowledge about inanimate objects and communicative knowledge about the human world. Indeed, he maintains that this crucial distinction is built into the design of the human brain, which may contain a "real system" specific to communication (Trevarthen & Hubley, 1978, p. 213).

Moreover, Trevarthen suggests that the maturation of this system can account for the emergence of new levels of communicative competence. According to the theory of innate cognition, maturation assures that new levels emerge at predictable times. One transformation-producing maturational event occurs at about 6 to 8 weeks of age, a claim that is consistent with the notion that a biobehavioral shift occurs at this time (see Chapter 5). A second major shift occurs at about 9 to 10 months of age. This shift expands an infant's intersubjectivity, pushing him or her to be interested in sharing objects as well as in interpersonal engagement.

Cross-cultural research is crucial for the evaluation of the claim that maturation is primarily responsible for the onset of intentional communication about objects. The few available studies are so far quite consistent with this claim. For example, Trevarthen (1988) reported that Yoruba infants of Lagos proceed eagerly along the same developmental path as the infants he had observed previously in Edinburgh, even though their mothers are strikingly different communicative partners when they play together with objects.

Bakeman, Adamson, Konner, and Barr (1990) reached a similar conclusion when they used systematic observations to chart the emergence of joint object involvement in the non-Western cultural setting of the !Kung San. As we noted in Chapter 4, !Kung childrearing practices differ markedly from our own. Ethnographic reports indicate that, unlike Western caregivers, !Kung caregivers neither restrain nor encourage object manipulation (Konner, 1972) except in the specific instance of ritualized object exchange (Lee, 1979). Yet, consistent with claims of universality in when object interest emerges, Bakeman and his colleagues found that !Kung infants first display sustained interest in objects at about 4 months of age, and at about 8 months, they begin to give objects to others. Moreover, they also found that although other people tend to ignore infants while they are playing with objects, they do communicate with infants when infants offer them objects. Thus, by the end of their first year, !Kung infants, like their American, Scottish, and Yoruba counterparts, are initiating and engaging in episodes of joint object involvement.

A New Level of Organization

So far, we have reviewed attempts to locate a single factor that might be primarily responsible for the onset of intentional object-focused communication. The final explanation we consider focuses on the orchestration of a variety of factors rather than on the characteristics of any single one.

Alan Fogel's (1985, 1990; Fogel & Thelen, 1987; Walker et al., 1992) *dynamic systems perspective* exemplifies this approach. He situates the cause of a new form of activity in the changing relations between numerous elements during periods of reorganization. These elements include the two factors that we have already considered, the maturation of an area of the central nervous system and a new cognitive insight. Further, factors related to the partner's contribution and to the inanimate environment are also considered.

From a dynamic systems perspective, although one element may usually be the *controlling factor* whose arrival ushers in a new accomplishment, other elements may serve this function. For example, the onset of communicative pointing often depends on the realization that an act can refer across space to a distant object. However, another element, such as a partner's interpretation of what pointing may mean, can play this role for some infants in some situations. Furthermore, any of a whole host of elements can limit an infant's performance in a particular situation. For example, the *rate-limiting element* for the production of a point might be an infant's notion of reference; her ability to perform specific motor acts such as extending the index finger; her postural control while sitting or standing; her partner's receptiveness to her actions; and the history of procedures for object reference that she shares with this partner. It may also be an idiosyncratic aspect of the current situation, such as the distance between the adult, infant, and target object.

This theoretical viewpoint demands the consideration of a daunting array of elements. Fogel (1990) argues that detailed case histories are needed to observe the changing relation between components from domains as diverse as the physiological, neuromotor, social, affective, and cognitive during the emergence of an action, be it walking or pointing. In a sense, he is urging researchers to couple the rich tradition of baby biographies to the modern methodology of systematic observation. Such data are crucial if we are to supplement studies that concentrate on one main taproot, even one as central as cognition or brain maturation, with information about the many particulars that converge to permit the onset of a new structure of communication.

Summary: Arranging Object-Focused Communication

During the latter half of their first year, infants gradually begin to master ways of managing object-focused communication. At first the path towards objects is cleared by adults who share an object topic with an infant without insisting that the infant help manage the triadic structuring of people and objects. By the end of infancy, infants are able to sustain periods of joint object involvement with equally (un)skilled peers. The pacing of infants' mastery of object-focused communication may be related to fundamental changes in cognition and to maturation, as well as to the orchestration of a complex of diverse elements.

Theme and Variation: Object Interest and Developmental Disorders

A central theme of this chapter is that a profound transformation of communication development occurs as infants become interested in objects and as adults react to and support this interest. In this section, we explore this theme further by examining how communication development is affected by variations in infants' interest in objects. We focus primarily on infants who have developmental disorders that delay or disturb the emergence of object interest. Then we close with a brief prospective look at communication during the last months of infancy to note how joint object involvement provides a source for the emergence of conventional communicative codes.

The Centrality of Infants' Interests

As we have seen in this chapter, infants' emerging interest in their immediate surroundings transforms interpersonal engagement into joint object involvement. This theme is, of course, varied daily. The intensity of an infant's curiosity in objects fluctuates as a function of countless personal and environmental factors. Furthermore, although almost all infants turn their attention outward toward objects, differences between infants certainly abound. They vary in how persistently they are drawn to objects and how receptive they are to a partner's influence.

One way to examine the effect of such variations on communication is to ask about how different levels of infant interest relate to different levels of adult assistance. Studies motivated by this question have demonstrated the overriding centrality of infants' interests in establishing the basic condition for object-focused communication. In other words, the infants' ongoing attention provides the focal point around which adults' attention-sustaining scaffolds are built.

This claim is well-illustrated in Parrinello and Ruff's (1988) experiment on the effect of adult intervention on infants' interest in objects. In this study, infants explored objects while an adult provided a low, a moderate, or a high level of support. The effect of this support depended on an infant's initial interest in the objects. Only infants who displayed relatively little spontaneous attention to objects during a baseline condition attended more to objects when the adult was involved than when she was not. Moreover, this effect held only when the adult provided a low or moderate, but not a high, level of intervention. In other words, it appears that an adult could subtly—but not brazenly—entice an initially reticent infant to become more involved with objects.

This study, coupled with subsequent naturalistic observations (Lawson, Parrinello, & Ruff, 1992), suggests that, at least within a sample of normally developing infants, the basic condition for object-focused communication can be established through different balances between infants' interest in objccts and adults' "intervention." Indeed, this generalization seems to hold true as well for many infants who are at-risk for experiencing developmental difficulties due to prematurity or a genetically based disorder such as Down syndrome. Object sharing has been found to be remarkably robust. For example, the duration of joint object involvement is often not affected by variations in infant status such as prematurity and Down syndrome (see, e.g., Landry & Chapieski, 1989; Lawson et al., 1992).

The robustness of joint object involvement highlights adults' ability to effect the best fit between their infants and objects. For example, Landry and Chapieski (1989) report that mothers of infants with Down syndrome are more likely to orient their infants physically to a toy, and mothers of preterm infants are more likely to hand toys to the infants. Correspondingly, infants with Down syndrome are less likely to explore objects on their own than preterm infants. Findings such as these suggest that, within a common frame of object sharing, different object-focused communicative functions such as requesting and referring may be differentially nurtured due to variations in infants' spontaneous tendencies to focus attention on different aspects of their environment.

Nevertheless, there may be limits to the efficacy of adult accommodations. In rare instances, an infant may manifest extremely little interest in object sharing (see, e.g., Yoder & Farran's 1986 study of two infants with profound handicaps). In others, joint object involvement may be achieved but not without distortions that may have an impact of subsequent communication development. This point is being rigorously pursued currently as a possible piece of two puzzling patterns of development.

The first pattern involves children with Down syndrome. These children often exhibit deficits in expressive language skills that are more severe than their cognitive limitations alone would lead researchers to predict (Lynch & Eilers, 1991; Mervis, 1990; for recent developmental research on children with Down syndrome, see Cicchetti & Beeghly, 1990). Mundy, Sigman, Kasari, and Yirmiya (1988) suggest that this pattern may have roots in the earlier periods of joint object involvement, during which a young child with Down syndrome may display relatively strong nonverbal social interaction skills such as turn taking and a concomitant deficit in object-requesting skills.

Young children with autism present a second puzzling pattern that may likewise have roots in episodes of joint object involvement. This developmental disorder is marked by pervasive problems, including a lack of responsiveness to others and, if speech is present, peculiar errors in pronoun use and echolalia (see Frith, 1989, for an excellent introduction to autism). Researchers have recently noted a distinct pattern of deficits within preverbal object-focused communication repertoires of young children with autism. They may use gestures to request adults' assistance with an object, but they do not use them to achieve joint attention with an object of shared interest. For example, compared to children with mental retardation or language delays, children with autism show a selective paucity of joint attention behaviors, such as pointing toward and showing objects, when the primary function of the exchange is to share attention to objects with another person (Loveland & Landry, 1986; Mundy, Sigman, Ungerer, & Sherman, 1986).

Children with autism may also be less receptive to a partner's attempts to convey object-focused messages. For example, Duncan McArthur and I recently found that young children with autism were less likely than children with specific language delay to open up a channel of communication when their adult partner tried to initiate communication about an object (Adamson & McArthur, in press). Richer (1978) has argued that when children with autism avoid "negotiations of shared understandings," they may fail "to acquire the skills for communication and cooperation" that are crucial for learning "the meaning of a culture's symbols, including language." This may result in "the partial noncommunication of culture to autistic children," leaving them "dyscultural" (p. 48).

These observations of how children with autism communicate about objects suggest that some crucial process may go awry during the movement from interpersonal engagement to joint object reference that may then hamper their mastery of symbolic communication (Mundy, Sigman, & Kasari, 1990). One recent notion is that young children with autism may have a profoundly deficient theory of mind. For a lively discussion of this possibility, see the exchange between Simon Baron-Cohen (1989) and Peter Mundy and Marian Sigman (1989a, b).

The study of variations in object sharing as extreme as those displayed by young children with autism raises questions about how adults best intervene in hopes of remediating their difficulties. Answers to these questions are far from firm. However, there have been interesting efforts of late to teach adults to supply extraordinary scaffolds to children with pervasive developmental disorders, in hopes of fostering early object sharing (see, e.g., Klinger & Dawson, 1992).

A Source for the Communicative Code

Although infants may enter episodes of joint object involvement primarily intent on exploring an environment whose contents are immediate and often tangible, they end up also encountering an abstract world whose temporal and spatial scope far exceeds the limits of the here and now. Caregivers inevitably open up this new developmental territory. As they help infants weave together their current social and object concerns, they continually thread future communicative acquisitions into their ongoing exchange.

The most striking of future acquisitions involve the use of the *communicative code,* which has two crucial attributes. First, it calls forth aspects of objects and events that are not immediately present. It is *symbolic* in that it provides ways to represent some entity or event from the past (e.g., the dog we saw yesterday) or to evoke some possible future occurrence (the puppy we'll pet tomorrow). Second, its form is *conventional.* Thus, it is due solely to custom that English-speaking adults call an immature dog a puppy. Such labeling is both arbitrary and mutually accepted.

The developmental task before the infant is enormous. She must learn not only how to use a new form of communicative acts, but also how they function and what they mean within the complex communicative context depicted in Figure 2.4. However, as with each of the prior transitions, the current communicative context provides a source for subsequent accomplishments. As a context for object sharing becomes well-established, patterns that are central for the next phase of communication development, with its focus on the communicative code, begin to emerge.

CHAPTER

7

The Emergence of the Symbolic Code

CHAPTER OUTLINE

The communicative code begins to surface during social interactions as infants enter their second year. Of particular note are symbols such as words that reside in this code. The emergence of symbols greatly expands the messages that infants can share with their social partners.

Unlike previously developed communicative acts such as smiles and points, symbols *represent* referents. With a smile or a point, an infant can communicate about an object, but this referent "remains 'stuck' in the concrete situation." With a symbol, the "characteristic features" of the referent are "lifted out, so to speak, and are realized in another material medium" such as sound or sight (Werner & Kaplan, 1963, p. 43). This process of "lifting out" is suggested in Figure 2.4 by the dotted circle used to indicate the *code*.

Prior to this developmental phase, the code stands in the background of communicative episodes. As it moves to the fore, it adds a new level of meaning to communicative episodes. Now, through the use of symbols, partners can introduce remote events from the past into the current situation. They can infuse the present with imagination, and they can help each other "experience the world by proxy" (Johnson-Laird, 1990, p. 11).

This momentous development continues well into childhood. In this chapter, we consider only the first symbolic stirrings that herald the end of infancy. The first section considers the extensive research related to how infants begin to produce and understand words. The next two sections focus on the code's integration into communication episodes. Here we examine how adults help infants to crack the communicative code and how dialogues are patterned to accommodate the use of symbols. In the final section, we emphasize the theme of shared symbolic conventions and illustrate its nuances by considering how infants who are congenitally deaf enter the realm of the symbolic code.

Infants' Approach to Language

We begin our consideration of the emergence of symbolic communication by recounting a widely accepted chronicle for the emergence of words from babbling, which begins at around 7 months of age, to the vocabulary spurt that occurs in the middle of the second year. Next we retrace these steps to describe how infants begin to comprehend language's sounds and meanings. This traditional two-part approach has several advantages. It allows us to clear a narrow path through the vast literature related to early language development. (For broader reviews, see Anisfeld, 1984; Bates et al., 1987; Foster, 1990; Ingram, 1989; Muma, 1986.) It also displays the impressive predictability in the infant's steps from coos to babbles, protowords, and words. However, an exclusive focus on milestones tends to sidestep difficult issues related to the emergence of symbolic communication. Therefore, we close this section with a consideration of alternative views of the same developmental territory. Here we consider the possibility that some infants may take a different route toward speech, and we ask what role concomitant nonvocal phenomena such as gestures and emotional expressions may play in the dawning of symbolic communication.

Toward the Production of Words

There is a predictable sequence in the emergence of the sounds that precede fluent speech. In Chapter 5, we discussed vocalizations such as coos and laughs that are within a 6-month-old infant's command. Now we continue our account by considering new vocal patterns that emerge during the next year of life.

Babbling

At around 7 months of age, infants suddenly begin to produce *canonical babbles* (Oller, 1980; Stark, 1980, 1986). Unlike earlier vocalizations, these first babbles are made by the repetition of well-formed syllables that are composed of a vowel and at least one consonant. Usually the same sound is *reduplicated,* as when an infant utters *bababa, dadada,* or *mamama. Nonreduplicated* sounds such as *ada* and *imi* are also often produced. By 11 or 12 months of age, infants also begin to utter *variegated babbles* in which different syllables are combined within the same stream of babbling (Oller, 1980). At this point, infants seem to sing pure gibberish as they emphatically string together a variety of speechlike syllables.

Babbling, as its name implies, is unintelligible. Yet adults often find it saturated with the shape of words and sentences. Two aspects of babbling contribute to its remarkable "speechiness" (Oller, 1980). First, babbles are composed of the same elements, *phonemes,* that are the building blocks of speech (Oller & Eilers, 1988, 1992). Second, a stream of babbling often flows like speech, following its distinctive intonational patterns of declarations, commands, and questions.

Although researchers concur that most preverbal infants babble profusely, they have not reached a consensus about how—or even if—babbling prepares the way for speech. Their disputes revolve around two issues: the reason why infants begin to babble when they do, and the nature of the link between babbling and speech. Thus far these issues are circled with fascinating data and theories that do not yet lead to a clear resolution.

Maturational factors weigh heavily in most accounts of babbling's sudden onset. To babble, infants must be able to repeatedly and rapidly make an efficient physical transition between consonant and vowel sounds. This skill depends on the maturation of the muscles that control the opening and closing of the vocal tract (Stark, 1980), as well as on the maturation of the central nervous system which controls rhythmic actions (Locke, 1989; Stark, 1986).

However, maturational factors alone do not account for the timing of babbling's onset. The experience of hearing speech may also prime its initial production. For a long time, developmentalists dismissed the importance of listening to speech because they thought that infants who are congenitally deaf begin to babble at the same time as hearing infants (Lenneberg, Rebelsky, & Nichols, 1965). However, in light of recent evidence, it appears that their data were misleading. Oller and Eilers (1988) have demonstrated that when canonical babbles are carefully sorted from nonbabbling (precanonical) sounds, deaf infants babble only after a marked delay. In a carefully executed study, they documented that although all of their many hearing subjects began to babble between 6 and 10 months of age, their nine deaf subjects did not reach this milestone until they were between 11 and 25 months old.

Such a striking delay casts doubt on claims that babbling is a *necessary* point along the route to symbolic communication. This doubt is amplified by two additional empirical findings and one well-regarded theory of phonological development. The first finding is that babbling, unlike first words, is not reserved primarily for intentional communication. Infants are more likely to babble when they explore objects on their own than when they interact with a caregiver (Bakeman & Adamson, 1986; Stark, 1980). Even when partners treat babbling as a conversational turn, infants do not routinely respond by looking toward their partners until babbles are blended with words and phrases (Stark, 1980).

The second finding is that hearing infants who never babble can nevertheless develop speech. This claim is supported by two case studies of hearing infants, Amy (Adamson & Dunbar, 1991) and Jenny (Locke & Pearson, 1990), whose vocalizations were inhibited by a tracheostomy before they began to babble and for several subsequent months. Two observations suggest that neither girl needed to babble before acquiring language. Both girls understood speech at a near age-appropriate level throughout the period when they could not vocalize (see also Lenneberg, 1962). Further, neither babbled when she was finally able to produce audible sounds. Each child entered the stream of vocal development close to the milestone associated with children of her age, and each was eventually able to produce fluent speech. These commonalities are all the more striking in light of substantial differences in how these two infants engaged in communicative episodes while their vocalizations were inhibited. Amy persistently used gestures and facial expressions to convey a variety of social-regulative and referential messages, and beginning at 22 months, she rapidly learned a manual sign language. At 30 months, when she was finally able to produce sounds with the aid of a specially designed "speaking trach," she immediately produced intelligible, although muted, words. In contrast, Jenny did not develop a way to convey messages about objects before she regained her voice. When she began to produce sounds at 20 months of age, her vocalizations were initially very restricted both in quality and quantity, and for several weeks she did not communicate referentially. But like Amy, Jenny ultimately mastered fluent speech without ever babbling.

In addition to these empirical findings, a now largely discredited *universal theory* of phonological development (which is most closely identified with Jakobson, 1968/1941; for a summary, see Ingram, 1989; Stark, 1986) also provided a conceptual rationale for postulating a discontinuity between the sounds of babbling and of speech. According to this theory, there is a qualitative difference in the way basic units of sound, phonemes, are combined in babbling and in speech. The combination of sounds during babbling is untempered by linguistic restrictions; theoretically, there can be a boundless mixture of sounds. In contrast, phonological laws govern the combination of sounds in speech.

This theory predicts that there may be a period of relative silence between babbling and the onset of speech. Moreover, it suggests that as infants gradually master phonological laws in a universal sequence, they gain linguistic control of sounds in a predictable order. For example, Jakobson proposed that infants first combine a forward articulated consonant stop and a vowel to produce the syllable [pa]. They then begin to contrast the nasal consonant [p] with an oral consonant [m] to form [ma].

Even with empirical and theoretical challenges to the link between babbling and speech, researchers have been hesitant to drop babbling from the path toward speech. There are several reasons for their reserve. For example, as infants practice with rhythmic movements, it is reasonable to assume that they may be acquiring control over the oral–motor activity necessary for speech (Locke, 1989). Further, as they delight in manipulating sounds, it makes sense to argue that they may be gaining a rudimentary appreciation of language's aesthetic and poetic potential (Lewis, 1936; see also Chapter 2). Recently, these reasons have been bolstered by research findings.

One source of these findings comes from the study of babbling's *prosody* rather than its specific sounds. Although the specific sounds produced by different infants seem remarkably similar (Locke, 1989), it is possible that the speech envelope in which they are placed may be shaped differently in different environments. This notion has received recent support from a study by Boysson-Bardies, Sagart, and Durand (1984), who found that French-speaking adults could reliably discriminate the babbles produced by infants who were being reared in a French-language environment from babbles of Arabic- and Chinese-immersed infants. This study suggests that babbling's intonation and rhythms may portend an infant's "mother tongue," although it is not yet clear exactly what cues of pitch and timing the adults used as they made these differentiations.

Detailed phonetic analyses of babbling provide a second source of new information. These analyses suggest that the combination of phonemes in babbling may be restricted. Only some syllables are common in babbling. Moreover, the most prevalent sound combinations of babbling and early speech may be quite similar (Locke, 1989; Oller, Wieman, Doyle, & Ross, 1975). These observations are consistent with a *refinement theory* of phonological development and counter to the universal theory (Oller, 1980; Oller & Eilers, 1992; Stark, 1980, 1986). According to the refinement theory, phonological development is best viewed as a movement through stages of vocalization. There is continuity in that earlier stages provide the basic building blocks used in later stages. Further, the initial set of sounds is gradually expanded as the child adds more and more sounds to the basic repertoire. This expansion is thought to be guided by several complementary mechanisms, including maturation (Locke, 1983), active exploration of sound production during vocal play (Oller, 1981), and listening to speech sounds (Boysson-Bardies et al., 1984).

In summary, when infants babble, they produce patterned but meaningless vocalizations. Although babbling sounds like a harbinger of speech, researchers have yet to secure its exact position along the course toward symbolic communication. Studies of infants who speak without ever babbling and observations of babbling outside of communicative contexts raise questions about the centrality of babbling in the path toward speech. However, it is possible that babbling helps infants to develop oral–motor control, to arrange phonemes into syllables, and to appreciate the melodies and poetry of language.

Protowords

The boundary between late babbles and early words is an ambiguous one. Although the quality of sound production is clearly transforming, infants continually mix old and emerging forms. To focus attention on new developments, several observers have abstracted transitional forms from the medley of vocalizations (e.g., Bates et al., 1975; Carter, 1978; Darwin, 1877; Dore et al., 1976; Halliday, 1975, 1979; Piaget, 1962/1945). They have been called by several different names, including *protowords* (Halliday, 1975), *phonetically consistent forms* (Dore et al., 1976), *sensorimotor morphemes* (Carter, 1979), *vocables* (Werner & Kaplan, 1963), and *vocal gestures* (Foster, 1990). For our current purposes, we will call them *protowords* to emphasize how they foreshadow first words.

Protowords differ from words in two main ways. First, they are typically idiosyncratic inventions. As Darwin noted, his son, Doddy, first created words, such as *mum* for food, "of a general nature invented by himself" well before he acquired "at a wonderfully quick rate [words] of a more precise nature imitated from those which he hears" (1877, p. 293). Thus, one infant's *ha* may be another infant's *didi* (see Chapter 6). Because protowords are so individualized, they may be understood only by members of an infant's intimate *meaning group* (Halliday, 1979, p. 175).

Second, unlike words, protowords are firmly attached to a specific context (Nelson, 1985). This context may be an action routine (e.g., producing *bam* when knocking down a tower or *brrr* when scooting a car;

Bates et al., 1975) or an emotional state (e.g., uttering *dada* when happy, *mama* when crying in anger; Bates et al., 1979). In any case, each protoword's use is confined to closely similar contexts. When it is lifted from its immediate communicative context, it is drained of meaning.

Nevertheless, once an infant begins to produce protowords, he or she is edging close to using words to communicate. Like words, protowords are relatively stable forms that can be used to serve specific communicative intentions. Initially these intentions usually involve interpersonal goals (Barrett, 1985, 1989). For example, Halliday (1975) found that his son, Nigel, used protowords primarily to obtain goods and services (a function he labeled *instrumental*), to communicate 'you do this!' (the *regulatory* function), to be in touch (the *interactional* function), and to express his likes and dislikes (the *personal* function). Infants then gradually begin to use protowords to accompany referential gestures. For example, Werner and Kaplan (1963) described how infants produce a specific *call sound* such as *ha-ha-ha* when straining toward an interesting object and a *demonstrative* sound such as *da!* while pointing.

In summary, protowords are used intentionally within a particular communicative context to regulate an ongoing social interaction or to indicate interest in a nearby object. They are idiosyncratic forms whose meaning may only be apparent to an infant's intimate partners.

First Words

Between 10 and 13 months of age, most infants begin to mix conventional words with their babbling and protowords. It is often difficult to zero in on precisely when an infant utters a first word (Bates et al., 1987; Menyuk, Menn, & Silber, 1986), in part because adults often assimilate infantile inventions such as *dada* and *mama* into their own vocabulary. To avoid being misled by such terms, researchers usually overlook the very first word and select for acclaim the milestone of a *10-word productive vocabulary*. Infants usually reach this landmark between the ages of 13 and 19 months (Nelson, 1973).

First words are a rather mundane collection. Vocabulary lists gathered using diaries (e.g., Mervis, Mervis, Johnson, & Bertrand, 1992), maternal interviews (e.g., Snyder, Bates, & Bretherton, 1981), maternal written records (Nelson, 1973), and systematic observations (e.g., Gopnik, 1981) typically include a prosaic assortment of names for objects, such as *car, duck, shoes,* and *teddy,* and social-regulative words, such as *no, more, bye,* and *that*. Essentially, infants' earliest vocabularies contain words for objects and occurrences that really interest them (Mervis, 1983; Nelson, 1973). Moreover, infants clearly enjoy producing words. Mervis (1987), for example, notes that even 12-month-old infants may label objects for the sheer pleasure of naming.

The production of first words is unquestionably a momentous achievement. With the advent of protowords, infants began to use sounds of their own invention to communicate intentionally; now they are also able to express these intentions using arbitrary cultural *conventions*. Their sounds serve communicative functions because a group of people agrees that they do, not because they have a natural or intrinsic force (Bakeman & Adamson, 1986; Bates et al., 1987). As they adopt a shared symbolic code, infants start to reap the benefits of language's extraordinary scope and precision.

Despite the indisputable significance of the conventionalization of vocalizations, some researchers urge caution. They charge that first words are a mere veneer of language. Griffiths, for example, suggests that infants may initially only "*appear* . . . to be acquiring words" (1986, p. 280; see also Dore, 1985; Nelson, 1985). To a mature listener, their new vocalizations may be mistaken for true words. But infants may still be using conventional sounds in the same context-dependent way in which they use other, more literal, communicative actions such as pouting or pointing. They may not yet appreciate that these sounds are *linguistic symbols*.

This charge draws our attention to the complexities of symbolization. When a word is used as a symbol, it gains meaning not only from its placement within an ongoing communicative event, but also from its location within a linguistic system. In terms of Figure 2.4, a 'true' or symbolic word is a unit within a *code*. This code stands in relation to—but is distinct from—a particular *message* within a specific communicative event. In this way, the advent of symbolization qualitatively transforms communicative events. It provides another level to messages, one that contains a culture's store of linguistic meaning. A key question with regard to first words is whether infants understand this arrangement between specific communicative events and the code. In other words, do they appreciate the *symbolic autonomy* of true words, which allows them to be drawn into ongoing communicative exchanges but to remain relatively independent from a specific event (Menyuk et al., 1986; Schwartz & Leonard, 1984; see also Werner & Kaplan, 1963)?

There is a fascinating debate over how best to answer this important question. One group of researchers contends that infants may not penetrate far into language's *semantic* (or meaning) system when they produce their first words. The second group counters that there are now convincing data indicating that from the start, word learners are able to follow some of the fundamental principles of vocabulary acquisition.

Two reasons are often offered by researchers who argue that first words may lack the symbolic autonomy requisite for true words. First, they note that early words are acquired very slowly; infants typically build a 10-word productive vocabulary by adding only one to three words a month (Nelson, 1973). At this rate, it is conceivable that they are merely learning to associate a conventional sound with one specific aspect of a communicative event. Second, many first words seem as *context-bound* as protowords (Barrett, 1989). A word may be used only within an action routine (e.g., *bam* when toppling a block tower; *boo* when reappearing during peekaboo), be tied to the occurrence of a particular event (*duck* when hitting a toy duck off the edge of a bath tub; *car* when seeing a vehicle move outside a window), or be reserved for the announcement of a particular desire or need (*go* or *no*).

However, other researchers note that some infants use at least some of their first 10 words in a range of contexts and for a variety of communicative purposes. Martyn Barrett (1989; Harris, Barrett, Jones, & Brookes, 1988; see also Goldfield & Reznick, 1990; Snyder et al., 1981) report that 10-word vocabularies always contain at least a few words that are used in situations other than the context in which they are originally produced. Further, Carolyn Mervis (Mervis et al., 1992) has recently published detailed documentation that shows that neither of her sons ever restricted any of his first words to a specific context.

One interpretation of this mix of findings is that first words and decontextualization may be related but not identical phenomena. In other words, first words are often produced around the same time that symbolic autonomy is first appreciated, but these two achievements are not necessarily entwined in one specific arrangement. Some first words may initially be closer to actions than to symbols. However, during the many weeks it takes for infants to acquire 10 words, they also come to understand that words can be used as symbols that can function flexibly across a range of contexts.

The decontextualization of words may well be "the hallmark of reference" (Golinkoff, Mervis, & Hirsh-Pasek, in press). It indicates that the infant is beginning to appreciate that a true word is mapped onto a representation of objects, actions, events, and attributes in the environment, not merely paired with a particular aspect of a recurring event. John McShane (1980; see also Dore, 1985) has called this realization the *naming insight.* He deliberately used the term "insight" to emphasize the infant's "relatively sudden realization of some previously unseen structural relationship" between a conventional label (a name) and a concept (p. 49).

An infant's fundamental insight into reference is usually less noticeable than her first words. However, some parent-linguists claim to have observed its moment of arrival. For example, Alan Kamhi recorded how his daughter, Alison, suddenly solved "the final piece of the puzzle in her development of referential speech" (1986, p. 160; see also Dore, 1985). Alison was a rather late talker who had mastered only two protowords during the first months of her second year. But then

> at 6 p.m. on the evening of 22 February, Alison realized that words could be used to name objects. It was dinner time and my wife and I were playing the 'What's that?' 'Who's this?' game with Alison. We had played this game many times in the past with no success. . . . Yet on this evening after a couple of rounds . . . , something different happened. Pointing to her mother, I asked Alison 'Who's this?' Alison paused (the insight?), looked at me, looked at my wife, pointed to her mother, and with rising intonation said, /mama/? 'Yes, mama,' my wife and I elatedly responded. My wife then asked Alison who I was. Alison pointed to me and with the same question intonation as before said /dada/? After adding a ball and dog to the naming game, we stopped to finish dinner. However, without any prompting from us, Alison continued to play. . . . (p. 159)

The naming insight places the infant in a new position to learn words. Now infants like Alison may actively seek names for things, and they may quickly realize that if objects have names, so too may attributes and actions be labeled using units from a conventional code (McShane, 1980). Further, they may begin to apply previously learned words more flexibly across contexts and situations (Barrett, 1989).

In summary, infants' first words mark an important step toward the conventionalization of communication. By the time they accumulate a 10-word productive vocabulary, infants also typically gain insight into the symbolic autonomy of words. This insight allows them to use words flexibly in different communicative contexts.

The Vocabulary Spurt

After the naming insight, it may take an infant many months to accumulate 30 to 50 words (Nelson, 1973). But then, often at about 17 to 19 months of age, an infant's vocabulary explodes (Goldfield & Reznick, 1990; Nelson, 1973), expanding at a rate of over 5 new words (and sometimes over 40 words, Mervis & Bertrand, in press) a week. This remarkable spurt then continues as a surge as the young child embarks on the developmental mission of acquiring a language's limitless lexicon (Goldfield & Reznick, 1990). By 18 months of age, infants have, on average, about 90 words in their productive vocabulary; by 24 months, they can be expected to produce about 320 words (Fenson et al., 1993). By age 6 years, the average child has learned over 14,000 words, a feat that Carey (1978) estimates works out to an average of about 9 new words a day, or almost 1 per waking hour. Before the end of high school, a person has usually acquired about 60,000 root words, at the mean rate of more than 10 words per day (Miller, 1991).

As the rate of vocabulary acquisition accelerates, infants master many new words that can symbolize a wide range of concepts. Although nouns often account for much of this spurt, some verbs (e.g., *play* and *kiss*), adjectives (*pretty* and *hot*), and adverbs (*up* and *more*) are also acquired (Bates et al., in press; Goldfield & Reznick, 1990).

Moreover, infants display a new appreciation of how words can be used to ask questions, answer questions, and offer comments (Barrett, 1989). For example, infants now begin to produce words to comment on events such as an object's disappearance (e.g., *gone*), on an object's salient attributes (*dirty*), and on their own actions and plans (*uh-oh;* Gopnik, 1988; Gopnik & Meltzoff, 1985, 1986). They also may repeatedly produce a phrase such as *what-da?* to request the name of an object, and they may please their partners with answers to yes/no questions and show off their words during games of "What's that?" An important quality of these new communicative functions is their reflectiveness. Infants are beginning to use language to learn language (a function Jakobson, 1960, called *metalingual;* see Chapter 2) and to learn about the social and material environment (a function Halliday, 1975, labeled *mathetic*).

However, even with fairly extensive vocabularies, just-verbal toddlers still are not fluent speakers. Their most striking limitation is that they typically utter only one word at a time (Bloom, 1973). Within communicative episodes, a single word often conveys a sentence's worth of meaning. For example, an infant might point to a cup and say *mommy,* which an adult might easily interpret in context as 'This is mommy's cup' or 'Mommy, give me the cup'. Because there often seems to be an implicit sentence beneath a single word, they have been called *holophrases* (De Laguna, 1927; Greenfield & Smith, 1976).

Before infants start to combine words, they often edge very close to this milestone by producing two related *successive single-word utterances* (e.g., *Cup. Hot.;* Greenfield & Smith, 1976; Scollon, 1976). Or they may begin to add an invented sound or *dummy word* such as *wida* to many single-word utterances, as if to reserve a place for a word not yet acquired (Bloom, 1973; Dore et al., 1976). In either case, they seem unable to string two or more words together to produce even simple sentences such as *mommy sock* and *no bed.*

Infants are usually about 20 months of age when they begin to use multiword utterances (as indicated by the use of 10 phrases; Nelson, 1973). It is not until their second birthday that they average about 2 words per sentence (as indexed by a measure called MLU or mean length of utterance; Nelson, 1973). For many psycholinguists, the milestone of 2-word utterances marks a major movement into language, and out of infancy. Now children relate words not only to concepts, but also to other words as elements in a linguistic system whose rules of *syntax* (i.e., grammar) govern how words are combined to form sentences (Brown, 1973).

The finding that infants can rapidly acquire words before they combine them into sentences raises perplexing questions about the status of single-word utterances. What sort of words are these? What do they mean? What principles guide the assignment of word meaning?

So far, these questions have provoked both heat and light. There has been more than ample fuel to ignite controversy over the issue of early word meaning. Investigators have approached this issue with vastly different ideas about the psychological and linguistic structure of adult languages. (See Miller, 1991, for a beautifully illustrated introduction to various descriptive systems.) External clues to infants' internal representations of words are difficult to abstract from the flux of early speech. Moreover, because the issue of word meaning is related to issues of cognition and culture, a fully satisfying answer will surely be extraordinarily complex.

Nevertheless, there is broad (but not universal; see Nelson, 1988) agreement that infants are systematically assigning meaning to words using some sort of implicit rules that are applied across contexts. These rules have been called *principles* (e.g., Golinkoff et al., in press) and *constraints* (Gelman, 1990).

One common research strategy for studying these rules is to document instances when infants' word assignments deviate from standard adult usage, in hopes that the logic of these "errors" might reveal the overall system of word assignment. Deviations are fairly common, particularly when vocabularies are small. By far the most common deviation involves the *overextension* of a word so that it labels objects that are not encompassed by an adult's definition (Rescorla, 1980). For example, the word *ball* may be overextended to label an observatory dome and crumpled pieces of paper used for a game of catch (Barrett, 1989) as well as an Easter egg, a round canister lid, and a round red balloon (Bowerman, 1978). Infants also may *underextend* a word (e.g., *duck* used only to name toy ducks) or even *mismatch* it to a concept (e.g., *catch* for the action of throwing; Barrett, 1989). Interestingly, the same word may be underextended by one child and overextended by another. For example, Bowerman (1976) observed that one of her daughters underextended *off* so that it referred only to the act of removing clothes, while another daughter overextended it to include several events involving separation, such as pulling cups apart or unfolding newspapers.

The "reasonableness" of most deviations supports the impression that infants follow rules as they assign words to concepts. But these rules have eluded researchers. Since the early 1970s, several rival models have been proposed. For example, Clark's (1973) *Semantic Feature Hypothesis* contends that assignments are most likely based on perceptual characteristics such as shape, sound, and smell. Nelson's (1974)

Functional Core Concept Model ties assignments more closely to infants' actions so that, for example, an infant may use the same term for all objects that she throws. However, each has fallen short of the data (for reviews, see Barrett, 1989; Griffiths, 1986; Ingram, 1989; Nelson & Lucariello, 1985).

Recently, many investigators have urged that a new site be explored in the study of early word meaning. Rather than seeking the criterion for the assignment (and seeming misassignment) of words to referents, they suggest that researchers probe the interrelation between words and concepts (Golinkoff et al., in press; Gopnik & Meltzoff, 1985; Nelson, 1991; Nelson & Lucariello, 1985). Central to this proposal is the familiar notion that there is a profound reorganization of thought at the end of infancy (Piaget, 1962/1945; see Chapter 1). As this cognitive reorganization proceeds, words are redirected. They no longer point to aspects of events that are currently occurring. Rather, they refer to (or *denote*) concepts of these events that reside on the emerging plane of thought (Dore, 1985; Nelson, 1985, 1991).

One outcome of cognitive reorganization is that the child gains new insight into the limitlessness of word assignment (Gopnik & Meltzoff, 1987, 1992; Reznick & Goldfield, 1992). Unlike the earlier-developed naming insight that things *can* be labeled, this new insight fuels the expectation that there *is* a word for every concept. Golinkoff and her colleagues (in press; see also Mervis & Bertrand, in press) have called this insight the *novel name–nameless category principle* (or N3C, for short). This insight allows the child to *fast map* novel words to categories for which the child does not yet have a name (Carey, 1978). For example, if a father says, "Give me the *wrench*" to an N3C-using child who sees both a hammer she knows the name of and a new tool, a wrench, that she has never seen before, she will correctly infer that *wrench* refers to the as-yet-unnamed referent.

Another outcome is that infants' semantic organization may change as their cognitive organization changes. This connection has often been characterized in terms of rather broad commonalities in the organization of language and thought. This notion has gained empirical support from several demonstrations that vocabulary expansion and reorganization of object knowledge tend to occur at about the same time. For example, there is a positive correlation between vocabulary size at 18 months of age and the tendency to produce *spontaneous exhaustive groupings* of objects (that is, to sort objects so that all objects of one kind are in one location and all objects of another kind are in another location; Gopnik & Meltzoff, 1987, 1992). The vocabulary spurt is also associated with the development of *specific constructions* (that is, the placement of objects which makes use of their particular properties in relation to one another, such as using a spoon to feed a doll or stringing beads; Bloom, Lifter, & Broughton, 1985; Lifter & Bloom, 1989).

The connection between cognitive and language development at the end of infancy has also recently been elaborated in terms of several links between the use of specific words to express certain meanings and the development of specific concepts. For example, Anisfeld (1984; see also Bloom, 1973; Corrigan, 1978) suggests that the crucial cognitive insight that objects continue to exist even when they are not currently perceived (a concept which Piaget, 1954/1937, called *object permanence*) allows infants to use words to represent concepts that stand free from specific sensorimotor actions and communicative contexts. In line with this *specificity hypothesis* (Gopnik & Meltzoff, 1986, 1992) are findings that young children first produce the word *gone* to indicate an object's disappearance when they achieve object permanence (e.g., Gopnik & Meltzoff, 1985, 1986; Tomasello & Farrar, 1984), and that they first produce words such as *uh-oh* to encode concepts of success and failure when they understand problems that involve means–ends relationships, such as using a stick to obtain an out-of-reach object (Gopnik & Meltzoff, 1986).

In summary, the vocabulary spurt marks infants' recognition of the vastness of their culture's conventional code. They now are positioned to produce a rapidly expanding number of single words from this code during communicative events. Further, these words have a new reflective quality. Infants may use them to denote their own concepts, to make comments about events, and to seek information, including new words.

Summary

The path we have traced from babbling to verbalization passes by several noteworthy milestones, each of which marks a significant accomplishment. With babbles, infants display a new level of control over the sound patterns of speech. With protowords, they start to harness sounds to communicative intentions such as requesting and referring. With first words, they begin to embrace their caregiver's conventional verbal code. Finally, with the vocabulary spurt, they expand both the scope and the depth of their appreciation of language's symbolic system.

Toward the Comprehension of Words

With the production of words, infants announce their movement into language. However, the cutting edge of the development of symbolic communication may well be hidden elsewhere, in the covert processes of comprehension. As listeners, infants may be introduced to the organization and conventions of a communicative code well before they can generate them on their own.

In this section, we consider studies that probe the developmental course of language comprehension during infancy. So far only two areas covered by this course, phonetic perception and single-word comprehension, have been examined extensively. But these investigations support the general claim that language comprehension precedes and may pave the way for language production.

Perceiving Phonemes

The earliest indication that an infant is acquiring a language may be a loss rather than a new attainment. During the first months of life, infants are sensitive to the full range of phonemes that compose human languages (Kuhl, 1987; see Chapter 4). Young infants may lose their *universal phonetic sensitivity* and become specialized listeners who attend selectively to only those sounds that are used in the particular language they hear.

Each language uses only a portion of the phonetic distinctions that young infants are able to hear. By adulthood, people are notoriously poor at discriminating between consonants that do not contrast meaning in the language(s) they have acquired. For example, English-speaking adults have difficulty hearing the difference between the two [p]s used in Thai; Japanese-speaking adults often initially confuse the English syllables of [ra] and [la], which are grouped together in Japanese.

Recent studies have demonstrated that linguistic experience may affect phonetic sensitivity before words are produced, and perhaps even before their meaning is understood. Janet Werker and her colleagues (1989; Werker & Lalonde, 1988; Werker & Tees, 1984) were the first to detect a decline in sensitivity in the first year of life. They conducted a series of carefully designed *cross-language* experiments using an infant *headturn learning paradigm*. In this paradigm, an infant who has been exposed to one of two languages (for example, English or Hindi) sits on his mother's lap next to a sound source. First, he learns that if he turns his head toward the sound source whenever he hears a new sound, he will be rewarded with the experimenter's praise and the sight of a fascinating toy. Then, once the infant is conditioned to respond to new sounds, the experimenter presents a string of sounds composed of two phonemes. The trick is that the phonemes are selected so that they mark a meaningful distinction in only one of the two languages. For example, the phonemes may be distinctive in English but not in Hindi (such as [ba] and [pa]), or they may be distinctive in Hindi but not in English (such as two *t* sounds, a dental [t] and a retroflex [t]). Werker found that her 6- to 8-month-old subjects consistently turned their heads whenever a new phoneme was introduced into the string. In contrast, 10- to 12-month-old infants discriminated only within pairs that contrasted meaning in their native language. English-learning infants discriminated between English—but not Hindi—syllables; Hindi-learning infants discriminated between Hindi—but not English—syllables.

Recently, Patricia Kuhl and her colleagues (Kuhl, Williams, Lacerda, Stevens, & Lindblom, 1992) demonstrated that as early as 6 months of age, infants' phonetic perception of vowel sounds may also be affected by the experience of listening to a specific language. Using a procedure similar to Werker's, they showed that the way infants in the United States and Sweden react to two vowels, the American English [i] as in *fee* and the Swedish [y] as in the Swedish word *fy,* was dependent on their native language.

In summary, a shift from *universal* to *language-specific* phonetic perception begins during the last half of the first year. Before infants produce the sounds of a particular language, they may be organizing their reception of sound in accord with their early listening experiences.

Understanding Words

The timetable for milestones in comprehension has been fairly well established. The first inklings of verbal understanding appear at about 9 to 10 months of age when infants start to respond reliably to a few words (e.g., *no;* their own name) and to follow verbal commands ("Say bye-bye"; "Clap your hands"), as long as they occur embedded within a specific context (Huttenlocher, 1974). By 11 months of age, infants usually have a receptive vocabulary of approximately 10 words, and they typically begin to understand these words across different contexts (Benedict, 1979). By 13 months of age, they understand on average 50 words (Benedict, 1979; Snyder et al., 1981). Soon afterward, they begin to carry out commands such as "Give mommy a cookie" and "Show daddy your bottle" that contain relational information between a direct and an indirect object (Greenfield & Smith, 1976; Huttenlocher, 1974).

There is considerable variability around each of these age norms. Thus, while an "average" 13-month-old infant may comprehend 50 words, it is not unusual for an infant of this age to have a considerably smaller or larger receptive vocabulary (e.g., Snyder et al., 1981, reported a range of 17 to 97 words). However, even with such a spread, infants reach milestones in comprehension far before they pass comparable milestones in production. Throughout the second year, receptive vocabularies are noticeably larger than productive vocabularies, often by a factor of 5 to 10 (Benedict, 1979). This generalization is particularly well-illustrated by a subset of reticent infants who convince others that they understand far more than they say; for example, one of Benedict's subjects understood 182 words, while producing only 10. Interestingly, researchers have yet to find any normally developing infants who say many different words while understanding relatively few (Snyder et al., 1981).

These observations support the widely held contention that comprehension precedes production during the developmental period when infants are acquiring words. This state of affairs makes intuitive sense. It is likely far easier to recognize a word than to generate it on one's own. But it also implies that data crucial to theories of early symbol formation are well hidden from view. To make inroads into covert areas, researchers have coupled methodological acumen with sharply pointed questions about the relation between the reception and the expression of meaning.

One productive line of inquiry has involved the comparison between the types of words found in early receptive and productive vocabularies. For example, Helen Benedict (1979) used both parental reports and observational procedures to compare the first 50 words infants understood with the first 50 words that they produced. She found that both vocabularies contained words from several classes of words. Further, names for things and action words dominated both vocabularies (see also Nelson, 1973). In light of these overriding similarities, slight differences in the two lexicons can provide insight into how meaning is first encoded. For example, Benedict noted that action words were more prevalent in early comprehension, particularly object-related words such as *give* and *kiss* and locative actions such as *come here*. She used this contrast to identify a subtle difference between how infants' spoken and heard words may intertwine with actions:

> Comprehension is an action-dominated mode, in the sense that the child's understanding of words triggers an action response. Although it is less obvious, production is also action-dominated, but here words accompany rather than trigger a response. To give an example, if the experimenter says *throw* to the child, typically the child will get the ball and throw it, thus showing his understanding of the action word. . . . At the same time the child says *ball,* a general nominal. In this case, the child does the action and uses his words, in their most general sense, as supplements or adjuncts to his action. (1979, p. 198)

A second strategy is to compare errors across production and comprehension to seek commonalities in the way in which infants construct categories. Although relevant data are rare (Ingram, 1989), it is evident that infants overextend words in comprehension as well as in production (Huttenlocher, 1974; Rescorla, 1980). By discerning the pattern of comprehension overextensions, researchers are gathering crucial evidence about the earliest organization of systems of word meaning. For example, Mervis (Mervis, 1984; Mervis & Canada, 1983) predicted and found an interesting pattern in how infants overextended the three words *kitty, car,* and *ball.* She used a standard probe during which an infant was asked if he saw a particular object (e.g., "Is there a kitty?") as he looked at an array of four different toys (e.g., a house cat, a tiger, a lion, and a duck). Infants tended to accept the experimenter's label for toys which were good exemplars of an adult's category (*kitty* for the house cat) and when it functioned as and was shaped like this exemplar (the tiger or the lion). However, they did not accept it for toys (the duck) that did not have the attributes of the good exemplar.

A third line of inquiry involves tracking the pattern of word comprehension over time. Sharon Oviatt (1980), for example, designed an experiment in which infants of different ages were provided equal exposure to a previously unknown name for an interesting object (such as a live animal) or for a simple action (such as pressing to activate a toy). After infants heard the word repeatedly for three minutes, their comprehension was probed to see if they would orient to the named object (e.g., *rabbit*) or perform the specified action (*press it*) when the new word—but not when another word or a nonsense word—was heard. Dramatic improvement occurred during the period from 9 to 17 months. Infants 9 to 11 months of age were as interested as others in the materials and naming, but few acted as if they understood the target word during the posttraining probes. In contrast, many 12- to 14-month-olds and most 15- to 17-month-olds were able to do so even after a 15-minute distraction period.

One interesting question is whether the pattern of vocabulary acquisition is similar for production and comprehension. Given that infants comprehend more words than they produce, the average rate of acquisition must, of course, be greater for comprehension than for production. However, the rate within each domain may not be constant, as the spurt in productive vocabulary indicates. Reznick and Goldfield (1992) asked whether there is a similar spurt in comprehension and, if there is, whether the receptive and productive vocabulary spurts are synchronized. Using a visual selection procedure in which comprehension was inferred from infants' fixation to slides in response to queries such as, "Do you see the [X]?", they found that many (but not all) children experience a spurt in their comprehension vocabulary. The timing of the *comprehension spurt* in Reznick and Goldfield's (1992) study is particularly intriguing. Although it sometimes occurs as early as 14 months, it is most likely to occur between 20 and 22 months of age. Further, infants tend to experience spurts in both their receptive and productive vocabularies at roughly the same time. These findings suggest that at the end of infancy, children begin to grasp some fundamental principle of language (such as the notion that all things can be and should be named) that informs the way in which they both understand and produce words.

A fourth approach to the development of language comprehension explores how infants begin to understand the meaning conveyed by word order. Although infancy ends before word combinations are produced, researchers have long suspected that the precursors of grammar might begin in infancy, hidden in comprehension. But they have puzzled over how to untangle comprehension from contextual supports and from production deficiencies. In everyday situations, it is often difficult to tell for sure if an infant understands word order. Non-linguistic hints often parallel information carried by word order. For example, context rather than syntax may help an infant determine who is doing the scrubbing when someone says, "Look, Cookie Monster is washing Big Bird." At other times, infants' motor immaturity hampers them from demonstrating comprehension of a command such as "Put the dolly on the chair." To control for both contextual cues and response demands, Hirsh-Pasek and Golinkoff (1991; see also Golinkoff, Hirsh-Pasek, Cauley, & Gordon, 1987) modified the *preferential looking paradigm* (described in Chapter 1) to test the language comprehension of infants as young as 12 months of age. In their procedure, an infant hears a speaker and sees two videotapes, one that matches and one that mismatches the speaker's message. Hirsh-Pasek and Golinkoff found that 16- to 18-month-old infants are most likely to look at the videotape that correctly depicts a sentence (such as 'Where is Cookie Monster washing Big Bird?') than at an equally plausible scene which reverses the subject and object. Moreover, they found that when a sentence conveys an odd arrangement (e.g., 'She is kissing the keys'), even 14-month-olds will look longer at an image that depicts this arrangement than one that merely contains the elements (such as kissing and keys) in a less unusual arrangement.

In summary, researchers are beginning to access infants' understanding of language during the period when language production is still quite limited. Although the available data are sparse, they establish early language comprehension as an organized process. Further, they suggest that although comprehension may precede production, it may be paced by common cognitive advances.

Alternative Views

So far we have viewed the emergence of symbolic communication development as a series of milestones leading to the spoken word. This approach placed phenomena as diverse as phonemic perception and the vocabulary spurt along the same developmental path. It also illuminated streams of change toward increasing conventionalization and decontextualization that are thought to underlie this path. As with any simplifying strategy, however, this focus on milestones may have smoothed over rough terrain or overshadowed potentially significant areas. In this section, we consider two alternative views. First, we discuss research aimed at exposing a second common path toward language, one in which the expression of messages rather than the referential use of words may dominate. Second, we examine how words become integrated with extant forms of communication such as affective expressions and manual gestures.

An Expressive Path toward Language

Like Piaget before them, pioneers in the area of early language development often used their own children as subjects (e.g., Bloom, 1973; Greenfield & Smith, 1976; Halliday, 1975; Mervis et al., 1992). Even when they recruited subjects from beyond their immediate families, they tended to seek out exceptionally articulate children. For example, Roger Brown admitted that he chose Adam, Eve, and Sarah, three preschoolers whose language inspired a generation of language researchers (Kessel, 1988), from "some thirty" candidates because "they were all just beginning to speak multiword utterances, had highly intelligible speech, and were highly voluble which meant we would not have to sit around forever to get usefully large transcriptions" (1973, p. 51).

This methodological decision allows relatively easy access to the copious details of early language acquisition. But it also weakens researchers' confidence in the generalizability of their findings. No matter how revealing a study of a few individuals may be, it can not quell the nagging concern that its highly amiable subjects may not be following a typical developmental path.

Katherine Nelson (1973) was among the first to fuel this concern with data. Although she found that the majority of the 18 children in her study of early language filled their 50-word vocabularies with single words that named objects, she also noted that a substantial minority of relatively late talkers seemed to detour around this traditional milestone. What was most striking about these infants' 50-word vocabularies was that they contained a considerable number of social-interactional words, such as *please* and *hello,* and several multiword formulas or giant words (Bates et al., 1987), such as *stop–it* and *I–want–it,* in addition to the expected assortment of nouns.

Nelson (1973) initially proposed that the content and form of these vocabularies indicated that these children were adopting an *expressive* style of language learning rather than the more commonly discussed *referential* style. Other researchers quickly concurred, adding both observations and new ways to characterize this alternate route toward language. For example, Dore contrasted *intonation* learners who mainly used a "message-oriented" style of language "to manipulate other people" with the more extensively studied *word-babies* who primarily used a "code-oriented" style to "declare things about the environment" (1974, p. 350). Bloom (1973) described *relational* children, who favor pronouns and terms that refer to relations (such as *all gone*), and *substantive* children, who are partial to nouns. Peters (1977) wrote about *gestalt* children, whose first unit of language tends to be well-intonated but sometimes under-articulated phrases (such as *I–like–read–Good–Night–Moon*) rather than the clearly articulated single words that characterize children who have an *analytic* language learning style.

There is now a vast literature about stylistic variations in early vocabulary (see Bates, Bretherton, & Snyder, 1988; McCabe, 1989; and Nelson, 1981, for reviews). It leaves little doubt that there are many variations to the basic themes of early language development. Further, it preserves thoughtful discussions of some of the most fundamental questions about variation and themes in developmental psychology. Two questions are particularly compelling. First, are the observed differences best conceptualized in the *qualitative* terms of distinct categories or in the *quantitative* terms of a single continuous scale? Second, are these differences best located within *infants,* who differ among themselves, or within *language,* which encompasses a range of form and content that all infants must master?

Initially, researchers seemed comfortable labeling an infant as either referential or expressive based primarily on the content and form of his or her early vocabulary. Moreover, they embraced the notion that during the second year there may be a temporary bifurcation in the developmental path that occurs because infants temporarily have difficulty integrating object and social realms (Nelson, 1979).

Soon, however, the appropriateness of categorizations was cast into doubt. Nelson (1981) once again led the charge. As she sifted through the mounting evidence related to individual differences in language development, she noted that it did not support an "argument for two distinct patterns, however intriguing such a possibility may be and however prevalent the tendency to dichotomize the data. Certain characteristics seem to go together . . . but most children present a mixture of these characteristics" (1981, p. 183).

Several researchers quickly confirmed Nelson's point. Peters (1983) described how her subject, Minh, switched daily from one style to another depending on the context of communication. Bates noted that her daughter, Julia, represented "a true dissociation between language styles, housed within a single child" (Bates et al., 1988, p. 259) when she provided "a rather clear example of high analytic, referential/nominal style in her acquisition of English" (p. 246) and then displayed the opposite strategy when she began to acquire Italian. Moreover, the findings of group studies (e.g., Bretherton, McNew, Snyder, & Bates, 1983) were consistent with these vivid case reports.

Researchers reacted to this evidence in three related ways. First, many of them started to think about style as a continuous dimension rather than as a dichotomy (e.g., Bates et al., 1988, and in press; McCabe, 1989). Thus infants began to be described as more or less referential, or more or less expressive, not as either expressive or referential.

Second, many investigators began to shift the focus of their labeling. Nelson suggested, for example, that the categories researchers were applying "may not be characteristic of individual children at all but of the same children at different times and in different contexts" (1981, p. 176). Each child may appreciate the fundamental variation that language contains, even though different children may emphasize some aspects more than others. This conceptual shift has led some researchers from the study of *children's* variations along the dimension of referential to expressive to the study of how they acquire referential and expressive *language* (Adamson, 1992; Goldfield, 1987).

Third, there has been an increasingly vigorous search for factors that influence different infants at different times to concentrate on one aspect of language over another. Explorations have included variables as diverse as birth order and brain organization, the characteristics of parental speech and attention-directing strategies, and the type of activities that a child and parent routinely share (Bates et al., 1988, and in press; Peters, 1983). Some interpreters of the rapidly accumulating evidence have been impressed by the importance of child-based factors (e.g., Bretherton et al., 1983), while others have stressed contextual variables (e.g., Furrow & Nelson, 1984; McCabe, 1989).

To summarize, as investigators have searched for a new path toward language, they have encountered many individual differences in the way infants develop language. Their findings indicate that there are likely several ways to pass the milestone of early words. These ways cannot be neatly categorized in terms of two separate paths, one taken by referential and one by expressive infants. Rather, each infant strikes a course which ultimately encompasses the variety inherent in early language, with its complex of forms and its range of communicative functions.

New Words among Old Forms

Considering how much attention researchers have paid to infants' words, it may come as a surprise how rarely most infants speak. For example, Bakeman and Adamson (1986) found that 15-month-old infants averaged less than one word a minute during mother–child play sessions that were otherwise brimming with communication. This observation suggests that words may not slip effortlessly into streams of social interaction to replace extant ways of communicating.

Recently, Lois Bloom and her colleagues spotted an intriguing negative relationship between speaking and expressing affect that indicates that it may initially take considerable cognitive effort to produce words during a social interaction. They found that infants who were the most emotionally expressive tended to reach the milestones of first words and a vocabulary spurt later than their more sober peers (Bloom & Capatides, 1987). Moreover, even though most infants are animated during periods of social interaction, they often dampen their affect during the moment they talk, especially if they are producing a new word. Bloom and Beckwith (1989) report that a 13-month-old infant's affect is most likely to surround rather than coincide with speech, peaking seconds after a word is produced. Moreover, when 20-month-old infants begin to overlap words and emotional expressions, they do so gradually, beginning with the relatively easy combinations of well-known words such as *mama* and *baby* with low intensity, positive affect and then only later attempting to articulate new words when upset.

Bloom's interpretation of her findings provides a fresh image of how much effort infants expend to reach the 10-word and 50-word milestones. She argues that reaching these milestones requires considerable cognitive effort. Infants must concentrate to produce a new word. Further, they may initially have difficulty straddling the reflective stance required for word learning and the evaluative stance inherent in emotional expression.

Investigations of how infants gesture as words emerge have also generated some provocative data. Several studies indicate that before infants speak, their gestures clarify unconventional vocal forms. By the end of the first year, infants intentionally produce deictic gestures of pointing, giving, and showing, as well as an assortment of gestures that are embedded in routines such as "wave bye-bye" (see Chapter 6). For at least some infants, these readily understood gestures are consistently combined with protowords to lend meaning to idiosyncratic vocalizations (e.g., Carter, 1979; Werner & Kaplan, 1963).

Yet infants' gestures are not merely a temporary support for vocalizations. Like vocalizations, gestures undergo a transformation toward symbolization, becoming both increasingly conventionalized and decontextualized. At about 12 to 13 months of age, infants typically begin to communicate spontaneously using symbolic gestures (Acredolo & Goodwyn, 1988, 1990; Bates, Thal, Whitesell, Fenson, & Oakes, 1989). Some infants develop a fairly extensive repertoire of gestural requests (e.g., knob-turning gestures for 'want out'), and gestural names (e.g., a sniff for 'flower'; panting for 'dog') and attributes (e.g., blowing for 'hot'). The timing, content, and function of symbolic gestures are remarkably similar to concurrent verbal vocabularies (Acredolo & Goodwyn, 1988, 1990). These findings fit readily into traditional theories of the transition to symbolization. They confirm Werner and Kaplan's (1963) suggestion that infants may enlist old forms, such as sensorimotor actions or vocalizations, to serve new functions, such as object naming, even before new forms are developed. Further, they are consistent with Piaget's (1962/1945) claim that the shift from sensorimotor to symbolic actions has many parallel manifestations in a toddler's behavior.

However, parallels between the development of symbolic gestures and verbal language may be short-lived. By the middle of the second year, verbalization usually begins to dominate. Infants become increasingly likely to produce a vocal label rather than a naming gesture (Bretherton, Bates, McNew, Shore, Williamson, & Beeghly-Smith, 1981), and speech may even "wrap around" gestural development to provide instructions for the acquisition of new symbolic gestures (Bates et al., 1989, p. 1016). There are several plausible reasons why the scale tips quickly in favor of speech (Acredolo & Goodwyn, 1988). Parents may selectively engage speech. Speech frees the infants' hands and can be understood even when the speaker is not in view. Perhaps most importantly, spoken symbols gain immeasurable stature from their placement within a linguistic system (Petitto, 1992).

Nevertheless, gestures are not simply discarded as an outmoded form of communication. Although few researchers have followed their development once speech reigns, the few available studies of the way in which gestures develop postinfancy indicate that they remain as elaborators and augmentors of speech which clarify failed requests and emphasize noteworthy references (Jancovic, Devoe, & Wiener, 1975; Petitto, 1992; Wilkinson & Rembold, 1981). Moreover, infants who understand speech but whose productive language is delayed may make up for their lack of words by using gestures communicatively (Adamson & Dunbar, 1991; Thal & Tobias, 1992; Whitehurst, Fischell, Arnold, & Lonigan, 1992).

In summary, researchers who have looked around language-defined milestones to observe how infants produce affective expressions and gestures have found that these earlier-developing forms are still vital parts of their communicative repertoire. Words gradually intertwine with these extant forms, gaining clarity from them and eventually carrying some of their message. But speech does not displace nonverbal means. As Greenfield and Smith once cogently remarked: "Children are able to communicate because they are not dependent solely on words but use their words with gestures, action, and intonation, within a context they share with their listener" (1976, p. 221).

Adults' Presentation of the Code

Adults often actively introduce infants to the symbolic codes of their culture. They modify their typical modes of speech in ways that make new forms particularly salient to infants. They time their delivery so that new forms are coordinated with infants' attention to objects and events. And, they interpret infants' rudimentary take-up of these forms, glossing their meaning as well as evaluating whether the clarity and conventionality of the infant's production is up to her current developmental par. In this section, we describe these modifications, coordinations, and interpretations. Then we weigh arguments about whether adults' speech to infants helps infants to crack the linguistic code.

Adults' Speech to Infants

In many cultures, adults address infants and young children using a peculiar speech register that has been called *baby talk* (Ferguson, 1977), *motherese* (Newport, Gleitman, & Gleitman, 1977), and more recently, *child-directed speech* (Snow, 1986). Several aspects of child-directed speech have been carefully described, often for several different languages. Throughout infancy, its prosody is higher pitched and more exaggerated and its grammar is simpler than adult-directed speech (Fernald, 1991; Snow, 1986; see Chapter 5).

One-year-old infants hear a particular version of child-directed speech that highlights words. It is grammatically simpler than speech addressed to slightly older children, and it contains a narrower range of vocabulary (Phillips, 1973). In addition, it is modulated in ways that make the units of language particularly salient. Toward the end of the first year, adults stress and repeat words (e.g., "See the . . . *doggie!*" or "*Show* mommy that"), so that they stand out as distinct and differentiated sound patterns (Fernald, 1991). In particular, adults may highlight nouns. For example, when showing picture books to word-learning infants, mothers consistently introduce new labels for unfamiliar objects at the peak of their intonation contours (Fernald & Mazzie, 1991; see also Goldfield, 1993). Aslin (1992) reports a similar phenomenon for Turkish mothers, who must violate the usual verb-final word order of Turkish to place nouns at the end of their child-directed sentences. Adults may also pause between clauses in a sentence, marking its major grammatical units (e.g., "This *dog* . . . goes *woof!*"; Garnica, 1977; Peters, 1983). Moreover, words are selected in accordance with infants' proclivity to produce reduplicated syllables such as *choo-choo, pee-pee,* and *bye-bye* (Locke, 1989) and their categorization propensities (see the aptly named study "Leopards are kitty-cats"; Mervis & Mervis, 1982).

Adults often place their speech directly on top of infants' actions in ways that tie words to objects and actions in the here and now (Bridges, 1986; Snow, 1977, 1986). Their timing is often precise as they concentrate speech inside episodes of joint attention to objects, producing shorter sentences and more comments than when they speak outside these episodes (Tomasello & Farrar, 1986). On an even more microscopic level, they synchronize verbal comments with the infants' manipulation of or gaze toward objects (Collis, 1977; Messer, 1978).

Furthermore, adults sometimes use their utterances to guide infants' attention toward words and their relation to other aspects of a communicative event. In certain contexts, such metalingual utterances may dominate an exchange. For example, when adults share a picture book with an infant, they may repeatedly use metalingual utterances to align labels with objects by calling attention to a picture ("Look!"), asking the infant for its name ("What are those?"), and providing the label ("Yes, they are rabbits"; Ninio, 1983; Ninio & Bruner, 1978; see also Jones & Adamson, 1987). They may also demonstrate how words can be integrated into social acts, even literally speaking for the infant to display the desired verbal response ("Do you want juice? . . . Yes? . . . Say please. . . . Please"; Deffebach & Adamson, 1994; see also Snow, 1977). For some infants, a particular metalingual utterance may come to mark a language-learning routine. For example, Kaluli mothers of Papua New Guinea often tell their young language-learning children what to say to a third person using the imperative phrase "Say like that" following the utterance to be repeated (Schieffelin, 1986).

In addition to modifying their own words, caregivers (and researchers) in our culture often enrich infants' first verbal attempts, interpreting protowords as words and words as sentences. They also interpret much of what 9- to 18-month-olds do as an indication that infants have communicative intentions (Gelman, 1983) and a special interest in objects (Bridges, 1986). As adults verbalize their interpretations, infants hear in words what an adult thinks an infant desires and intends, as well as how an infant might shape his or her utterances so that they conform to cultural expectations (Bruner, 1984).

In summary, during the period of early language development, caregivers accommodate their speech to their infants. Adults display new forms of communication with exceptional clarity, shape conversations to place words near their referents, and verbalize infants' communicative intentions.

The Effect of Adults' Adjustments

The literature on adults' speech to young children has an unsettled quality. Investigators have acted as if it is a widespread and interesting phenomenon, one worthy of sustained research effort (see, e.g., Snow & Ferguson, 1977). Yet they also have argued continually about its significance, debating whether child-directed speech merely accompanies infants' development or whether it penetrates deeply into the process of language development (compare, e.g., Shatz, 1982, with Tomasello, 1992).

The center of the debate has shifted repeatedly (see Snow, 1986, for a historical review). For a long time, the effect of adults' input on language development was considered primarily during grand theoretical disputes about the ultimate source of children's grammatical competence (see, e.g., Chomsky's 1959 review of Skinner's book *Verbal Behavior* and his debate with Piaget in Piattelli-Palmarini, 1980). On this stage, events during infancy seem peripheral. More recently, however, researchers who argue about the emergence of symbolic communication have engaged in skirmishes about whether child-directed speech might play a crucial role in facilitating infants' earliest grasp of word meanings.

There are several ways that this role can be conceived (McCall, 1979). It can be considered *normative*. That is, one can ask whether a certain form of adult input is necessary or sufficient for a particular aspect of language development. Or, adult input can be considered within the frame of *individual differences*. That is, one might ask whether certain amounts or types of adult input facilitate the mastery of a particular aspect of language. In most skirmishes over early word learning, the role of adults' input has been considered within this latter frame.

Currently, there is broad consensus that the most effective adult adjustments are those that are timed so that they coincide with the vicissitudes of infants' attention. As Schaffer states, "Starting where the child is, and providing verbal input within the context of the child's rather than the adult's interest, appears . . . to be an important ingredient to early language acquisition" (1989, p. 9; see also Bruner, 1983b). Tomasello has honed this idea into a sharply focused research agenda. He claims that episodes of joint attention are most likely to be "hot spots" for the learning of words, especially when adults follow rather than direct infants' attentional focus (1988, p. 74; see also Nelson, 1981, 1985).

Studies of the relation between naturally occurring variations in maternal activities and variations in infants' language support Tomasello's contention. Most generally, infants whose mothers speak to them more often during daily activities tend to have larger vocabularies (Huttenlocher, Haight, Bryk, Seltzer, & Lyons, 1991). More specifically, an association between the propensity to engage in joint attention and infants' use of conventional means of communication has been found. The more mothers encourage infants' attention to objects and events, the higher the infants' performance on a number of concurrent measures of very early language (Tomasello & Todd, 1983; Vibbert & Bornstein, 1989). Further, there appears to be a positive relation between the amount of mother–infant joint attention that infants experience and their vocabulary acquisition months later (Dunham & Dunham, 1992; Smith, Adamson, & Bakeman, 1988; Tomasello, Mannle, & Kruger, 1986).

Despite these many demonstrations, it is still difficult to evaluate the importance of child-centered adult input on word learning. For one, the studies are correlational, not experimental. Thus, it is conceivable that the results are due in part to children's influence on the mothers who adjust their speech in response to infants' feedback (see Chapter 5). Variations in how caregivers provide facilitative speech may thus reflect variations in infants' flair for vocal production, eagerness to sustain attention to objects, or enthusiasm for word-learning exchanges such as naming games. Garton has recently recommended that researchers might do well to rename child-directed speech *child interactive speech* (1992, p. 41), to acknowledge children's crucial role in promoting adult adjustments.

In addition, the correlation between maternal and infant variables may arise because of the influence of some unspecified third variable. Among interesting third variables are a myriad of culturally mediated environmental factors such as the type of props and common events that might affect both how adults speak to children and how children develop speech (Jones & Adamson, 1987; O'Brien & Nagle, 1987; see also Lemish & Rice, 1986, on shared television viewing).

In an attempt to circumvent the interpretative problems of correlational studies, Tomasello and Farrar (1986) designed a clever *lexical training study* in which they compared how well 14- to 23-month-old infants would learn new words under two conditions. In the Follow-In condition, the experimenter referred to an object on which the child's attention was already focused (saying, e.g., "You have the *clip!*"); in the Direct condition, the experimenter referred to an unfamiliar object while attempting to direct the child's attention to it (e.g., "Here's the *clip*"). Consistent with the theory that child-centered speech would promote word learning, children understood words better when they were exposed to them in the Follow-In as compared to the Direct condition.

Even with the clarity of this experimental confirmation, we need to be careful. Although child-centered speech can be facilitative, it may nevertheless be neither necessary nor sufficient for early word learning. For many successful word learners, adult speech adjustments may be a rare (or even a nonexistent) occurrence. Even in studies of middle-class Western mothers, minor variations in child status or in experimenter instruction can influence how adults speak with toddlers. For example, Jones and Adamson (1987) found that birth order was an important factor in accounting for the way in which mothers used speech. Mothers speaking to later-born infants used far fewer metalingual utterances than mothers speaking to firstborns, even when reading a picture book with no sibling present. Although all of these mothers shared a cultural belief that toddlers are capable of reciprocal conversations (Snow, 1977), they may have differed in how energetically they turned playful dialogues to word-learning lessons.

As researchers broaden their observational scope, doubts have arisen about the status of any single form of child-directed speech in facilitating language acquisition. Across cultures, there are wide variations in adults' beliefs and concerns about infants that inform the way in which they talk to their infants (Ochs, 1988; Schieffelin & Ochs, 1986; for reviews, see Ingram, 1989; Rogoff, 1990). These sociocultural differences include assumptions about whether infants are communicative partners and whether adults have to teach speech in order for children to learn to talk. In her ethnography of language socialization in a Samoan village, Elinor Ochs (1987, 1988) has provided a particularly compelling counterimage to our culture's preoccupation with the benefits of child-centered speech. Samoan adults shower infants with affection, cuddles, and songs. However, they do not view infants as conversational partners who should be treated as active speaker/listeners, nor do they believe that they have to teach children to talk. Rather, they maintain that infants are better served if adults resist children's egocentric tendencies and expose them directly to social events. Thus Samoan infants are often positioned facing outward so that they hear lots of multiparty—and little, if any, child-directed—talk. Yet, even without a large dose of adult input that accommodates their current capacities or starts with their current attentional focus, Samoan children still develop language.

For researchers who have searched for the conditions of language acquisition in episodes of joint attention with an accommodating adult, such observations are simultaneously troubling and enticing. Schaffer, for example, concludes his survey of recent research on joint involvement episodes and language development by noting that a "pessimistic note has crept into the literature on language acquisition" because "conditions previously thought of as essential are in fact *not* likely to assume such a role" for many infants (1989, p. 16). Yet he also calls attention to the lure of a new conceptual challenge. Perhaps because the research has displayed *one* possible way that adults may facilitate early language development, we can now begin to more fully appreciate how this way emanates from a specific culture that informs caregivers' actions (Bruner, 1982). In other words, adults seem to custom-tailor their activities as they bring conventional means of communication to their infants. Moreover, a broader sociocultural view of language development may force a deeper examination of how different types of input may advantage different aspects of language acquisition. For example, although child-directed speech may hasten vocabulary development, overhearing others talking may help children to gain an understanding of speaker/listener roles (Schaffer, 1989), and interacting with less than accommodating partners, such as siblings, may provide opportunities for learning how to use language for social-regulative purposes (Dunn & Shatz, 1989).

Symbolic Communication as a Collective Activity

Weaving the symbolic code into an ongoing interaction is a collective activity. The code must be positioned within an intricate arrangement of a particular communicative event so that its strands can be tied to aspects of this event in a way that makes sense to both participants (see Figure 2.4). This is a creative and challenging process. At times, the partners create a fabric elaborate with shared meaning. At other times, they confront knots of misunderstanding.

We begin this section with a discussion of the general characteristics of the first code-permeated dialogues. Our basic point is that the structure of these events is continuous with earlier communicative structures. Then we inspect some interesting patterns that infants and adults often follow as they draw symbols into communication.

Continuities with Presymbolic Communication

Symbolic communication vastly expands and ultimately revolutionizes infants' interactions with other people. But during the last months of infancy, many investigators have been more impressed by continuity than by change. Instead of finding that the foundation for communication has suddenly shifted, they have observed that words and symbolic gestures settle into the established arrangement of joint object involvement.

Several forms of continuities have been identified (Bruner, 1975, 1983b; Schaffer, 1984). In early symbolic communicative episodes, partners often take turns as speaker and listener, much as they did during the interpersonal exchanges of early infancy (Barrett, 1985; Kaye, 1982a). They continue to convey messages that refer to and request objects as they have been doing for many months. The asymmetry and complementarity between adults' and infants' contributions persist. Interpersonal routines such as object give-and-take that were negotiated during earlier interactions provide ready formats for symbolic communication.

In light of these continuities, many researchers conclude that words do not force an abrupt reorganization of social interactions (see Bruner, 1975, 1983b). Instead, infants and partners elaborate prior structures to allow new conventional forms to serve old communicative functions. This state of affairs allows infants to say and hear words without also having to internalize the structure of dialogue that upholds their use.

John Dore (1985) captures this process particularly well in his *dialogic model* of early word use. A basic premise of Dore's model is that the infant's first use of conventional means of communication is a joint accomplishment, rather than an individual achievement. Here he is clearly indebted to Vygotsky's sociohistorical theory of development that provides a view of communication as education (see Chapter 2). Dore then elaborates this premise with more contemporary notions of intersubjectivity (Trevarthen, 1977, 1988) that emphasize interpersonal processes such as affective attunement and introjection (Stern, 1985; see Chapter 5).

From the perspective of the dialogic model, an infant's word is surrounded by an adult who acts continually "to project, introject and retroject the meaning status of forms before, during and after the baby's use of them" (Dore, 1985, p. 31). The adult thereby provides a personalized reading of the infant's behavior. This reading may be primarily affective, as when the mother attunes her actions to her infant and expresses "their shared states with conventional forms" (p. 56). Or, the reading may be primarily didactic, as when a mother recasts the infant's behavior into a more conventional form, displaying for the infant a way to communicate that is slightly in advance of his current developmental level.

The dialogic model is not, by itself, a complete account of the early emergence of word meaning. At minimum, it needs to be complemented by a model of how the child acquires internal semantic representations for words (Barrett, 1985). However, it does highlight the importance of preverbal patterns of dialogue for subsequent communication development. Infants' first use of language occurs within an interpersonal process that endows the infant's behavior with meaning. Further, this meaning is cultivated by the caregiver, who locates it within a specific cultural context.

Patterns for Dialogues

During the last months of infancy, many patterns for dialogues can be abstracted from communicative episodes. These patterns are often quite fluid as infants and their partners alter the content and order of elements. Nevertheless, they provide a stable framework for communication during a period of rapid development. In this section, we examine these patterns from two angles. First, we consider some of the designs that are used to create interactional routines in our culture. Then we focus on one motif, topic-comment, which can be found in many of these designs.

Interactional Routines

By the end of the first year, infants and caregivers have usually negotiated several interactional routines which are highly ritualized and frequently repeated. These routines provide a predictable setting for practicing the elements of dialogue, such as turn taking, as well as the production of words. In addition, they provide a local introduction to a range of cultural practices dealing with the use of objects and the regulation of speech.

These routines start to take form well before infants begin to integrate symbolic forms into dialogues. Episodes of joint object involvement are often formatted to facilitate the expression of new communicative intentions, such as requesting and referring (see Chapter 6). During the first half of their second year, infants' language begins to infuse these interactional routines.

Many of these early language routines begin as small-scale constructions. Peters and Boggs (1986) described several language *miniroutines* that are composed of one speaker's turn and a partner's limited set of responses. Among their illustrations are two miniroutines that were used repeatedly by a 14-month-old infant learning English. The first was a summons/response routine ("Mommy!" + "What?/Huh?"), during which the infant produced some variant of *mommy* (including "mami," "nanEh," and "mommy"), and his mother responded with some version of *What?* or *Huh?* with or without a follow-up guess at the topic (e.g., "What–Hm. . . . Want me t'chew it up for you?"). The second routine was a topic-nominating routine ("Ooh!" + guess at topic) that was characterized by the infant's production of some form of *Ooh* uttered in a low, intense, and somewhat breathy voice, and the mother's attempt to figure out what the infant was interested in. These routines are like miniscripts where both the caregiver and the infants "know all the 'lines' " (p. 86). To engage in a dialogue, all that is needed is a cue for which routine is being used.

Miniroutines can serve as interactive building blocks for more complex constructions. In the simplest instance, two miniroutines can join together. For example, the mother and infant described above soon combined the summons/response and topic-nominating routines to produce the following exchange (Peters & Boggs, 1986, p. 90):

CHILD: ma::nih. [A summons]
MOTHER: Wha' do you want? [A response]
CHILD: 'ew: -. (breathy). uwu:. (breathy)
MOTHER: That machine scare you? Hm?
CHILD: 'o:h (breathy)
MOTHER: Duzzat scare you? Hm? Izzat why you say "oh"?

Earlier developing routines may also be transformed in other ways. The infant and the adult may reverse roles, or they may expand the scope of their routine to include a third person or a new object. They may also renegotiate their respective roles so that the adult can transfer more and more of the responsibility for structuring the routine to the child (Rogoff, 1990).

Eventually, it may be difficult to identify the stable pattern across different enactments unless one knows the history of an infant's routines. However, some routines are still readily recognizable because their main theme is drawn from the caregiver's culture. These routines include a wide array of *conventional rituals* which in our culture include such shared activities as book reading and "telephoning." From 6 to 18 months, mothers and infants increasingly use such rituals to structure their play (Adamson & Bakeman, 1984), and these rituals become a particularly popular context for the infants' first words and gestures (Adamson, Bakeman, & Smith, 1990; Bakeman & Adamson, 1986).

As infants become increasingly verbal, conventional rituals may become a center for learning more about language, including both its specific words and the modes of speech that are appropriate to one's culture (Peters & Boggs, 1986). For example, joint picture book reading can serve both as a "multiple vocabulary acquisition device" (Ninio, 1983, p. 445) and as a context for learning specific ways to talk about a given situation (Snow & Goldfield, 1983). The ubiquitous question-and-answer action routines that delight 1-year-olds and their parents ("Where's your nose? . . . Where's your toes?" "What's on dolly's head? . . . Can you put it on instead?") can simultaneously link words with objects and provide an introduction to our cultural style of making a request by asking a rhetorical question. During these routines, adults tend to leave a lot of space for the infant to answer with new information. Should an infant remain unresponsive or reveal a lack of understanding by repeating old information ("dolly"), the adult can then supply the answer (be it a tweak of nose and toes or a child-directed, "She has on her silly *hat!*").

Topics and Comments

Because it is impossible to talk about every aspect of a topic simultaneously, all speakers must decide what to talk about. They must decide what can be assumed as a given and what new information deserves articulation. Since infants are initially limited to one-word utterances, it might seem that they should have a particularly difficult time deciding what to include in a turn. However, rarely do they seem stymied by indecision.

Researchers have identified two attentional processes that may help infants select words for particular occasions. The first process can be found at the level of dialogues (Snow, 1986). Adult partners typically share responsibility for selecting a topic and then sustain it through an exchange of comments. During caregiver–infant dialogues, adults can intervene to ease the infant's burden. First, they can let the infant's interests dominate topic selection. Then they can do most of the talking, producing comments that help to sustain the infant's attention to the topic. In this way, an infant can introduce a topic with only a word, and his partner can expand it with comments.

The second process involves infants' long-standing tendency to attend to novel aspects of a situation (see Chapter 5). Patricia Greenfield (1978, 1982; Greenfield & Smith, 1976; Greenfield & Zukow, 1978; see also Furrow & James, 1985) has proposed that young children tend to coordinate their early utterances with their ongoing attention. This coordination leads them to choose to talk about what is new to them, particularly what they have just noticed.

Greenfield's intriguing proposal has two interesting implications for the topic-comment structure of early dialogues. First, it suggests that infants are already able to follow some of the *principles of informativeness* that underlie adults' commenting. That is, they are primed to express what from their point of view is most uncertain in a situation. Greenfield (1978) has developed several predictions that derive from these principles. For example, she predicted that when an object is not in a child's possession, it becomes more uncertain and will thus be likely to be encoded verbally (e.g., "I want my *shoe*"). However, when an object that is already securely possessed undergoes a change, the object is relatively certain and so goes unmentioned while the new action or state change is labeled (e.g., "Mommy is taking my shoe *off*"). Greenfield has found her claims supported by both observational and experimental studies (Greenfield & Smith, 1976; Greenfield & Zukow, 1978).

Second, Greenfield's proposal highlights the importance of adults' assumption of early topic management. When an infant marks only what is *new* in a situation, it falls to the adult to maintain what is *given* and to weave these words into a conversation so that a topic threads through an ongoing dialogue. Adults' analysis of a situation is eased by the way that infants' interests stay within the here and now (Greenfield, 1978; Snow, 1986). Nevertheless, caregivers must often be quite creative. Consider, for example, the following conversation (Snow, 1977, p. 18) between Ann, an 18-month-old, and her mother.

ANN: (blowing noises)
MOTHER: That's a bit rude.
ANN: Mouth.

MOTHER: Mouth, that's right.
ANN: Face.
MOTHER: Face, yes, mouth is in your face.
What else have you got in your face?
ANN: Face. (closing eyes)
MOTHER: You're making a face, aren't you?

Although this exchange is at most a simple conversation, it is a major triumph. Ann has begun to add conventional terms to mark the focus of her attention during each communication turn. Ann's mother has surrounded these turns with comments, filling them with meaning during their dialogue.

Theme and Variation: Symbolic Codes and Deafness

One of this chapter's major themes is that *symbol*-using infants are introduced to a conventional *code* as they communicate with their *intimate* partners. Each of the three keynotes in this theme entered researchers' repertoires decades ago during theoretical discussions about development and communication. Piaget located the emergence of *symbolic* activity at the end of infancy as the culmination of a constructive process of cognitive development that begins with the newborn's interactions with the environment (see Chapter 1). Linguists such as Jakobson described how communicative events contain *codes,* a culture's organized systems of conventional symbols, of which verbal languages are predominant examples (see Chapter 2). Developmentalists, including Werner and Vygotsky, noted how infants initially communicate with *intimate* caregivers who guide them toward these codes (see Chapters 1 and 2).

In this section, we begin by commenting on how these three keynotes usually resonate in unison during the last months of infancy. Then, we consider how their tone may vary when an infant's access to a conventional code is blocked by a profound hearing impairment. Finally, we close with a glance forward to the conversations of early childhood.

Communication and Conventions

At the end of infancy, there is usually an auspicious convergence of cognitive, interpersonal, and cultural processes. An infant who is beginning to appreciate symbols is typically also one who communicates intentionally with intimate caregivers who are sophisticated users of their culture's code. The near-universality of this convergence is matched by the seeming inevitability of one of its outcomes, the mastery of language. Despite wide variations in patterns of interpersonal communication, in specific language, and in infants' intelligence, virtually every child in every culture will acquire its conventional codes.

Such developmental robustness leaves researchers little room to maneuver in answering questions about how component processes affect one another during the first half of infants' second year. Describing the relation between components can display the kaleidoscope of closely knit patterns that caregivers, children, and culture can create. Yet such documentation does not reveal whether components that are always present are crucial to the emergence of other omnipresent components. For example, although studies that correlate certain aspects of caregivers' speech input with certain aspects of infants' early language production provide important information about the way in which components typically interpenetrate, they do not reveal if such input is necessary for such production to occur (Schaffer, 1984).

Without a method that allows a component to be deleted, researchers can never be sure whether other components of a complex pattern are truly dependent upon it. This methodological quandary has led many researchers interested in the limits of language development to use a *deprivation paradigm* (Gleitman, 1986). Within this paradigm, one component that is typically present is absent, and the development of other components is carefully scrutinized. For ethical reasons, investigators cannot design their own deprivation studies. Rather, they must rely on *experiments of nature* (Bronfenbrenner, 1979), where a component has been radically altered by factors beyond their control.

The necessity to rely on natural experiments greatly complicates interpretation. Rarely do unfortunate situations cleave components in ways that conform to the joints in our theories of early communication. Most situations involve children whose deprivation has tragically affected all components of communication (see, e.g., Curtiss's 1977 study of Genie) or children whose severe language impairments are concomitant to severe mental retardation (e.g., Romski & Sevcik, 1992). However, there is one prominent exception: infants who are congenitally deaf but otherwise healthy.

Research with deaf infants is allowing researchers to study communication development under conditions that selectively deprive access to a conventional code. Other than their lack of oral language input, infants with a profound hearing loss form a diverse population (see Meadow, 1980; Moores, 1987, for an introduction). One contrast in linguistic circumstance—the absence or presence of a formal visual–gestural language—provides the crucial research contrast. The grand majority of deaf infants is born to hearing parents who use only oral language and do not expose their infants to a non-oral communicative code. A far smaller number of deaf infants are born to deaf parents who are fluent in a sign language such as American Sign Language (ASL) whose linguistic structure is not derived from oral language (Klima & Bellugi, 1979;

Sacks, 1989). Infants from these two groups can be recruited to fill two conditions in a natural experiment about the effect of a conventional code on social interactions and on symbol formation. Infants who are not provided with a code form the experimental group; infants who have access to sign language form a control group.

Although rarely are both groups included in the same research project, the literature now contains several complementary investigations. (See the volume edited by Volterra and Erting, 1990, for a broad sample of studies.) Taken together, these studies provide a compelling testimony to the flexibility and complexity inherent in the emergence of a shared symbolic code.

The communication development of infants in the control group—deaf infants who are exposed to sign language from birth—is remarkably similar to that of hearing infants who are exposed to oral language (Erting & Volterra, 1990). For example, Petitto and Marentette (1991; see also Petitto, 1990) report that two profoundly deaf infants of ASL-using parents began to babble in the manual mode by the time they were 10 months old. These babbles were comprised of handshapes that are phonetic units in ASL and other sign languages. At first, these handshapes were often reduplicated. Then, at around 12 months of age, both infants began to produce sentencelike sequences of variegated babbles and first signs.

Furthermore, deaf caregivers who sign as their first and preferred language begin to prepare for their infants' induction into language months before their infants produce first signs or even manual babbles. For example, Erting, Prezioso, and O'Grady Hynes (1990) observed that when deaf mothers interacted with their 3- to 6-month-old deaf infants, they varied patterns of touch and facial expressions to gain and maintain attention even more than hearing mothers did. Moreover, they consistently placed gestures and signs within the bounds of the infant's visual field, and they produced a baby talk version of ASL that was slower, more exaggerated, and grammatically less complex than adult-directed signing. Masataka has also reported that deaf mothers who are fluent in Japanese Sign Language produce "motherese in the manual mode" (1992, p. 459) as they interact with their 8- to 11-month-old deaf infants.

The unimpeded communication development of deaf infants who have access to a sign language (as well as the comparable success of hearing infants of deaf ASL-signing parents; see Folven & Bonvillian, 1991) clearly demonstrates that human communication is not modality-specific. Development toward a shared symbolic code can be fueled by partner input and marked by milestones that are composed by visible as well as by auditory elements.

An important question remains: How is the transition to symbolic communication affected when caregivers are not able to readily import a conventional code from a surrounding linguistic culture? In other words, does the communication development of the so-called experimental group of hearing-impaired infants with speaking caregivers match the control group's success?

This question cannot yet be answered in detail. Too little is known about the prelinguistic development of infants with hearing losses that are sufficient to block access to their hearing parents' oral language. However, it is clear that the onset of conventional communication is often delayed (Meadow, 1980). Indeed, one of the primary concerns that can lead to the diagnosis of deafness in healthy infants who are born into families without a history of deafness is a delay in speech. Given the code-learning success of ASL-immersed infants, the language delays and deficiencies often reported for deaf children of hearing parents are especially troubling (and have prompted a move toward universal hearing screenings to detect hearing loss at birth).

Available studies suggest that the lack of a common code can pervade prelinguistic social interactions. Deaf infants with hearing parents have been found to be more passive and less likely to participate actively in interactions than hearing infants (Spencer & Gutfreund, 1990; Wedell-Monnig & Lumley, 1980; but also see Lederberg, 1993). Moreover, their mothers have been reported to make fewer references to the child's activities and focus of attention and to give fewer acknowledgments to their children's actions (Cross, Nienhuys, & Kirkman, 1985).

However, two thin strands of evidence suggest that even when infants lack access to a conventional code, meaning-filled dialogues and symbols can still arise relatively unimpaired. The first strand can be abstracted from Patricia Spencer's (1993) study of the communicative acts of infants with hearing loss and their hearing mothers. Spencer observed 36 hearing mothers interacting with their healthy infants when the children were 12 months old and then again when they were 18 months old. Half of the infants were hearing, and half were diagnosed with a hearing loss before their ninth month. To recruit so many deaf infants of hearing parents so young, Spencer and her colleagues at Gallaudet University had to search for two years in five major metropolitan areas. Their efforts paid off, providing a promising view of how infants and adults can communicate despite a lack of a common conventional code.

Spencer found that, in contrast with previous reports, hearing mothers and their deaf infants did engage in lively, object-focused, communication-filled exchanges. They produced gestural and vocal intentional communicative acts at a rate comparable to that of hearing mothers and hearing infants. Further, the mothers with deaf infants seemed to make reasonable adjustments to their infants' need to rely more on vision than on audition for receptive communication as they elevated their production of object-focused actions such as showing objects and demonstrating actions on objects. Based on these fresh observations, it appears that object-focused communication need not be compromised by the lack of a conventional code, especially when caregivers find out early that an infant has limited access to their oral code and they have the cultural support of intervention services.

However, the results of Spencer's study do not quiet concerns that deaf infants of hearing parents may have difficulty acquiring language. As a group, 18-month-old infants with hearing loss did not produce as much expressive language (either spoken or, in rare instances, signed) as their hearing peers. However, and here Spencer sounds a welcome note of optimism, 6 of the 18 deaf toddlers in her study were beginning to produce some linguistic-level expressions. As she suggests, it is now crucial that research focus on these relatively successful youngsters and their caregivers to identify factors that support their acquisition of language.

The second strand comes from studies of the gestures of deaf children whose hearing parents decide to educate them orally. In a series of fascinating reports, Goldin-Meadow and her colleagues (Feldman, Goldin-Meadow, & Gleitman, 1978; Goldin-Meadow & Mylander, 1984, 1991) have documented how 10 deaf toddlers and preschoolers created idiosyncratic *home signs*. These signs were used both one at a time and in combinations to point to objects and to characterize actions (such as 'hit', a fist swat in air) and attributes (such as 'round', an index finger and thumb forming a circle in the air).

Goldin-Meadow and Mylander concluded that each child appeared able to discover several properties of language "without the helping hand of a conventional language model" (1984, p. 114). This claim has provoked considerable controversy about whether these youngsters are discovering some resilient linguistic properties on their own (see, e.g., Bates and Volterra, 1984; de Villiers, 1984). However, all commentators seem to agree on one crucial point: these children provide a vivid illustration of the power and creativity of human infants as they strive to communicate with others using whatever means may be available (Acredolo & Goodwyn, 1990; Schaffer, 1989).

Toward Community and Conversations

As they interact with their caregivers, developing infants experience human communication as communion, as transmission, and as education (see Chapter 2). Over a period of some 18 months, their inchoate shared attentiveness transforms into patterned, meaning-filled dialogues.

So much is accomplished during infancy that it is tempting to see all of later development foreshadowed in its final dialogues. But there is, of course, still a long path between an infant who utters single words to his interpretation-prone parent and a 4-year-old who chatters freely with an unfamiliar, same-aged friend, much less an adult who reads a book about the beginnings of communication. Thus, we end our account of communication development during infancy with a few comments about what lies ahead.

First, the just-verbal infant is poised to tackle the complexities of language. As Gleitman and Wanner noted sharply in their introduction to a collection of essays on the state of theories of language acquisition, "It is massively overexuberant to hope that knowing meaning is tantamount to knowing language" (1982, p. 14). Clearly, many moves remain before a child makes significant inroads into the inner structure of grammar. Brown (1973) and Ingram (1989), among many others, provide excellent guides to how children begin this incomparable journey.

Second, infants are now ready to use their burgeoning communication skills to cultivate their coordinations with other people. At the end of infancy, speech has only just begun to be integrated into dialogues. Over the next many months, conversations begin to be structured where speech can follow quickly upon speech (Halliday, 1975; Lewis, 1936; Schaffer, 1984). Furthermore, the toddler literally begins to walk into a broader community of partners. With increased mobility come new communicative challenges as the child enters a sphere of peers and outsiders who, by dint of age or familiarity, are less inclined than intimate caregivers to coddle their communicative attempts (see, e.g., Eckerman, Davis, & Didow, 1989).

Finally, children begin to communicate with others about their innermost thoughts and feelings (Bretherton & Beeghly, 1982; Brown & Dunn, 1992) and about the process of social interaction itself. The development of this *meta-sociability* (Schaffer, 1984) blends self-consciousness with ongoing activities (Shotter, 1974) and endows communication with unprecedented depth. Children's conversations gradually come to carry explicit reference to shared experiences, as well as increasingly coherent reflections upon themselves, their partners, and their cultural context.

REFERENCES

Acredolo, L. P., & Goodwyn, S. W. (1988). Symbolic gesturing in normal infants. *Child Development*, *59*, 450–466.

Acredolo, L. P., & Goodwyn, S. W. (1990). Sign language in babies: The significance of symbolic gesturing for understanding language development. In R. Vasta (Ed.), *Annals of Child Development* (Vol. 7, pp. 1–42). London: Kingsley.

Adamson, L. B. (1992). Variations in the early use of language. In L. T. Winegar & J. Valsiner (Eds.), *Children's development within social context: Vol. 1. Metatheory and theory* (pp. 123–141). Hillsdale, NJ: Erlbaum.

Adamson, L. B., Als, H., Tronick, E., & Brazelton, T. B. (1977). The development of social reciprocity between a sighted infant and her blind parents. *Journal of the Academy of Child Psychiatry*, *16*, 194–207.

Adamson, L. B., & Bakeman, R. (1982). Affectivity and reference: Concepts, methods and techniques in the study of communication development of six to eighteen month old infants. In T. M. Field & A. Fogel (Eds.), *Emotion and interaction* (pp. 213–236). Hillsdale, NJ: Erlbaum.

Adamson, L. B., & Bakeman, R. (1984). Mothers' communicative acts: Changes during infancy. *Infant Behavior and Development*, *7*, 467–478.

Adamson, L. B., & Bakeman, R. (1985). Affect and attention: Infants observed with mothers and peers. *Child Development*, *56*, 582–593.

Adamson, L. B., & Bakeman, R. (1991). The development of shared attention during infancy. In R. Vasta (Ed.), *Annals of Child Development* (Vol. 8, pp. 1–41). London: Kingsley.

Adamson, L. B., Bakeman, R., & Smith, C. B. (1990). Gestures, words, and early object sharing. In V. Volterra & C. Erting (Eds.), *From gesture to language in hearing and deaf children* (pp. 31–41). New York: Springer-Verlag.

Adamson, L. B., Bakeman, R., Smith, C. B., & Walters, A. S. (1987). Adults' interpretation of infants' acts. *Developmental Psychology*, *23*, 383–387.

Adamson, L. B., & Dunbar, B. (1991). Communication development of young children with tracheostomies. *Augmentative and Alternative Communication*, *7*, 275–283.

Adamson, L. B., & McArthur, D. (in press.) Joint attention, affect, and culture. In C. Moore & P. Dunham (Eds.), *Joint attention: Its origin and role in development*. Hillsdale, NJ: Erlbaum.

Ainsworth, M. D. S. (1967). *Infancy in Uganda: Infant care and the growth of love*. Baltimore: The Johns Hopkins University Press.

Als, H. (1979). Social interaction: Dynamic matrix for developing behavioral organization. In I. Č. Užgiris (Ed.), *Social interaction and communication during infancy: Vol. 4. New Directions for Child Development* (pp. 21–41). San Francisco: Jossey-Bass.

Als, H. (1982). The unfolding of behavioral organization in the face of a biological violation. In E. Z. Tronick (Ed.), *Social interchange in infancy: Affect, cognition, and communication* (pp. 125–160). Baltimore: University Park Press.

Anderson, B. J., Vietze, P., & Dokecki, P. R. (1978). Interpersonal distance and vocal behavior in the mother–infant dyad. *Infant Behavior and Development*, *1*, 381–391.

Anisfeld, M. (1984). *Language development from birth to three*. Hillsdale, NJ: Erlbaum.

Anisfeld, M. (1991). Neonatal imitation: A review. *Developmental Review*, *11*, 60–97.

Argyle, M., & Cook, M. (1976). *Gaze and mutual gaze*. Cambridge, England: Cambridge University Press.

Aronson, E., & Rosenbloom, S. (1971). Space perception in early infancy: Perception within a common auditory-visual space. *Science*, *172*, 1161–1163.

Aslin, R. N. (1987). Visual and auditory development in infancy. In J. D. Osofsky (Ed.), *Handbook of infant development* (2nd ed., pp. 5–97). New York: Wiley.

Aslin, R. N. (1992). Segmentation of fluent speech into words: Learning models and the role of maternal input. In B. de Boysson-Bardies, P. Jusczyk, P. MacNeilage, J. Morton, & S. de Schonen (Eds.), *Developmental neurocognition: Speech and face processing in the first year of life* (pp. 305–315). Dordrecht, Netherlands: Kluwer.

Astington, J. W., Harris, P. L., & Olson, D. R. (Eds.). (1988). *Developing theories of the mind*. Cambridge, England: Cambridge University Press.

Baars, B. J. (1986). *The cognitive revolution in psychology*. New York: Guilford.

Bakeman, R., & Adamson, L. B. (1984). Coordinating attention to people and objects in mother–infant and peer–infant interaction. *Child Development*, *55*, 1278–1289.

Bakeman, R., & Adamson, L. B. (1986). Infants' conventionalized acts: Gestures and words with mothers and peers. *Infant Behavior and Development*, *9*, 215–230.

Bakeman, R., Adamson, L. B., Konner, M., & Barr, R. G. (1990). !Kung infancy: The social context of object exploration. *Child Development*, *61*, 794–809.

Bakeman, R., & Brown, J. V. (1977). Behavioral dialogues: An approach to the assessment of mother–infant interaction. *Child Development*, *48*, 195–203.

Bakeman, R., & Brown, J. V. (1980). Analyzing behavioral sequences: Differences between preterm and full-term infant–mother dyads during the first months of life. In D. B. Sawin, R. C. Hawkins II, L. O. Walker, & J. H. Penticuff (Eds.), *Exceptional infant: Vol. 4. Psychological risks in infant–environment transactions* (pp. 271–299). New York: Brunner/Mazel.

Bakeman, R., & Gottman, J. M. (1986). *Observing interaction: An introduction to sequential analysis.* New York: Cambridge University Press.

Baron-Cohen, S. (1989). Joint-attention deficits in autism: Towards a cognitive analysis. *Development and Psychopathology*, *1*, 185–189.

Barr, R. G. (1990). The normal crying curve: What do we really know? *Developmental Medicine and Child Neurology*, *32*, 368–374.

Barr, R. G., Konner, M., Bakeman, R., & Adamson, L. B. (1991). Crying in !Kung San infants: A test of the cultural specificity hypothesis. *Developmental Medicine and Child Neurology*, *33*, 601–611.

Barrett, M. (1985). Issues in the study of children's single-word speech. In M. Barrett (Ed.), *Children's single-word speech* (pp. 1–19). New York: Wiley.

Barrett, M. (1989). Early language development. In A. Slater & G. Bremner (Eds.), *Infant development* (pp. 211–241). Hillsdale, NJ: Erlbaum.

Bates, E., Benigni, L., Bretherton, I., Camaioni, L., & Volterra, V. (1979). *The emergence of symbols: Cognition and communication in infancy*. New York: Academic Press.

Bates, E., Bretherton, I., & Snyder, L. (1988). *From first words to grammar: Individual differences and dissociable mechanisms*. Cambridge, England: Cambridge University Press.

Bates, E., Camaioni, L., & Volterra, V. (1975). The acquisition of performatives prior to speech. *Merrill-Palmer Quarterly*, *21*, 205–226.

Bates, E., Marchman, V., Thal, D., Fenson, L., Dale, P., Reznick, J. S., Reilly, J., & Hartung, J. (in press). Developmental and stylistic variation in the composition of early vocabulary. *Journal of Child Language*.

Bates, E., O'Connell, B., & Shore, C. (1987). Language and communication in infancy. In J. D. Osofsky (Ed.), *Handbook of infant development* (2nd ed., pp. 149–203). New York: Wiley.

Bates, E., Thal, D., Whitesell, K., Fenson, L., & Oakes, L. (1989). Integrating language and gesture in infancy. *Developmental Psychology*, *25*, 1004–1019.

Bates, E., & Volterra, V. (1984). On the invention of language: An alternative view. *Monographs of the Society for Research in Child Development*, *49* (3–4, Serial No. 207), 130–142.

Baum, W. M., & Heath, J. L. (1992). Behavioral explanations and intentional explanations in psychology. *American Psychologist*, *47*, 1312–1317.

Bayley, N. (1969). *Bayley scales of infant development*. Cleveland, OH: Psychological Corporation.

Beebe, B., & Gerstman, L. J. (1980). The "packaging" of maternal stimulation in relation to infant facial–visual engagement: A case study at four months. *Merrill-Palmer Quarterly*, *26*, 321–339.

Bell, R. Q. (1968). A reinterpretation of the direction of effects in studies of socialization. *Psychological Review*, *75*, 81–95.

Benedict, H. (1979). Early lexical development: Comprehension and production. *Journal of Child Language*, *6*, 183–200.

Berg, W. K., Adkinson, C. D. P., & Strock, B. D. (1973). Duration and frequency of periods of alertness in neonates. *Developmental Psychology*, *9*, 434.

Block, J. H. (1984). *Sex role identity and ego development*. San Francisco: Jossey-Bass.

Bloom, L. (1973). *One word at a time: The use of single word utterances before syntax*. The Hague: Mouton.

Bloom, L., & Beckwith, R. (1989). Talking with feeling: Integrating affective and linguistic expression in early language development. *Cognition and Emotion, 3*, 313–342.

Bloom, L., & Capatides, J. (1987). Expression of affect and the emergence of language. *Child Development, 58*, 1513–1522.

Bloom, L., Lifter, K., & Broughton, J. (1985). The convergence of early cognition and language in the second year of life: Problems in conceptualization and measurement. In M. Barrett (Ed.), *Children's single-word speech* (pp. 149–180). New York: Wiley.

Bornstein, M. H., Tal, J., Rahn, C., Galperín, C. Z., Pêcheux, M-G., Lamour, M., Toda, S., Azuma, H., Ogino, M., & Tamis-LeMonda, C. S. (1992). Functional analysis of the contents of maternal speech to infants of 5 and 13 months in four cultures: Argentina, France, Japan, and the United States. *Developmental Psychology, 28*, 593–603.

Bower, T. G. R. (1989). *The rational infant*. New York: Freeman.

Bower, T. G. R., Broughton, J. M., & Moore, M. K. (1970). The coordination of vision and touch in infancy. *Perception and Psychophysics, 8*, 51–53.

Bowerman, M. (1976). Semantic factors in the acquisition of rules for word use and sentence construction. In D. M. Morehead & A. E. Morehead (Eds.), *Normal and deficient child language* (pp. 99–179). Baltimore: University Park Press.

Bowerman, M. (1978). The acquisition of word meaning: An investigation into some current conflicts. In N. Waterson & C. Snow (Eds.), *The development of communication* (pp. 263–287). Chichester, England: Wiley.

Bowlby, J. (1969). *Attachment and loss: Vol. 1. Attachment*. New York: Basic Books.

Boysson-Bardies, B., Sagart, L., & Durand, C. (1984). Discernible differences in the babbling of infants according to target language. *Journal of Child Language, 11*, 1–15.

Brazelton, T. B. (1962). Crying in infancy. *Pediatrics, 29*, 579–588.

Brazelton, T. B. (1973). *Neonatal behavioral assessment scale*. London: Spastics International Medical Publications.

Brazelton, T. B. (1979). Evidence of communication during neonatal behavioral assessment. In M. Bullowa (Ed.), *Before speech: The beginning of interpersonal communication* (pp. 79–88). Cambridge, England: Cambridge University Press.

Brazelton, T. B. (1982). Joint regulation in neonate-parent behavior. In E. Z. Tronick (Ed.), *Social interchange in infancy: Affect, cognition, and communication* (pp. 7–22). Baltimore: University Park Press.

Brazelton, T. B., Koslowski, B., & Main, M. (1974). The origins of reciprocity: The early mother–infant interaction. In M. Lewis & L. Rosenblum (Eds.), *The effect of the infant on its caregiver* (pp. 49–76). New York: Wiley.

Brazelton, T. B., Tronick, E., Adamson, L. B., Als, H., & Wise, S. (1975). Early mother–infant reciprocity. In M. A. Hofer (Ed.), *Parent–infant interaction* (pp. 137–154). Amsterdam: ASP CIBA Foundation.

Bretherton, I. (1992). Social referencing, intentional communication, and the interfacing of minds in infancy. In S. Feinman (Ed.), *Social referencing and the social construction of reality in infancy* (pp. 57–77). New York: Plenum.

Bretherton, I., Bates, E., McNew, S., Shore, C., Williamson, C., & Beeghly-Smith, M. (1981). Comprehension and production of symbols in infancy: An experimental study. *Developmental Psychology*, *17*, 728–736.

Bretherton, I., & Beeghly, M. (1982). Talking about internal states: The acquisition of an explicit theory of mind. *Developmental Psychology*, *18*, 906–921.

Bretherton, I., McNew, S., Snyder, L., & Bates, E. (1983). Individual differences at 20 months: Analytic and holistic strategies in language acquisition. *Journal of Child Language*, *10*, 293–320.

Bridges, A. (1986). Actions and things: What adults talk about to 1-year-olds. In S. A. Kuczaj II & M. D. Barrett (Eds.), *The development of word meaning* (pp. 225–255). New York: Springer-Verlag.

Broerse, J., Peltola, C., & Crassini, B. (1983). Infants' reactions to perceptual paradox during mother–infant interaction. *Developmental Psychology*, *19*, 310–316.

Bronfenbrenner, U. (1979). *The ecology of human development: Experiments by nature and design*. Cambridge, MA: Harvard University Press.

Brown, J. (1973). Non-nutritive sucking in great ape and human newborns. In J. Bosma (Ed.), *Oral sensation and perception: Development of the fetus and infant* (pp. 118–131). Bethesda, MD: U. S. Department of Health, Education, and Welfare.

Brown, J. R., & Dunn, J. (1992). Talk with your mother or your sibling? Developmental changes in early family conversations about feelings. *Child Development*, *63*, 336–349.

Brown, R. (1973). *A first language: The early stages*. Cambridge, MA: Harvard University Press.

Bruner, J. (1969). Eye, hand, and mind. In D. Elkind & J. H. Flavell (Eds.), *Studies in cognitive development: Essays in honor of Jean Piaget* (pp. 223–235). New York: Oxford University Press.

Bruner, J. (1972). Nature and uses of immaturity. *American Psychologist*, *27*, 687–708.

Bruner, J. (1975). From communication to language: A psychological perspective. *Cognition*, *3*, 255–287.

Bruner, J. (1982). The formats of language acquisition. *American Journal of Semiotics*, *1*, 1–16.

Bruner, J. (1983a). In *A tribute to Roman Jakobson 1896–1982* (pp. 88–92). Berlin: Mouton.

Bruner, J. (1983b). *Child's talk: Learning to use language*. New York: Norton.

Bruner, J. (1983c). *In search of mind: Essays in autobiography*. New York: Harper Colophon.

Bruner, J. (1984). Interaction, communication, and self. *Journal of the American Academy of Child Psychiatry*, *23*, 1–7.

Bruner, J. (1985). Vygotsky: A historical and conceptual perspective. In J. V. Wertsch (Ed.), *Culture, communication, and cognition: Vygotskian perspectives* (pp. 21–34). Cambridge, England: Cambridge University Press.

Bruner, J. (1990). *Acts of meaning*. Cambridge, MA: Harvard University Press.

Bruner, J., & Haste, H. (1987). Introduction. In J. Bruner & H. Haste (Eds.), *Making sense: The child's construction of the world* (pp. 1–25). London: Methuen.

Bruner, J., Roy, C., & Ratner, N. (1982). The beginnings of request. In K. E. Nelson (Ed.), *Children's language* (Vol. 3, pp. 91–138). Hillsdale, NJ: Erlbaum.

Bühler, K. (1982). The axiomatization of the language sciences. In R. E. Innis (Ed.), *Karl Bühler: Semiotic foundations of language theory* (pp. 75–164). New York: Plenum. (Original work published 1933)

Bullowa, M. (1979). Introduction: Prelinguistic communication: A field for scientific research. In M. Bullowa (Ed.), *Before speech: The beginning of interpersonal communication* (pp. 1–62). Cambridge, England: Cambridge University Press.

Butterfield, H. (1957). *The origins of modern science*. New York: Macmillan.

Butterworth, G. (1987). Some benefits of egocentrism. In J. Bruner & H. Haste (Eds.), *Making sense: The child's construction of the world* (pp. 62–80). London: Methuen.

Butterworth, G., & Cochran, E. (1980). Towards a mechanism of joint visual attention in human infancy. *International Journal of Behavioral Development*, *3*, 253–272.

Butterworth, G., & Grover, L. (1990). Joint visual attention, manual pointing, and preverbal communication in human infancy. In M. Jeannerod (Ed.), *Attention and performance XIII* (pp. 605–624). Hillsdale, NJ: Erlbaum.

Campos, J. J., & Stenberg, C. R. (1981). Perception, appraisal, and emotion: The onset of social referencing. In M. E. Lamb & L. R. Sherrod (Eds.), *Infant social cognition: Empirical and theoretical considerations* (pp. 273–314). Hillsdale, NJ: Erlbaum.

Carey, S. (1978). The child as word learner. In M. Halle, J. Bresnan, & G. A. Miller (Eds.), *Linguistic theory and psychological reality* (pp. 264–293). Cambridge, MA: MIT Press.

Carlile, K. S., & Holstrum, W. J. (1989). Parental involvement behaviors: A comparison of Chamorro and Caucasian parents. *Infant Behavior and Development*, *12*, 479–494.

Carter, A. L. (1978). The development of systematic vocalizations prior to words: A case study. In N. Waterson & C. Snow (Eds.), *The development of communication* (pp. 127–138). Chichester, England: Wiley.

Carter, A. L. (1979). Prespeech meaning relations: An outline of one infant's sensorimotor morpheme development. In P. Fletcher & M. Garman (Eds.), *Language acquisition: Studies in first language development* (1st ed., pp. 71–92). Cambridge, England: Cambridge University Press.

Cernoch, J. M., & Porter, R. H. (1985). Recognition of maternal axillary odors by infants. *Child Development*, *56*, 1593–1598.

Chapman, M. (1988). *Constructive evolution: Origins and development of Piaget's thought*. Cambridge, England: Cambridge University Press.

Chappell, P. F., & Sander, L. W. (1979). Mutual regulation of the neonatal-maternal interactive process: Context for the origins of communication. In M. Bullowa (Ed.), *Before speech: The beginning of interpersonal communication* (pp. 89–109). Cambridge, England: Cambridge University Press.

Chomsky, N. (1959). Review of *Verbal Behavior* by B. F. Skinner. *Language*, *35*, 26–58.

Cicchetti, D., & Beeghly, M. (Eds.). (1990). *Children with Down syndrome: A developmental perspective*. Cambridge, England: Cambridge University Press.

Clark, E. V. (1973). What's in a word? On the child's acquisition of semantics in his first language. In T. E. Moore (Ed.), *Cognitive development and the acquisition of language* (pp. 65–110). New York: Academic Press.

Clark, R. A. (1978). The transition from action to gesture. In A. Lock (Ed.), *Action, gesture, and symbol* (pp. 231–257). London: Academic Press.

Clarke-Stewart, K. A. (1973). Interactions between mothers and their young children: Characteristics and consequences. *Monographs of the Society for Research in Child Development, 38* (6–7, Serial No. 153).

Cohn, J. F., Campbell, S. B., Matias, R., & Hopkins, J. (1990). Face-to-face interactions of postpartum depressed and nondepressed mother–infant pairs at 2 months. *Developmental Psychology, 26*, 15–23.

Cohn, J. F., & Elmore, M. (1988). Effect of contingent changes in mothers' affective expression on the organization of behavior in 3-month-old infants. *Infant Behavior and Development, 11*, 493–505.

Cohn, J. F., Matias, R., Tronick, E. Z., Lyons-Ruth, K., & Connell, D. (1986). Face-to-face interactions, spontaneous and structured, of mothers with depressive symptoms. In T. Field & E. Z. Tronick (Eds.), *Maternal depression and child development: Vol. 34. New Directions for Child Development* (pp. 31–46). San Francisco: Jossey-Bass.

Cohn, J. F., & Tronick, E. Z. (1983). Three-month-old infants' reaction to simulated maternal depression. *Child Development, 54*, 185-193.

Cohn, J. F., & Tronick, E. Z. (1988a). Discrete versus scaling approaches to the description of mother–infant face-to-face interaction: Convergent validity and divergent applications. *Developmental Psychology, 24*, 396–397.

Cohn, J. F., & Tronick, E. Z. (1988b). Mother–infant face-to-face interaction: Influence is bidirectional and unrelated to periodic cycles in either partner's behavior. *Developmental Psychology, 24*, 386–392.

Cole, M. (1985). The zone of proximal development: Where culture and cognition create each other. In J. V. Wertsch (Ed.), *Culture, communication, and cognition: Vygotskian perspectives* (pp. 146–161). Cambridge, England: Cambridge University Press.

Cole, M., & Scribner, S. (1978). Introduction to L. S. Vygotsky's *Mind in Society* (pp. 1–14). Cambridge, MA: Harvard University Press.

Collins, W. A. (Ed.). (1982). *The concept of development: The Minnesota symposia on child psychology* (Vol. 15). Hillsdale, NJ: Erlbaum.

Collis, G. M. (1977). Visual co-orientation and maternal speech. In H. R. Schaffer (Ed.), *Studies in mother–infant interaction* (pp. 355–375). London: Academic Press.

Condon, W., & Sander, L. (1974). Neonate movement is synchronized with adult speech: Interactional participation and language acquisition. *Science, 183*, 99–101.

Condry, S. M., Haltom, M., & Neisser, U. (1977). Infant sensitivity to audio-visual discrepancy: A failure to replicate. *Bulletin of the Psychonomic Society, 9*, 431–432.

Cooper, R. P., & Aslin, R. N. (1990). Preference for infant-directed speech in the first month after birth. *Child Development, 61*, 1584–1595.

Corrigan, R. (1978). Language development as related to Stage 6 object permanence development. *Journal of Child Language, 5*, 173–189.

Cross, T. G., Nienhuys, T. G., & Kirkman, M. (1985). Parent-child interaction with receptively disabled children: Some determinants of maternal speech style. In K. Nelson (Ed.), *Children's language* (Vol. 5, pp. 247–290). Hillsdale, NJ: Erlbaum.

Crow, B. M., & Gowers, J. I. (1979). The smiling age of preterm babies. *Developmental Medicine and Child Neurology, 21*, 174–177.

Curtiss, S. (1977). *Genie: A psycholinguistc study of a modern-day "Wild-Child."* New York: Academic Press.

Darwin, C. (1859). *On the origin of species by means of natural selection.* London: John Murray.

Darwin, C. (1877). A biographical sketch of an infant. *Mind, 2,* 285–294.

Deaux, K., & Major, B. (1987). Putting gender in context: An interactive model of gender-related behavior. *Psychological Review, 94*, 369–389.

DeCasper, A. J., & Fifer, W. P. (1980). Of human bonding: Newborns prefer their mothers' voices. *Science, 208,* 1174–1176.

DeCasper, A. J., & Spence, M. J. (1986). Prenatal maternal speech influences newborns' perception of speech sounds. *Infant Behavior and Development, 9*, 133–150.

Deffebach, K., & Adamson, L. B. (1994). *Teaching referential and social-regulative words to toddlers: Mothers' use of metalingual language.* Manuscript submitted for publication.

De Laguna, G. A. (1927). *Speech: Its function and development.* New Haven: Yale University Press.

Demetriou, A. (Ed.). (1988). *The neo-Piagetian theories of cognitive development: Toward an integration.* Amsterdam: Elsevier Science.

Dennis, W. (1936). A bibliography of baby biographies. *Child Development, 7*, 71–73.

de Villiers, J. (1984). Limited input? Limited structure. *Monographs of the Society for Research in Child Development, 49* (3–4, Serial No. 207), 122–129.

DeWitt, N. J. (1957). Organism and humanism: An empirical view. In D. B. Harris (Ed.), *The concept of development: An issue in the study of human behavior* (pp. 177–198). Minneapolis: University of Minnesota Press.

Dickstein, S., & Parke, R. D. (1988). Social referencing in infancy: A glance at fathers and marriage. *Child Development, 59*, 506–511.

Dixon, S., Tronick, E. Z., Keefer, C., & Brazelton, T. B. (1981). Mother–infant interaction among the Gusii of Kenya. In T. M. Field, A. M. Sostek, P. Vietze, & P. H. Leiderman (Eds.), *Culture and early interactions* (pp. 149–170). Hillsdale, NJ: Erlbaum.

Dixon, S., Yogman, M., Tronick, E., Adamson, L. B., Als, H., & Brazelton, T. B. (1981). Early infant social interaction with parents and strangers. *Journal of the American Academy of Child Psychiatry, 20*, 32–52.

Donaldson, M. (1978). *Children's minds.* New York: Norton.

Dore, J. (1974). A pragmatic description of early language development. *Journal of Psycholinguistic Research, 3*, 343–350.

Dore, J. (1985). Holophrases revisited: Their 'logical' development from dialog. In M. Barrett (Ed.), *Children's single-word speech* (pp. 23–58). New York: Wiley.

Dore, J., Franklin, M. B., Miller, R. T., & Ramer, A. L. H. (1976). Transitional phenomena in early language acquisition. *Journal of Child Language, 3*, 13–28.

Dowd, J. M., & Tronick, E. Z. (1986). Temporal coordination of arm movements in early infancy: Do infants move in synchrony with adult speech? *Child Development, 57*, 762–776.

Dunham, P., & Dunham, F. (1992). Lexical development during middle infancy: A mutually driven infant–caregiver process. *Developmental Psychology, 28*, 414–420.

Dunn, J., & Shatz, M. (1989). Becoming a conversationalist despite (or because of) having an older sibling. *Child Development, 60*, 399–410.

Eckerman, C. O., Davis, C. C., & Didow, S. M. (1989). Toddlers' emerging ways of achieving social coordinations with a peer. *Child Development, 60*, 440–453.

Eckerman, C. O., & Whatley, J. L. (1977). Toys and social interaction between infant peers. *Child Development*, *48*, 1645–1656.

Eckerman, C. O., Whatley, J. L., & Kutz, S. L. (1975). Growth of social play with peers during the second year of life. *Developmental Psychology*, *11*, 42–49.

Eckerman, C. O., Whatley, J. L., & McGehee, L. J. (1979). Approaching and contacting the object another manipulates: A social skill of the 1-year-old. *Developmental Psychology*, *15*, 585–593.

Eibl-Eibesfeldt, I. (1989). *Human ethology*. New York: Aldine de Gruyter.

Eimas, P. D., Siqueland, E. R., Jusczyk, P., & Vigorito, J. (1971). Speech perception in infants. *Science*, *171*, 303–306.

Ellsworth, C. P., Muir, D. W., & Hains, S. M. J. (1993). Social competence and person-object differentiation: An analysis of the still-face effect. *Developmental Psychology*, *29*, 63–73.

Emde, R. N. (1992). Social referencing research: Uncertainty, self, and the search for meaning. In S. Feinman (Ed.), *Social referencing and the social construction of reality in infancy* (pp. 79–94). New York: Plenum.

Emde, R. N., Gaensbauer, T. J., & Harmon, R. J. (1976). Emotional expression in infancy: A biobehavioral study. *Psychological Issues* (Monograph 37). New York: International Universities Press.

Emde, R. N., & Robinson, J. (1979). The first two months: Recent research in developmental psychobiology and the changing view of the newborn. In J. Noshpitz (Ed.), *Basic Handbook of Child Psychiatry* (pp. 72–105). New York: Basic Books.

Erting, C. J., Prezioso, C., & O'Grady Hynes, M. (1990). The interactional context of deaf mother–infant communication. In V. Volterra & C. J. Erting (Eds.), *From gesture to language in hearing and deaf children* (pp. 97–106). New York: Springer-Verlag.

Erting, C. J., & Volterra, V. (1990). Conclusion. In V. Volterra & C. J. Erting (Eds.), *From gesture to language in hearing and deaf children* (pp. 299–303). New York: Springer-Verlag.

Fantz, R. L. (1958). Pattern vision in young infants. *Psychological Record*, *8*, 43–47.

Feinman, S. (Ed.). (1992). *Social referencing and the social construction of reality in infancy.* New York: Plenum.

Feinman, S., & Lewis, M. (1983). Social referencing at ten months: A second-order effect on infants' responses to strangers. *Child Development*, *54*, 878–887.

Feldman, H., Goldin-Meadow, S., & Gleitman, L. R. (1978). Beyond Herodotus: The creation of language by linguistically deprived deaf children. In A. Lock (Ed.), *Action, gesture, and symbol* (pp. 351–414). London: Academic Press.

Fenson, L., Dale, P. S., Reznick, J. S., Thal, D., Bates, E., Hartung, J. P., Pethick, S., & Reilly, J. S. (1993). *Technical manual for the MacArthur Communication Development Inventory*. San Diego, CA: Singular Press.

Ferguson, C. A. (1977). Baby talk as a simplified register. In C. E. Snow & C. A. Ferguson (Eds.), *Talking to children: Language input and acquisition* (pp. 209–235). Cambridge, England: Cambridge University Press.

Fernald, A. (1991). Prosody in speech to children: Prelinguistic and linguistic functions. In R. Vasta (Ed.), *Annals of Child Development* (Vol. 8, pp. 43–80). London: Kingsley.

Fernald, A., & Mazzie, C. (1991). Prosody and focus in speech to infants and adults. *Developmental Psychology*, *27*, 209–221.

Fernald, A., & Simon, T. (1984). Expanded intonation contours in mothers' speech to newborns. *Developmental Psychology*, *20*, 104–113.

Field, T. M. (1977a). Effects of early separation, interactive deficits, and experimental manipulations on infant–mother face-to-face interaction. *Child Development*, *48*, 763–771.

Field, T. M. (1977b). Maternal stimulation during infant feeding. *Developmental Psychology*, *13*, 539–540.

Field, T. M., Cohen, D., Garcia, R., & Greenberg, R. (1984). Mother-stranger face discrimination by the newborn. *Infant Behavior and Development*, *7*, 19–25.

Field, T., Healy, B., Goldstein, S., & Guthertz, M. (1990). Behavior-state matching and synchrony in mother–infant interactions of nondepressed versus depressed dyads. *Developmental Psychology*, *26*, 7–14.

Field, T., Healy, B., Goldstein, S., Perry, S., Bendell, D., Schanberg, S., Zimmerman, E. A., & Kuhn, C. (1988). Infants of depressed mothers show "depressed" behavior even with nondepressed adults. *Child Development*, *59*, 1569–1579.

Field, T., Vega-Lahr, N., Scafidi, F., & Goldstein, S. (1986). Effects of maternal unavailability on mother–infant interactions. *Infant Behavior and Development*, *9*, 473–478.

Field, T. M., Woodson, R., Greenberg, R., & Cohen, D. (1982). Discrimination and imitation of facial expressions by neonates. *Science*, *218*, 179–181.

Fischer, K. W., & Farrar, M. J. (1988). Generalizations about generalization: How a theory of skill development explains both generality and specificity. In A. Demetriou (Ed.), *The neo-Piagetian theories of cognitive development: Toward an integration* (pp. 137–171). Amsterdam: Elsevier Science.

Fischer, K. W., & Hogan, A. E. (1989). The big picture for infant development: Levels and variations. In J. J. Lockman & N. L. Hazen (Eds.), *Action in social context: Perspectives on early development* (pp. 275–305). New York: Plenum.

Flavell, J. (1963). *The developmental psychology of Jean Piaget*. Princeton, NJ: Van Nostrand.

Fogel, A. (1977). Temporal organization in mother–infant face-to-face interaction. In H. R. Schaffer (Ed.), *Studies in mother–infant interaction* (pp. 119–151). London: Academic Press.

Fogel, A. (1985). Coordinative structures in the development of expressive behavior in early infancy. In G. Zivin (Ed.), *The development of expressive behavior: Biology–environment interactions* (pp. 249–267). Orlando, FL: Academic Press.

Fogel, A. (1988). Cyclicity and stability in mother–infant face-to-face interaction: A comment on Cohn & Tronick (1988). *Developmental Psychology*, *24*, 393–395.

Fogel, A. (1990). The process of developmental change in infant communicative action: Using dynamic systems theory to study individual ontogenies. In J. Colombo & J. Fagen (Eds.), *Individual differences in infancy: Reliability, stability, prediction* (pp. 341–358). Hillsdale, NJ: Erlbaum.

Fogel, A., Diamond, G. R., Langhorst, B. H., & Demos, V. (1982). Affective and cognitive aspects of the 2-month-old's participation in face-to-face interaction with the mother. In E. Z. Tronick (Ed.), *Social interchange in infancy: Affect, cognition, and communication* (pp. 37–57). Baltimore: University Park Press.

Fogel, A., & Hannan, T. E. (1985). Manual actions of nine- to fifteen-week-old human infants during face-to-face interaction with their mothers. *Child Development, 56,* 1271–1279.

Fogel, A., & Thelen, E. (1987). Development of early expressive and communicative action: Reinterpreting the evidence from a dynamic systems perspective. *Developmental Psychology, 23,* 747–761.

Fogel, A., Toda, S., & Kawai, M. (1988). Mother-infant face-to-face interaction in Japan and the United States: A laboratory comparison using 3-month-old infants. *Developmental Psychology, 24,* 398–406.

Folven, R. J., & Bonvillian, J. D. (1991). The transition from nonreferential to referential language in children acquiring American Sign Language. *Developmental Psychology, 27,* 806–816.

Foster, S. H. (1990). *The communicative competence of young children: A modular approach.* New York: Longman.

Fraiberg, S. (1971). Smiling and stranger reaction in blind infants. In J. Hellmuth (Ed.), *Exceptional infant* (Vol. 2, pp. 110–127). New York: Brunner/Mazel.

Freud, S. (1958). Formulations on the two principles of mental functioning. In J. Strachey (Ed.), *The standard edition of the complete psychological works of Sigmund Freud* (Vol. 12, pp. 218–226). London: Hogarth Press. (Original work published 1911)

Frith, U. (1989). *Autism: Explaining the enigma.* Oxford: Basil Blackwell.

Frodi, A. M. (1985). When empathy fails: Aversive infant crying and child abuse. In B. M. Lester & C. F. Z. Boukydis (Eds.), *Infant crying: Theoretical and research perspectives* (pp. 217–277). New York: Plenum.

Frodi, A. M., & Lamb, M. E. (1980). Child abusers' responses to infant smiles and cries. *Child Development, 51,* 238–241.

Frodi, A. M., Lamb, M. E., Leavitt, L. A., & Donovan, W. L. (1978). Fathers' and mothers' responses to infant smiles and cries. *Infant Behavior and Development, 1,* 187–198.

Frodi, A. M., Lamb, M. E., Leavitt, L. A., Donovan, W. L., Neff, C., & Sherry, D. (1978). Fathers' and mothers' responses to the faces and cries of normal and premature infants. *Development Psychology, 14,* 490–498.

Frye, D., & Moore, C. (Eds.). (1991). *Children's theories of mind: Mental states and social understanding.* Hillsdale, NJ: Erlbaum.

Frye, D., Rawling, P., Moore, C., & Myers, I. (1983). Object–person discrimination and communication at 3 and 10 months. *Developmental Psychology, 19,* 303–309.

Furrow, D., & James, P. (1985). Attentional change and vocalizations: Evidence for a relation. *Child Development, 56,* 1179–1183.

Furrow, D., & Nelson, K. (1984). Environmental correlates of individual differences in language acquisition. *Journal of Child Language, 11,* 523–534.

Garnica, O. K. (1977). Some prosodic and paralinguistic features of speech to young children. In C. E. Snow & C. A. Ferguson (Eds.), *Talking to children: Language input and acquisition* (pp. 63–88). Cambridge, England: Cambridge University Press.

Garton, A. (1992). *Social interaction and the development of language and cognition.* Hove, England: Erlbaum.

Gelman, R. (1983). Reconsidering the transition from prelinguistic to linguistic communication. In R. M. Golinkoff (Ed.), *The transition from prelinguistic to linguistic communication* (pp. 275–279). Hillsdale, NJ: Erlbaum.

Gelman, R. (1990). Structural constraints on cognitive development: Introduction to a special issue of *Cognitive Science. Cognitive Science, 14*, 3–10.

Gesell, A. (1945). *The embryology of behavior: The beginnings of the human mind.* New York: Harper & Brothers.

Gianino, A., & Tronick, E. Z. (1988). The mutual regulation model: The infant's self and interactive regulation and coping and defensive capacities. In T. M. Field, P. M. McCabe, & N. Schneiderman (Eds.), *Stress and coping across development* (pp. 47-68). Hillsdale, NJ: Erlbaum.

Gibson, E. J. (1988). Exploratory behavior in the development of perceiving, acting, and the acquiring of knowledge. *Annual Review of Psychology, 19*, 1–41.

Gibson, J. J. (1979). *The ecological approach to visual perception.* Boston: Houghton Mifflin.

Ginsburg, H. P., & Opper, S. (1988). *Piaget's theory of intellectual development* (3rd ed.). Englewood Cliffs, NJ: Prentice Hall.

Gleitman, L. R. (1986). Biological dispositions to learn language. In W. Demopolous & A. Marras (Eds.), *Language learning and concept acquisition* (pp. 3–28). Norwood, NJ: Ablex.

Gleitman, L. R., & Wanner, E. (1982). Language acquisition: The state of the state of the art. In E. Wanner & L. R. Gleitman (Eds.), *Language acquisition: The state of the art* (pp. 3–48). Cambridge, England: Cambridge University Press.

Goldberg, S. (1977). Social competence in infancy: A model of parent–infant interaction. *Merrill-Palmer Quarterly, 23*, 163–177.

Goldberg, S., & DiVitto, B. A. (1983). *Born too soon: Preterm birth and early development.* San Francisco: Freeman.

Goldfield, B. A. (1987). The contributions of child and caregiver to referential and expressive language. *Applied Psycholinguistics, 8*, 267–280.

Goldfield, B. A. (1993). Noun bias in maternal speech to one-year-olds. *Journal of Child Language, 20*, 85–99.

Goldfield, B. A., & Reznick, J. S. (1990). Early lexical acquisition: Rate, content, and the vocabulary spurt. *Journal of Child Language, 17*, 171–183.

Goldin-Meadow, S., & Mylander, C. (1984). Gestural communication in deaf children: The effects and noneffects of parental input on early language development. *Monographs of the Society for Research in Child Development, 49* (3–4, Serial No. 207).

Goldin-Meadow, S., & Mylander, C. (1991). Levels of structure in a communication system developed without a language model. In K. R. Gibson & A. C. Petersen (Eds.), *Brain maturation and cognitive development: Comparative and cross-cultural perspectives* (pp. 315–344). New York: Aldinede Gruyter.

Golinkoff, R. M. (1986). 'I beg your pardon?': The preverbal negotiation of failed messages. *Journal of Child Language, 13*, 455–476.

Golinkoff, R. M., & Gordon, L. (1988). What makes communication run? Characteristics of immediate successes. *First Language, 8*, 103–124.

Golinkoff, R. M., Hirsh-Pasek, K., Cauley, K. M., & Gordon, L. (1987). The eyes have it: Lexical and syntactic comprehension in a new paradigm. *Journal of Child Language, 14*, 23–45.

Golinkoff, R. M., Mervis, C. B., & Hirsh-Pasek, K. (in press). Early object labels: The case for a developmental lexical principles framework. *Journal of Child Language.*

Golub, H. L., & Corwin, M. J. (1985). A physioacoustic model of the infant cry. In B. M. Lester & C. F. Z. Boukydis (Eds.), *Infant crying: Theoretical and research perspectives* (pp. 59–82). New York: Plenum.

Gopnik, A. (1981). Development of non-nominal expressions in 1–2-year-olds: Why the first words aren't about things. In P. S. Dale & D. Ingram (Eds.), *Child language: An international perspective* (pp. 93–104). Baltimore: University Park Press.

Gopnik, A. (1988). Three types of early word: The emergence of social words, names and cognitive-relational words in the one-word stage and their relation to cognitive development. *First Language*, *8*, 49–70.

Gopnik, A., & Meltzoff, A. N. (1985). From people, to plans, to objects: Changes in the meaning of early words and their relation to cognitive development. *Journal of Pragmatics*, *9*, 495–512.

Gopnik, A., & Meltzoff, A. N. (1986). Relations between semantic and cognitive development in the one-word stage: The specificity hypothesis. *Child Development*, *57*, 1040–1053.

Gopnik, A., & Meltzoff, A. N. (1987). The development of categorization in the second year and its relation to other cognitive and linguistic developments. *Child Development*, *58*, 1523–1531.

Gopnik, A., & Meltzoff, A. N. (1992). Categorization and naming: Basic-level sorting in eighteen-month-olds and its relation to language. *Child Development*, *63*, 1091–1103.

Greenfield, P. M. (1978). Informativeness, presupposition, and semantic choice in single-word utterances. In N. Waterson & C. Snow (Eds.), *The development of communication* (pp. 443–467). Chichester, England: Wiley.

Greenfield, P. M. (1982). The role of perceived variability in the transition to language. *Journal of Child Language*, *9*, 1–12.

Greenfield, P. M., & Smith, J. H. (1976). *The structure of communication in early language development*. New York: Academic Press.

Greenfield, P. M., & Zukow, P. G. (1978). Why do children say what they say when they say it?: An experimental approach to the psychogenesis of presupposition. In K. E. Nelson (Ed.), *Children's language* (Vol. 1, pp. 287–336). New York: Gardner Press.

Griffiths, P. (1986). Early vocabulary. In P. Fletcher & M. Garman (Eds.), *Language acquisition: Studies in first language development* (2nd ed., pp. 279–306). Cambridge, England: Cambridge University Press.

Gunnar, M. R. (1980). Control, warning signals, and distress in infancy. *Developmental Psychology*, *16*, 281-289.

Gunnar, M. R., Senior, K., & Hartup, W. W. (1984). Peer presence and the exploratory behavior of eighteen- and thirty-month-old children. *Child Development*, *55*, 1103–1109.

Gunnar, M. R., & Stone, C. (1984). The effects of positive maternal affect on infant responses to pleasant, ambiguous, and fear-provoking toys. *Child Development*, *55*, 1231–1236.

Gusella, J. L., Muir, D., & Tronick, E. Z. (1988). The effect of manipulating maternal behavior during an interaction on three- and six-month-olds' affect and attention. *Child Development*, *59*, 1111–1124.

Gustafson, G. E., & Green, J. A. (1989). On the importance of fundamental frequency and other acoustic features in cry perception and infant development. *Child Development*, *60*, 772–780.

Gustafson, G. E., & Green, J. A. (1991). Developmental coordination of cry sounds with visual regard and gestures. *Infant Behavior and Development, 14*, 51–57.

Gustafson, G. E., Green, J. A., & West, M. J. (1979). The infant's changing role in mother–infant games: The growth of social skills. *Infant Behavior and Development, 2*, 301–308.

Gustafson, G. E., & Harris, K. L. (1990). Women's responses to young infants' cries. *Developmental Psychology, 26*, 144–152.

Haith, M. M., Bergman, T., & Moore, M. J. (1977). Eye contact and face scanning in early infancy. *Science, 198*, 853–855.

Halliday, M. A. K. (1975). *Learning how to mean*. London: Edwin Arnold.

Halliday, M. A. K. (1979). One child's protolanguage. In M. Bullowa (Ed.), *Before speech: The beginning of interpersonal communication* (pp. 171–190). Cambridge, England: Cambridge University Press.

Harding, C. (1984). Acting with intention: A framework for examining the development of the intention to communicate. In L. Feagans, C. Garvey, & R. Golinkoff (Eds.), *The origins and growth of communication* (pp. 123–135). Norwood, NJ: Ablex.

Harding, C., & Golinkoff, R. M. (1979). The origins of intentional vocalizations in prelinguistic infants. *Child Development, 50*, 33–40.

Harris, D. B. (Ed.). (1957). *The concept of development: An issue in the study of human behavior*. Minneapolis: University of Minnesota Press.

Harris, M. B., Barrett, M., Jones, D., & Brookes, S. (1988). Linguistic input and early word mappings. *Journal of Child Language, 15*, 77–94.

Haviland, J. M., & Lelwica, M. (1987). The induced affect response: 10-week-old infants' responses to three emotion expressions. *Developmental Psychology, 23*, 97–104.

Hay, D. F., Stimson, C. A., & Castle, J. (1991). A meeting of minds in infancy: Imitation and desire. In D. Frye & C. Moore (Eds.), *Children's theories of mind: Mental states and social understanding* (pp. 115–137). Hillsdale, NJ: Erlbaum.

Hayes, L. A., & Watson, J. S. (1981). Neonatal imitation: Fact or artifact? *Developmental Psychology, 17*, 655–660.

Heaton, H. (1957). Clio puts the question. In D. B. Harris (Ed.), *The concept of development: An issue in the study of human behavior* (pp. 199–213). Minneapolis: University of Minnesota Press.

Hirshberg, L. M., & Svejda, M. (1990). When infants look to their parents: I. Infants' social referencing of mothers compared to fathers. *Child Development, 61*, 1175–1186.

Hirsh-Pasek, K., & Golinkoff, R. M. (1991). Language comprehension: A new look at some old themes. In N. A. Krasnegor, D. M. Rumbaugh, R. L. Schiefelbusch, & M. Studdert-Kennedy (Eds.), *Biological and behavioral determinants of language development* (pp. 301–320). Hillsdale, NJ: Erlbaum.

Hodapp, R. M., Goldfield, E. C., & Boyatzis, C. J. (1984). The use and effectiveness of maternal scaffolding in mother–infant games. *Child Development, 55*, 772–781.

Holenstein, E. (1976). *Roman Jakobson's approach to language*. Bloomington, IN: Indiana University Press.

Hornik, R., & Gunnar, M. R. (1988). A descriptive analysis of infant social referencing. *Child Development, 59*, 626–634.

Hornik, R., Risenhoover, N., & Gunnar, M. (1987). The effects of maternal positive, neutral, and negative affective communications on infant responses to new toys. *Child Development, 58*, 937–944.

Huttenlocher, J. (1974). The origins of language comprehension. In R. L. Solso (Ed.), *Theories in cognitive psychology: The Loyola symposium* (pp. 331–368). Hillsdale, NJ: Erlbaum.

Huttenlocher, J., Haight, W., Bryk, A., Seltzer, M., & Lyons, T. (1991). Early vocabulary growth: Relation to language input and gender. *Developmental Psychology, 27*, 236–248.

Hyche, J. K., Bakeman, R., & Adamson, L. B. (1992). Understanding communicative cues of infants with Down Syndrome: Effects of mothers' experience and infants' age. *Journal of Applied Developmental Psychology, 13*, 1–16.

Ingram, D. (1989). *First language acquisition: Method, description, and explanation.* Cambridge, England: Cambridge University Press.

Jacklin, C. N., Maccoby, E. E., & Doering, C. H. (1983). Neonatal sex-steroid hormones and timidity in 6–18-month-old boys and girls. *Developmental Psychobiology, 16*, 163–168.

Jacobson, J. L. (1981). The role of inanimate objects in early peer interaction. *Child Development, 52*, 618–626.

Jacobson, S. W. (1979). Matching behavior in the young infant. *Child Development, 50*, 425–430.

Jakobson, R. (1960). Linguistics and poetics. In T. A. Sebeok (Ed.), *Style in language* (pp. 350–377). New York: Wiley.

Jakobson, R. (1968). *Child language aphasia and phonological universals.* The Hague: Mouton. (Original work published 1941)

James, W. (1890). *The principles of psychology* (Vol. 1). New York: Holt.

Jancovic, M., Devoe, S., & Wiener, M. (1975). Age-related changes in hand and arm movements as nonverbal communication: Some conceptualizations and an empirical exploration. *Child Development, 46*, 922–928.

Johnson-Laird, P. N. (1990). Introduction: What is communication? In D. H. Mellor (Ed.), *Ways of communicating* (pp. 1–13). Cambridge, England: Cambridge University Press.

Jones, C. P., & Adamson, L. B. (1987). Language use in mother–infant and mother–child–sibling interactions. *Child Development, 58*, 356–366.

Kagan, J., & Lamb, S. (Eds.). (1987). *The emergence of morality in young children.* Chicago: University of Chicago Press.

Kamhi, A. G. (1986). The elusive first word: The importance of the naming insight for the development of referential speech. *Journal of Child Language, 13*, 155–161.

Katz, J. J. (1973). The realm of meaning. In G. A. Miller (Ed.), *Communication, language, and meaning: Psychological perspectives* (pp. 36–48). New York: Basic Books.

Kaye, K. (1977). Toward the origin of dialogue. In H. R. Schaffer (Ed.), *Studies in mother–infant interaction* (pp. 89–117). London: Academic Press.

Kaye, K. (1979). Thickening thin data: The maternal role in developing communication and language. In M. Bullowa (Ed.), *Before speech: The beginning of interpersonal communication* (pp. 191–206). Cambridge, England: Cambridge University Press.

Kaye, K. (1982a). *The mental and social life of babies: How parents create persons.* Chicago: University of Chicago Press.

Kaye, K. (1982b). Organism, apprentice, and person. In E. Z. Tronick (Ed.), *Social interchange in infancy: Affect, cognition, and communication* (pp. 183–196). Baltimore: University Park Press.

Kaye, K., & Fogel, A. (1980). The temporal structure of face-to-face communication between mothers and infants. *Developmental Psychology, 16*, 454–464.

Kaye, K., & Wells, A. (1980). Mothers' jiggling and the burst-pause pattern in neonatal sucking. *Infant Behavior and Development, 3*, 29–46.

Kent, R. D. (1981). Sensorimotor aspects of speech development. In R. N. Aslin, J. R. Alberts, & M. R. Petersen (Eds.), *Development of perception: Psychobiological perspectives* (Vol. 1, pp. 161–189). New York: Academic Press.

Kessel, F. S. (Ed.). (1988). *The development of language and language researchers: Essays in honor of Roger Brown.* Hillsdale, NJ: Erlbaum.

Kessen, W. (1966). Questions for a theory of cognitive development. In H. W. Stevenson (Ed.), Concept of development, *Monographs of the Society for Research in Child Development, 31*, (55–70, Serial No. 107).

Kessen, W. (1979). The American child and other cultural inventions. *American Psychologist, 34*, 815–820.

Klima, E., & Bellugi, U. (1979). *The signs of language*. Cambridge, MA: Harvard University Press.

Klinger, L. G., & Dawson, G. (1992). Facilitating early social and communicative development in children with autism. In S. F. Warren & J. Reichle (Eds.), *Causes and effects in communication and language intervention* (pp. 157–186). Baltimore: Brookes.

Klinnert, M. D. (1984). The regulation of infant behavior by maternal facial expression. *Infant Behavior and Development, 7*, 447–465.

Klinnert, M. D., Campos, J. J., Sorce, J. F., Emde, R. N., & Svejda, M. (1983). Emotions as behavior regulators: Social referencing in infancy. In R. Plutchik & H. Kellerman (Eds.), *Emotion: Theory, research and experience* (Vol. 2, pp. 57–86). New York: Academic Press.

Klinnert, M. D., Emde, R. N., Butterfield, P., & Campos, J. J. (1986). Social referencing: The infant's use of emotional signals from a friendly adult with mother present. *Developmental Psychology, 22*, 427–432.

Koepke, J. E., Hamm, M., Legerstee, M., & Russell, M. (1983). Neonatal imitation: Two failures to replicate. *Infant Behavior and Development, 6*, 97–102.

Köhler, W. (1940). *Dynamics in psychology*. New York: Liveright.

Konner, M. (1972). Aspects of the developmental ethology of a foraging people. In N. Blurton Jones (Ed.), *Ethological studies of child behavior* (pp. 285–304). Cambridge, England: Cambridge University Press.

Konner, M. (1976). Maternal care, infant behavior and development among the !Kung. In R. B. Lee & I. DeVore (Eds.), *Kalahari hunter–gatherers* (pp. 218–245). Cambridge, MA: Harvard University Press.

Konner, M. (1977). Infancy among the Kalahari Desert San. In P. H. Leiderman, S. R. Tulkin, & A. Rosenfeld (Eds.), *Culture and infancy* (pp. 287–328). New York: Academic Press.

Korner, A. F. (1972). State as variable, as obstacle, and as mediator of stimulation in infant research. *Merrill-Palmer Quarterly, 18*, 77–94.

Korner, A. F., Brown, B. W., Reade, E. P., Stevenson, D. K., Fernbach, S. A., & Thom, V. A. (1988). State behavior of preterm infants as a function of development, individual and sex differences. *Infant Behavior and Development*, *11*, 111–124.

Korner, A. F., & Grobstein, R. (1966). Visual alertness as related to soothing in neonates: Implications for maternal stimulation and early deprivation. *Child Development*, *37*, 867–876.

Korner, A. F., & Thoman, E. B. (1970). Visual alertness in neonates as evoked by maternal care. *Journal of Experimental Child Psychology*, *10*, 67–78.

Kuchuk, A., Vibbert, M., & Bornstein, M. H. (1986). The perception of smiling and its experiential correlates in three-month-old infants. *Child Development*, *57*, 1054–1061.

Kuhl, P. K. (1987). Perception of speech and sound in early infancy. In P. Salapatek & L. Cohen (Eds.), *Handbook of infant perception* (Vol. 2, pp. 275–382). Orlando, FL: Academic Press.

Kuhl, P. K., & Meltzoff, A. N. (1982). The bimodal perception of speech in infancy. *Science*, *218*, 1138–1141.

Kuhl, P. K., & Miller, J. D. (1975). Speech perception by the chinchilla: Voiced–voiceless distinction in alveolar plosive consonants. *Science*, *190*, 69–72.

Kuhl, P. K., Williams, K. A., Lacerda, F., Stevens, K. N., & Lindblom, B. (1992). Linguistic experience alters phonetic perception in infants by 6 months of age. *Science*, *255*, 606–608.

Kuhn, T. S. (1970). *The structure of scientific revolutions* (2nd ed.). Chicago: University of Chicago Press.

Lamb, M. E., Morrison, D. C., & Malkin, C. M. (1987). The development of infant social expectations in face-to-face interaction: A longitudinal study. *Merrill-Palmer Quarterly*, *33*, 241–254.

Landau, R. (1976). Extent that the mother represents the social stimulation to which the infant is exposed: Findings from a cross-cultural study. *Developmental Psychology*, *12*, 399–405.

Landry, S. H., & Chapieski, M. L. (1989). Joint attention and infant toy exploration: Effects of Down syndrome and prematurity. *Child Development*, *60*, 103–118.

Lawson, K. R., Parrinello, R., & Ruff, H. A. (1992). Maternal behavior and infant attention. *Infant Behavior and Development*, *15*, 209–229.

Lederberg, A. R. (1993). The impact of deafness on mother–child and peer relationships. In M. Marschark & D. Clark (Eds.), *Psychological perspectives on deafness* (pp. 93–119). Hillsdale, NJ: Erlbaum.

Lee, R. B. (1979). *The !Kung San: Men, women, and work in a foraging society*. Cambridge, England: Cambridge University Press.

Legerstee, M. (1990). Infants use multimodal information to imitate speech sounds. *Infant Behavior and Development*, *13*, 343–354.

Legerstee, M., Corter, C., & Kienapple, K. (1990). Hand, arm, and facial actions of young infants to a social and nonsocial stimulus. *Child Development*, *61*, 774–784.

Legerstee, M., Pomerleau, A., Malcuit, G., & Feider, H. (1987). The development of infants' responses to people and a doll: Implications for research in communication. *Infant Behavior and Development*, *10*, 81–95.

Lemish, D., & Rice, M. L. (1986). Television as a talking picture book: A prop for language acquisition. *Journal of Child Language*, *13*, 251–274.

Lenneberg, E. H. (1962). Understanding language without ability to speak: A case report. *Journal of Abnormal and Social Psychology, 65*, 419–425.

Lenneberg, E. H., Rebelsky, F. G., & Nichols, I. A. (1965). The vocalization of infants born to deaf and to hearing parents. *Human Development, 8*, 23–37.

Lester, B. M. (1985). Introduction: There's more to crying than meets the ear. In B. M. Lester & C. F. Z. Boukydis (Eds.), *Infant crying: Theoretical and research perspectives* (pp. 1–27). New York: Plenum.

Lester, B. M., & Boukydis, C. F. Z. (Eds.). (1985). *Infant crying: Theoretical and research perspectives*. New York: Plenum.

Lester, B. M., Emory, E. K., Hoffman, S. L., & Eitzman, D. V. (1976). A multivariate study of the effects of high-risk factors on performance on the Brazelton Neonatal Assessment Scale. *Child Development, 47*, 515–517.

Lester, B. M., Hoffman, J., & Brazelton, T. B. (1985). The rhythmic structure of mother–infant interaction in term and preterm infants. *Child Development, 56*, 15–27.

Leung, E. H. L., & Rheingold, H. L. (1981). Development of pointing as a social gesture. *Developmental Psychology, 17*, 215–220.

LeVine, R. A. (1990). Infant environments in psychoanalysis: A cross-cultural view. In J. W. Stigler, R. A. Shweder, & G. Herdt (Eds.), *Cultural psychology: Essays on comparative human development* (pp. 454–474). Cambridge, England: Cambridge University Press.

Lewis, M. M. (1936). *Infant speech: A study of the beginnings of language*. New York: Harcourt, Brace.

Lewis, M., & Rosenblum, L. A. (Eds.). (1974). *The effect of the infant on its caregiver*. New York: Wiley.

Lifter, K., & Bloom, L. (1989). Object knowledge and the emergence of language. *Infant Behavior and Development, 12*, 395–423.

Lock, A. (1980). *The guided reinvention of language*. London: Academic Press.

Locke, A., Young, A., Service, V., & Chandler, P. (1990). Some observations on the origins of the pointing gesture. In V. Volterra & C. Erting (Eds.), *From gesture to language in hearing and deaf children* (pp. 42–55). New York: Springer-Verlag.

Locke, J. L. (1983). *Phonological acquisition and change*. New York: Academic Press.

Locke, J. L. (1989). Babbling and early speech: Continuity and individual differences. *First Language, 9*, 191–206.

Locke, J. L., & Pearson, D. M. (1990). Linguistic significance of babbling: Evidence from a tracheostomized infant. *Journal of Child Language, 17*, 1–16.

Lorenz, K. (1943). Die angeborenen formem möglicher erfahrung. *Zeitschrift für Tierpsychologie, 5*, 233–409. (Cited in Eibl-Eibesfeldt, 1989.)

Lorenz, K. (1970). Companions as factors in the bird's development. In K. Lorenz (Ed.), *Studies in animal and human behavior* (Vol. 1, pp. 101–258). Cambridge, MA: Harvard University Press. (Original work published 1935)

Loveland, K. A., & Landry, S. H. (1986). Joint attention and language in autism and developmental language delay. *Journal of Autism and Developmental Disorders, 16*, 335–349.

Lynch, M. P., & Eilers, R. E. (1991). Perspectives on early language from typical development and Down syndrome. *International Review of Research in Mental Retardation, 17*, 55–90.

Lyons, J. (1977). *Semantics* (Vol. 1). Cambridge, England: Cambridge University Press.

Macfarlane, A. (1977). *The psychology of childbirth*. Cambridge, MA: Harvard University Press.

MacKain, K., Studdert-Kennedy, M., Spieker, S., & Stern, D. (1983). Infant intermodal speech perception is a left-hemisphere function. *Science, 219*, 1347–1349.

Marcos, H., & Chanu, M. K. (1992). Learning how to insist and clarify in the second year: Reformulation of requests in different contexts. *International Journal of Behavioral Development, 15*, 359–376.

Marean, G. C., Werner, L. A., & Kuhl, P. K. (1992). Vowel categorization by very young infants. *Developmental Psychology, 28*, 396–405.

Masataka, N. (1992). Motherese in a signed language. *Infant Behavior and Development, 15*, 453–460.

Masur, E. F. (1983). Gestural development, dual-directional signaling, and the transition to words. *Journal of Psycholinguistic Research, 12*, 93–109.

Maurer, D. (1985). Infants' perception of facedness. In T. M. Field & N. A. Fox (Eds.), *Social perception in infants* (pp. 73–100). Norwood, NJ: Ablex.

Maurer, D., & Salapatek, P. (1976). Developmental changes in the scanning of faces by young infants. *Child Development, 47*, 523–527.

McCabe, A. E. (1989). Differential language learning styles in young children: The importance of context. *Developmental Review, 9*, 1–20.

McCall, R. B. (1979). Qualitative transitions in behavioral development in the first two years of life. In M. H. Bornstein & W. Kessen (Eds.), *Psychological development from infancy* (pp. 183–224). Hillsdale, NJ: Erlbaum.

McGehee, L. J., & Eckerman, C. O. (1983). The preterm infant as a social partner: Responsive but unreadable. *Infant Behavior and Development, 6*, 461–470.

McGurk, H., & Lewis, M. (1974). Space perception in early infancy: Perception within a common auditory-visual space? *Science, 186*, 649–650.

McShane, J. (1980). *Learning to talk*. Cambridge, England: Cambridge University Press.

Meadow, K. P. (1980). *Deafness and child development*. Berkeley, CA: University of California Press.

Meltzoff, A. N. (1985). The roots of social and cognitive development: Models of man's original nature. In T. M. Field & N. A. Fox (Eds.), *Social perception in infants* (pp. 1–30). Norwood, NJ: Ablex.

Meltzoff, A. N., & Kuhl, P. K. (1989). Infants' perception of faces and speech sounds: Challenges to developmental theory. In P. R. Zelazo & R. G. Barr (Eds.), *Challenges to developmental paradigms* (pp. 67–91). Hillsdale, NJ: Erlbaum.

Meltzoff, A. N., & Moore, M. K. (1977). Imitation of facial and manual gestures by human neonates. *Science, 198*, 75–78.

Meltzoff, A. N., & Moore, M. K. (1983). Newborn infants imitate adult facial gestures. *Child Development, 54*, 702–709.

Menyuk, P., Menn, L., & Silber, R. (1986). Early strategies for the perception and production of words and sounds. In P. Fletcher & M. Garman (Eds.), *Language acquisition: Studies in first language development* (2nd ed., pp. 198–222). Cambridge, England: Cambridge University Press.

Mervis, C. B. (1983). Acquisition of a lexicon. *Contemporary Educational Psychology, 8*, 210–236.

Mervis, C. B. (1984). Early lexical development: The contributions of mother and child. In C. Sophian (Ed.), *Origins of cognitive skills* (pp. 339–370). Hillsdale, NJ: Erlbaum.

Mervis, C. B. (1987). Child-basic object categories and early lexical development. In U. Neisser (Ed.), *Concepts and conceptual development: Ecological and intellectual factors in categorization* (pp. 201–233). Cambridge, England: Cambridge University Press.

Mervis, C. B. (1990). Early conceptual development of children with Down syndrome. In D. Cicchetti & M. Beeghly (Eds.), *Children with Down syndrome: A developmental perspective* (pp. 252–301). Cambridge, England: Cambridge University Press.

Mervis, C. B., & Bertrand, J. (in press). Acquisition of the novel name–nameless category (N3C) principle. *Child Development.*

Mervis, C. B., & Bertrand, J. (in press). Early lexical acquisition and the vocabulary spurt: A response to Goldfield & Reznick. *Journal of Child Language.*

Mervis, C. B., & Canada, K. (1983). On the existence of competence errors in early comprehension: A reply to Fremgen & Fay and Chapman & Thomson. *Journal of Child Language, 10*, 431–440.

Mervis, C. B., & Mervis, C. A. (1982). Leopards are kitty-cats: Object labeling by mothers for their thirteen-month-olds. *Child Development, 53*, 267–273.

Mervis, C. B., Mervis, C. A., Johnson, K. E., & Bertrand, J. (1992). Studying early lexical development: The value of the systematic diary method. In C. Rovee-Collier & L. P. Lipsitt (Eds.), *Advances in infancy research* (Vol. 7, pp. 291–378). Norwood, NJ: Ablex.

Messer, D. J. (1978). The integration of mothers' referential speech with joint play. *Child Development, 49*, 781–787.

Messer, D. J., & Vietze, P. M. (1984). Timing and transitions in mother–infant gaze. *Infant Behavior and Development, 7*, 167–181.

Messer, D. J., & Vietze, P. M. (1988). Does mutual influence occur during mother–infant social gaze? *Infant Behavior and Development, 11*, 97–110.

Miller, G. A. (1981). *Language and speech.* San Francisco: Freeman.

Miller, G. A. (1991). *The science of words.* New York: Scientific American Library.

Moore, C., & Corkum, V. L. (in press). Social understanding at the end of the first year of life. *Developmental Review.*

Moores, D. F. (1987). *Educating the deaf: Psychology, principles, and practices* (3rd ed.). Boston: Houghton Mifflin.

Mueller, E. C., & Vandell, D. (1979). Infant–infant interaction. In J. D. Osofsky (Ed.), *Handbook of infant development* (pp. 591–622). New York: Wiley.

Muir, D., & Field, J. (1979). Newborn infants orient to sounds. *Child Development, 50*, 431–436.

Muma, J. R. (1986). *Language acquisition: A functionalistic perspective.* Austin, TX: Pro-ed.

Mundy, P., & Sigman, M. (1989a). Second thoughts on the nature of autism. *Development and Psychopathology, 1*, 213–217.

Mundy, P., & Sigman, M. (1989b). The theoretical implications of joint-attention deficits in autism. *Development and Psychopathology, 1*, 173–183.

Mundy, P., Sigman, M., & Kasari, C. (1990). A longitudinal study of joint attention and language development in autistic children. *Journal of Autism and Developmental Disorders, 20*, 115–128.

Mundy, P., Sigman, M., Kasari, C., & Yirmiya, N. (1988). Nonverbal communication skills in Down syndrome children. *Child Development*, *59*, 235–249.

Mundy, P., Sigman, M., Ungerer, J., & Sherman, T. (1986). Defining the social deficits of autism: The contribution of nonverbal communication measures. *Journal of Child Psychology and Psychiatry*, *27*, 657–669.

Murphy, C. M., & Messer, D. J. (1977). Mothers, infants and pointing: A study of a gesture. In H. R. Schaffer (Ed.), *Studies in mother–infant interaction* (pp. 325–354). London: Academic Press.

Murray, A. D. (1979). Infant crying as an elicitor of parental behavior: An examination of two models. *Psychological Bulletin*, *86*, 191–215.

Murray, A. D. (1985). Aversiveness is in the mind of the beholder: Perception of infant crying by adults. In B. M. Lester & C. F. Z. Boukydis (Eds.), *Infant crying: Theoretical and research perspectives* (pp. 217–239). New York: Plenum.

Murray, L., & Trevarthen, C. (1985). Emotional regulation of interactions between two-month-olds and their mothers. In T. M. Field & N. Fox (Eds.), *Social perception in infants* (pp. 177–197). Norwood, NJ: Ablex.

Neisser, U. (1967). *Cognitive psychology*. New York: Appleton-Century-Crofts.

Neisser, U. (1976). *Cognition and reality: Principles and implications for cognitive psychology*. San Francisco: W. H. Freeman.

Nelson, C. A. (1985). The perception and recognition of facial expressions in infancy. In T. M. Field & N. A. Fox (Eds.), *Social perception in infants* (pp. 101–125). Norwood, NJ: Ablex.

Nelson, C. A., & Horowitz, F. D. (1983). The perception of facial expressions and stimulus motion by two- and five-month-old infants using holographic stimuli. *Child Development*, *54*, 868–877.

Nelson, C. A., & Horowitz, F. D. (1987). Visual motion perception in infancy: A review and synthesis. In P. Salapatek & L. Cohen (Eds.), *Handbook of infant perception* (Vol. 2, pp. 123–153). Orlando, FL: Academic Press.

Nelson, K. (1973). Structure and strategy in learning to talk. *Monographs of the Society for Research in Child Development*, *38* (1–2, Serial No. 149).

Nelson, K. (1974). Concept, word, and sentence: Interrelations in acquisition and development. *Psychological Review*, *81*, 267–285.

Nelson, K. (1979). The role of language in infant development. In M. H. Bornstein & W. Kessen (Eds.), *Psychological development from infancy: Image to intention* (pp. 307–337). Hillsdale, NJ: Erlbaum.

Nelson, K. (1981). Individual differences in language development: Implications for development and language. *Developmental Psychology*, *17*, 170–187.

Nelson, K. (1985). *Making sense: The acquisition of shared meaning*. Orlando, FL: Academic Press.

Nelson, K. (1988). Constraints on word learning? *Cognitive Development*, *3*, 221–246.

Nelson, K. (1991). Concepts and meaning in language development. In N. A. Krasnegor, D. M. Rumbaugh, R. L. Schiefelbusch, & M. Studdert-Kennedy (Eds.), *Biological and behavioral determinants of language development* (pp. 89–115). Hillsdale, NJ: Erlbaum.

Nelson, K., & Lucariello, J. (1985). The development of meaning in first words. In M. Barrett (Ed.), *Children's single-word speech* (pp. 59–86). New York: Wiley.

Newport, E. L., Gleitman, H., & Gleitman, L. R. (1977). Mother, I'd rather do it myself: Some effects and non-effects of maternal speech style. In C. E. Snow & C. A. Ferguson (Eds.), *Talking to children: Language input and acquisition* (pp. 109–149). Cambridge, England: Cambridge University Press.

Newson, J. (1978). Dialogue and development. In A. Lock (Ed.), *Action, gesture, and symbol* (pp. 31–42). London: Academic Press.

Newson, J., & Newson, E. (1975). Intersubjectivity and the transmission of culture. *Bulletin of the British Psychological Society, 28*, 437–446.

Ninio, A. (1979). The naive theory of the infant and other maternal attitudes in two subgroups in Israel. *Child Development, 50*, 976–980.

Ninio, A. (1983). Joint book reading as a multiple vocabulary acquisition device. *Developmental Psychology, 19*, 445–451.

Ninio, A., & Bruner, J. (1978). The achievement and antecedents of labeling. *Journal of Child Language, 5*, 1–15.

O'Brien, M., & Nagle, K. J. (1987). Parents' speech to toddlers: The effect of play context. *Journal of Child Language, 14*, 269–279.

Ochs, E. (1987). Input: A socio-cultural perspective. In M. Hickmann (Ed.), *Social and functional approaches to language and thought* (pp. 305–319). Orlando, FL: Academic Press.

Ochs, E. (1988). *Culture and language development: Language acquisition and language socialization in a Samoan village*. Cambridge, England: Cambridge University Press.

Oller, D. K. (1980). The emergence of the sounds of speech in infancy. In G. H. Yeni-Komshian, J. F. Kavanagh, & C. A. Ferguson (Eds.), *Child phonology, Vol. 1: Production* (pp. 93–112). New York: Academic Press.

Oller, D. K. (1981). Infant vocalizations: Exploration and reflexivity. In R. E. Stark (Ed.), *Language behavior in infancy and early childhood* (pp. 85–103). New York: Elsevier North Holland.

Oller, D. K., & Eilers, R. E. (1988). The role of audition in infant babbling. *Child Development, 59*, 441–449.

Oller, D. K., & Eilers, R. E. (1992). Development of vocal signaling in human infants: Toward a methodology for cross-species vocalization comparisons. In H. Papoušek, U. Jurgens, & M. Papoušek (Eds.), *Nonverbal vocal communication: Comparative and developmental approaches* (pp. 174–191). Cambridge, England: Cambridge University Press.

Oller, D. K., Wieman, L. A., Doyle, W. J., & Ross, C. (1975). Infant babbling and speech. *Journal of Child Language, 3*, 1–11.

Oster, H. (1981). "Recognition" of emotional expression in infancy? In M. E. Lamb & L. R. Sherrod (Eds.), *Infant social cognition: Empirical and theoretical considerations* (pp. 85–125). Hillsdale, NJ: Erlbaum.

Oster, H., & Ekman, P. (1978). Facial behavior in child development. In W. A. Collins (Ed.), *Minnesota Symposia on Child Psychology* (Vol. 11, pp. 231–279). Hillsdale, NJ: Erlbaum.

Ostwald, P. (1972). The sounds of infancy. *Developmental Medicine and Child Neurology, 14*, 350–361.

Oviatt, S. L. (1980). The emerging ability to comprehend language: An experimental approach. *Child Development, 51*, 97–106.

Papoušek, H., & Bornstein, M. H. (1992). Didactic interactions: Intuitive parental support of vocal and verbal development in human infants. In H. Papoušek, U. Jurgens, & M. Papoušek (Eds.), *Nonverbal vocal communication: Comparative and developmental approaches* (pp. 209–229). Cambridge, England: Cambridge University Press.

Papoušek, H., & Papoušek, M. (1977). Mothering and the cognitive headstart: Psychobiological considerations. In H. R. Schaffer (Ed.), *Studies in mother–infant interaction* (pp. 63–88). London: Academic Press.

Papoušek, H., & Papoušek, M. (1987). Intuitive parenting: A dialectic counterpart to the infant's integrative competence. In J. D. Osofsky (Ed.), *Handbook of infant development* (2nd ed., pp. 669–720). New York: Wiley.

Papoušek, M., Papoušek, H., & Symmes, D. (1991). The meanings of melodies in motherese in tone and stress languages. *Infant Behavior and Development*, *14*, 415–440.

Parrinello, R. M., & Ruff, H. A. (1988). The influence of adult intervention on infants' level of attention. *Child Development*, *59*, 1125–1135.

Pepper, S. C. (1942). *World hypotheses: A study in evidence*. Berkeley, CA: University of California Press.

Peters, A. M. (1977). Language learning strategies: Does the whole equal the sum of the parts? *Language*, *53*, 560–573.

Peters, A. M. (1983). *The units of language acquisition*. Cambridge, England: Cambridge University Press.

Peters, A. M., & Boggs, S. T. (1986). Interactional routines as cultural influences upon language acquisition. In B. B. Schieffelin & E. Ochs (Eds.), *Language socialization across cultures* (pp. 80–96). Cambridge, England: Cambridge University Press.

Petitto, L. A. (1990). The transition from gesture to symbol in American Sign Language. In V. Volterra & C. J. Erting (Eds.), *From gesture to language in hearing and deaf children* (pp. 153–161). New York: Springer-Verlag.

Petitto, L. A. (1992). Modularity and constraints in early lexical acquisition: Evidence from children's early language and gesture. In M. R. Gunnar & M. Maratsos (Eds.), *Modularity and constraints in language and cognition: The Minnesota symposia on child psychology* (Vol. 25, pp. 25–58). Hillsdale, NJ: Erlbaum.

Petitto, L. A., & Marentette, P. F. (1991). Babbling in the manual mode: Evidence for the ontogeny of language. *Science*, *251*, 1493–1496.

Phillips, J. R. (1973). Syntax and vocabulary of mothers' speech to young children: Age and sex comparisons. *Child Development*, *44*, 182–185.

Phillips, W. E. (1993). *Prospective parents' beliefs about infant behavior and cognitive abilities, perceived parenting self-efficiacy and the relation to maternal postpartum depression*. Unpublished master's thesis, Georgia State University.

Piaget, J. (1954). *The construction of reality in the child*. New York: Ballantine. (Original work published 1937)

Piaget, J. (1962). *Play, dreams, and imitation in childhood*. New York: Norton. (Original work published 1945 as *La formation de symbole*)

Piaget, J. (1963). *The origins of intelligence in children*. New York: Norton. (Original work published 1936)

Piaget, J. (1971). *Biology and knowledge: An essay on the relations between organic regulations and cognitive processes*. Chicago: University of Chicago Press. (Original work published 1967)

Piattelli-Palmarini, M. (Ed.). (1980). *Language and learning: The debate between Jean Piaget and Noam Chomsky*. Cambridge, MA: Harvard University Press.

Popper, K. R. (1968). *The logic of scientific discovery* (2nd ed.). New York: Harper & Row.

Reddy, V. (1991). Playing with others' expectations: Teasing and mucking about in the first year. In A. Whiten (Ed.), *Natural theories of mind: Evolution, development and simulation of everyday mindreading* (pp. 143–158). Cambridge, MA: Blackwell.

Rescorla, L. A. (1980). Overextension in early language development. *Journal of Child Language*, *7*, 321–335.

Reznick, J. S., & Goldfield, B. A. (1992). Rapid change in lexical development in comprehension and production. *Developmental Psychology*, *28*, 406–413.

Rheingold, H. L. (1969). The social and socializing infant. In D. A. Goslin (Ed.), *Handbook of socialization theory and research* (pp. 779–790). Chicago: Rand McNally.

Rheingold, H. L., & Adams, J. L. (1980). The significance of speech to newborns. *Developmental Psychology*, *16*, 397–403.

Rheingold, H. L., Gewirtz, J. L., & Ross, H. W. (1959). Social conditioning of vocalizations in the infant. *Journal of Comparative and Physiological Psychology*, *52*, 68–73.

Richards, M. P. M. (1974a). The development of psychological communication in the first year of life. In K. J. Connolly & J. S. Bruner (Eds.), *The growth of competence* (pp. 119–132). London: Academic Press.

Richards, M. P. M. (1974b). First steps in becoming social. In M. P. M. Richards (Ed.), *The integration of a child into a social world* (pp. 83–97). London: Cambridge University Press.

Richards, M. P. M. (Ed.). (1974c). *The integration of a child into a social world*. London: Cambridge University Press.

Richer, J. (1978). The partial noncommunication of culture to autistic children: An application of human ethology. In M. Rutter & E. Schopler (Eds.), *Autism: A reappraisal of concepts and treatment* (pp. 47–61). New York: Plenum.

Richman, A. L., Miller, P. M., & LeVine, R. A. (1992). Cultural and educational variations in maternal responsiveness. *Developmental Psychology*, *28*, 614–621.

Robson, K. S. (1967). The role of eye-to-eye contact in maternal–infant attachment. *Journal of Child Psychology and Psychiatry and Allied Disciplines*, *8*, 13–25.

Rogoff, B. (1990). *Apprenticeship in thinking: Cognitive development in social context*. New York: Oxford University Press.

Rogoff, B., Mistry, J., Göncü, A., & Mosier, C. (1993). Guided participation in cultural activity by toddlers and caregivers. *Monograph of the Society for Research in Child Development*, *58* (8, Serial No. 236).

Rogoff, B., Mistry, J., Radziszewska, B., & Germond, J. (1992). Infants' instrumental social interaction with adults. In S. Feinman (Ed.), *Social referencing and the social construction of reality in infancy* (pp. 323–348). New York: Plenum.

Romski, M. A., & Sevcik, R. A. (1992). Developing augmented language in children with severe mental retardation. In S. F. Warren & J. Reichle (Eds.), *Causes and effects in communication and language intervention* (pp. 113–130). Baltimore: Brookes.

Rose, S. A., & Ruff, H. A. (1987). Cross-modal abilities in human infants. In J. D. Osofsky (Ed.), *Handbook of infant development* (2nd ed., pp. 318–362). New York: Wiley.

Rosen, W. D., Adamson, L. B., & Bakeman, R. (1992). An experimental investigation of infant social referencing: Mothers' messages and gender differences. *Developmental Psychology, 28*, 1172–1178.

Rosenstein, D., & Oster, H. (1988). Differential facial responses to four basic tastes in newborns. *Child Development, 59*, 1555–1568.

Ross, H. S., & Goldman, B. M. (1977). Establishing new social relations in infancy. In T. Alloway, P. Pliner, & L. Krames (Eds.), *Advances in the study of communication and affect: Vol. 3. Attachment behavior* (pp. 61–79). New York: Plenum.

Ross, H. S., & Lollis, S. P. (1987). Communication within infant social games. *Developmental Psychology, 23*, 241–248.

Rovee-Collier, C. (1987). Learning and memory in infancy. In J. D. Osofsky (Ed.), *Handbook of infant development* (2nd ed., pp. 98–148). New York: Wiley.

Rovee-Collier, C. (1990). The "memory system" of prelinguistic infants. In A. Diamond (Ed.), *The development and neural bases of higher cognitive functions. Annals of the New York Academy of Sciences, 608*, 517–542.

Rutter, D. R., & Durkin, K. (1987). Turn-taking in mother–infant interaction: An examination of vocalizations and gaze. *Developmental Psychology, 23*, 54–61.

Ryan, J. (1974). Early language development: Towards a communicational analysis. In M. P. M. Richards (Ed.), *The integration of a child into a social world* (pp. 185–213). London: Cambridge University Press.

Sacks, O. (1989). *Seeing voices.* Berkeley, CA: University of California Press.

Sagi, A., & Hoffman, M. L. (1976). Empathic distress in the newborn. *Developmental Psychology, 12*, 175–176.

Sander, L. W. (1962). Issues in early mother–child interaction. *Journal of the American Academy of Child Psychiatry, 1*, 141–166.

Sander, L. W. (1977). The regulation of exchange in the infant–caretaker system and some aspects of the context-content relationship. In M. Lewis & L. A. Rosenblum (Eds.), *Interaction, conversation, and the development of language* (pp. 133–156). New York: Wiley.

Sander, L. W., Chappell, P. F., & Snyder, P. A. (1982). An investigation of change in the infant-caregiver system over the first week of life. In R. N. Emde & R. J. Harmon (Eds.), *The development of attachment and affiliative systems* (pp. 119–136). New York: Plenum.

Sander, L. W., Stechler, G., Burns, P., & Julia, H. (1970). Early mother–infant interaction and 24-hour patterns of activity and sleep. *The Journal of the American Academy of Child Psychiatry, 9*, 103–123.

Sander, L. W., Stechler, G., Burns, P., & Lee, A. (1979). Change in infant and caregiver variables over the first two months of life: Integration of action in early development. In E. B. Thoman (Ed.), *Origins of the infant's social responsiveness* (pp. 349–407). Hillsdale, NJ: Erlbaum.

Savage-Rumbaugh, S., McDonald, K., Sevcik, R., Hopkins, W., & Rupert, E. (1986). Spontaneous symbol acquisition and communicative use by Pygmy Chimpanzees (*Pan paniscus*). *Journal of Experimental Psychology: General, 115*, 211–235.

Scaife, M., & Bruner, J. S. (1975). The capacity for joint visual attention in the infant. *Nature, 253*, 265–266.

Schaffer, H. R. (Ed.). (1977). *Studies in mother–infant interaction.* London: Academic Press.

Schaffer, H. R. (1984). *The child's entry into a social world.* London: Academic Press.

Schaffer, H. R. (1989). Language development in context. In S. von Tetzchner, L. S. Siegel, & L. Smith (Eds.), *The social and cognitive aspects of normal and atypical language development* (pp. 1–22). New York: Springer-Verlag.

Schaffer, H. R., Collis, G. M., & Parsons, G. (1977). Vocal interchange and visual regard in verbal and preverbal children. In H. R. Schaffer (Ed.), *Studies in mother–infant interaction* (pp. 291–324). London: Academic Press.

Schieffelin, B. B. (1986). Teasing and shaming in Kaluli children's interactions. In B. B. Schieffelin & E. Ochs (Eds.), *Language socialization across cultures* (pp. 165–181). Cambridge, England: Cambridge University Press.

Schieffelin, B. B., & Ochs, E. (Eds.). (1986). *Language socialization across cultures.* Cambridge, England: Cambridge University Press.

Schwartz, R. G., & Leonard, L. B. (1984). Words, objects, and actions in early lexical acquisition. *Journal of Speech and Hearing Research, 27,* 119–127.

Scollon, R. (1976). *Conversations with a one-year-old.* Honolulu: University Press of Hawaii.

Scoville, R. (1984). Development of the intention to communicate: The eye of the beholder. In L. Feagans, C. Garvey, & R. Golinkoff (Eds.), *The origins and growth of communication* (pp. 109–122). Norwood, NJ: Ablex.

Sebeok, T. A., & Rosenthal, R. (Eds.). (1981). The Clever Hans phenomenon: Communication with horses, whales, apes, and people. *Annals of the New York Academy of Sciences, 364.*

Shannon, C. E., & Weaver, W. (1949). *The mathematical theory of communication.* Urbana, IL: University of Illinois Press.

Shatz, M. (1982). On mechanisms of language acquisition: Can features of the communicative environment account for development? In E. Wanner & L. R. Gleitman (Eds.), *Language acquisition: The state of the art* (pp. 102–127). Cambridge, England: Cambridge University Press.

Shereshefsky, P. M., & Yarrow, L. J. (Eds.). (1973). *Psychological aspects of a first pregnancy and early postnatal adaptation.* New York: Raven Press.

Sherrod, L. R. (1981). Issues in cognitive perceptual development: The special case of social stimuli. In M. E. Lamb & L. R. Sherrod (Eds.), *Infant social cognition: Empirical and theoretical considerations* (pp. 11–36). Hillsdale, NJ: Erlbaum.

Shinn, M. W. (1900). *The biography of a baby.* Boston: Houghton-Mifflin.

Shotter, J. (1974). The development of personal powers. In M. P. M. Richards (Ed.), *The integration of a child into a social world* (pp. 215–244). London: Cambridge University Press.

Sigel, I. E. (Ed.). (1985). *Parental belief systems: The psychological consequences for children.* Hillsdale, NJ: Erlbaum.

Simner, M. L. (1971). Newborn's response to the cry of another infant. *Developmental Psychology, 5,* 136–150.

Simon, H. A. (1971). Spurious correlation: A causal interpretation. In H. M. Blalock, Jr. (Ed.), *Causal models in the social sciences* (pp. 5–17). Chicago: Aldine.

Skinner, B. F. (1938). *The behavior of organisms.* New York: Appleton-Century-Crofts.

Smith, C. B., Adamson, L. B., & Bakeman, R. (1988). Interactional predictors of early language. *First Language, 8,* 143–156.

Snow, C. E. (1977). The development of conversation between mothers and babies. *Journal of Child Language*, *4*, 1–22.

Snow, C. E. (1986). Conversations with children. In P. Fletcher & M. Garman (Eds.), *Language acquisition: Studies in first language development* (2nd ed., pp. 69–89). Cambridge, England: Cambridge University Press.

Snow, C. E., & Ferguson, C. A. (Eds.). (1977). *Talking to children: Language input and acquisition.* Cambridge, England: Cambridge University Press.

Snow, C. E., & Goldfield, B. A. (1983). Turn the page please: Situation-specific language acquisition. *Journal of Child Language*, *10*, 551–569.

Snyder, L. S., Bates, E., & Bretherton, I. (1981). Content and context in early lexical development. *Journal of Child Language*, *8*, 565–582.

Society for Research in Child Development, Committee for Ethical Conduct in Child Development Research (1990, Winter). SRCD ethical standards for research with children. *SRCD Newsletter*.

Sorce, J. F., & Emde, R. N. (1982). The meaning of infant emotional expressions: Regularities in caregiving responses in normal and Down's syndrome infants. *Journal of Child Psychology and Psychiatry*, *23*, 145–158.

Sorce, J. F., Emde, R. N., Campos, J., & Klinnert, M. D. (1985). Maternal emotional signaling: Its effect on the visual cliff behavior of 1-year-olds. *Developmental Psychology*, *21*, 195–200.

Sostek, A. M., Vietze, P., Zaslow, M., Kreiss, L., van der Waals, F., & Rubinstein, D. (1981). Social context in caregiver-infant interaction: A film study of Fais and the United States. In T. M. Field, A. M. Sostek, P. Vietze, & P. H. Leiderman (Eds.), *Culture and early interactions* (pp. 21–37). Hillsdale, NJ: Erlbaum.

Spelke, E. S. (1987). The development of intermodal perception. In P. Salapatek & L. Cohen (Eds.), *Handbook of infant perception* (Vol. 2, pp. 233–273). Orlando, FL: Academic Press.

Spencer, P. E. (1993). Communication behaviors of infants with hearing loss and their hearing mothers. *Journal of Speech and Hearing Research*, *36*, 311–321.

Spencer, P. E., & Gutfreund, M. K. (1990). Characteristics of "dialogues" between mothers and prelinguistic hearing-impaired and normally hearing infants. *Volta Review*, *92*, 351–359.

Spiker, C. C. (1966). The concept of development: Relevant and irrelevant issues. In H. W. Stevenson (Ed.), Concept of development, *Monographs of the Society for Research in Child Development*, *31* (pp. 40–54, Serial No. 107).

Spitz, R. A. (1957). *No and yes: On the beginnings of human communication*. New York: International Universities Press.

Spitz, R. A., & Wolf, K. M. (1946). The smiling response: A contribution to the ontogenesis of social relations. *Genetic Psychology Monographs*, *34*, 57–125.

Sroufe, L. A., & Waters, E. (1976). The ontogenesis of smiling and laughter: A perspective on the organization of development in infancy. *Psychological Review*, *83*, 173–189.

Stack, D. M., & Muir, D. W. (1990). Tactile stimulation as a component of social interchange: New interpretations for the still-face effect. *British Journal of Developmental Psychology*, *8*, 131–145.

Stack, D. M., & Muir, D. W. (1992). Adult tactile stimulation during face-to-face interactions modulates five-month-olds' affect and attention. *Child Development*, *63*, 1509–1525.

Stankiewicz, E. (1983). Roman Jakobson, teacher and scholar. In *A tribute to Roman Jakobson 1896–1982* (pp. 17–26). Berlin: Mouton.

Stark, R. E. (1978). Features of infant sounds: The emergence of cooing. *Journal of Child Language*, *5*, 379–390.

Stark, R. E. (1980). Stages of speech development in the first year of life. In G. H. Yeni-Komshian, J. F. Kavanagh, & C. A. Ferguson (Eds.), *Child phonology: Vol. 1. Production* (pp. 73–92). New York: Academic Press.

Stark, R. E. (1986). Prespeech segmental feature development. In P. Fletcher & M. Garman (Eds.), *Language acquisition: Studies in first language development* (2nd ed., pp. 149–173). Cambridge, England: Cambridge University Press.

Sterman, M. B., & Hoppenbrouwers, T. (1971). The development of sleep-waking and rest-activity patterns from fetus to adult in man. In M. B. Sterman, D. McGinty, & A. Adinolfi (Eds.), *Brain development and behavior* (pp. 203–227). New York: Academic Press.

Stern, D. N. (1974). Mother and infant at play: The dyadic interaction involving facial, vocal and gaze behaviors. In M. Lewis & L. A. Rosenblum (Eds.), *The effect of the infant on its caregiver* (pp. 187–213). New York: Wiley.

Stern, D. N. (1977). *The first relationship: Infant and mother*. Cambridge, MA: Harvard University Press.

Stern, D. N. (1985). *The interpersonal world of the infant: A view from psychoanalysis and developmental psychology*. New York: Basic Books.

Stern, D. N., Beebe, B., Jaffe, J., & Bennett, S. L. (1977). The infant's stimulus world during social interaction: A study of caregiver behaviors with particular reference to repetition and timing. In H. R. Schaffer (Ed.), *Studies in mother–infant interaction* (pp. 177–202). London: Academic Press.

Stern, D. N., & Gibbon, J. (1979). Temporal expectancies of social behaviors in mother–infant play. In E. B. Thoman (Ed.), *Origins of the infant's social responsiveness* (pp. 409–429). Hillsdale, NJ: Erlbaum.

Stern, D. N., Spieker, S., Barnett, R. K., & MacKain, K. (1983). The prosody of maternal speech: Infant age and context related changes. *Journal of Child Language*, *10*, 1–15.

Stern, D. N., Spieker, S., & MacKain, K. (1982). Intonation contours as signals in maternal speech to prelinguistic infants. *Developmental Psychology*, *18*, 727–735.

Stevenson, H. W. (Ed.). (1966). Concept of development. *Monographs of the Society for Research in Child Development*, *31* (Serial No. 107).

Stevenson, M. B., Ver Hoeve, J. N., Roach, M. A., & Leavitt, L. A. (1986). The beginning of conversation: Early patterns of mother–infant vocal responsiveness. *Infant Behavior and Development*, *9*, 423–440.

Stifter, C. A., & Moyer, D. (1991). The regulation of positive affect: Gaze aversion activity during mother–infant interaction. *Infant Behavior and Development*, *14*, 111–123.

Stone, L. J., Smith, H. T., & Murphy, L. B. (1973). *The competent infant: Research and commentary*. New York: Basic Books.

Sugarman-Bell, S. (1978). Some organizational aspects of preverbal communication. In I. Markova (Ed.), *The social context of language* (pp. 49–66). Chichester, England: Wiley.

Symons, D. K., & Moran, G. (1987). The behavioral dynamics of mutual responsiveness in early face-to-face mother–infant interactions. *Child Development, 58*, 1488–1495.

Thal, D. J., & Tobias, S. (1992). Communicative gestures in children with delayed onset of oral expressive vocabulary. *Journal of Speech and Hearing Research, 35*, 1281–1289.

Tinbergen, N. (1951). *The study of instinct*. London: Oxford University Press.

Tomasello, M. (1988). The role of joint attentional processes in early language development. *Language Sciences, 10*, 69–88.

Tomasello, M. (1992). The social bases of language acquisition. *Social Development, 1*, 67–87.

Tomasello, M., & Farrar, M. J. (1984). Cognitive bases of lexical development: Object permanence and relational words. *Journal of Child Language, 11*, 477–493.

Tomasello, M., & Farrar, M. J. (1986). Joint attention and early language. *Child Development, 57*, 1454–1463.

Tomasello, M., Mannle, S., & Kruger, A. C. (1986). Linguistic environment of 1- to 2-year-old twins. *Developmental Psychology, 22*, 169–176.

Tomasello, M., & Todd, J. (1983). Joint attention and lexical acquisition style. *First Language, 4*, 197–212.

Trevarthen, C. (1977). Descriptive analyses of infant communicative behaviour. In H. R. Schaffer (Ed.), *Studies in mother–infant interaction* (pp. 227–270). London: Academic Press.

Trevarthen, C. (1979). Communication and cooperation in early infancy: A description of primary intersubjectivity. In M. Bullowa (Ed.), *Before speech: The beginning of interpersonal communication* (pp. 321–347). Cambridge, England: Cambridge University Press.

Trevarthen, C. (1988). Universal co-operative motives: How infants begin to know the language and culture of their parents. In G. Jahoda & I. M. Lewis (Eds.), *Acquiring culture: Cross cultural studies in child development* (pp. 37–90). London: Croom Helm.

Trevarthen, C., & Hubley, P. (1978). Secondary intersubjectivity: Confidence, confiding and acts of meaning in the first year. In A. Lock (Ed.), *Action, gestures and symbol* (pp. 183–229). London: Academic Press.

Tronick, E. Z. (1982). Affectivity and sharing. In E. Z. Tronick (Ed.), *Social interchange in infancy: Affect, cognition, and communication* (pp. 1–6). Baltimore: University Park Press.

Tronick, E. Z. (1992). Special section: Cross-cultural studies of development. *Developmental Psychology, 28*, 566–567.

Tronick, E., Als, H., & Adamson, L. B. (1979). The communicative structure of early face-to-face interaction. In M. Bullowa (Ed.), *Before speech: The beginnings of interpersonal communication* (pp. 349–372). Cambridge, England: Cambridge University Press.

Tronick, E., Als, H., Adamson, L. B., Wise, S., & Brazelton, T. B. (1978). The infant's response to entrapment between contradictory messages in face-to-face interaction. *Journal of the American Academy of Child Psychiatry, 17*, 1–13.

Tronick, E., Als, H., & Brazelton, T. B. (1980). Monadic phases: A structural descriptive analysis of infant–mother face-to-face interaction. *Merrill-Palmer Quarterly, 26*, 3–24.

Tronick, E. Z., & Cohn, J. F. (1989). Infant–mother face-to-face interaction: Age and gender differences in coordination and the occurrence of miscoordination. *Child Development, 60*, 85–92.

Tronick, E. Z., Morelli, G. A., & Ivey, P. K. (1992). The Efé forager infant and toddler's pattern of social relationships: Multiple and simultaneous. *Developmental Psychology, 28,* 568–577.

Tronick, E. Z., Ricks, M., & Cohn, J. F. (1982). Maternal and infant affective exchange: Patterns of adaptation. In T. Field & A. Fogel (Eds.), *Emotion and early interaction* (pp. 83–100). Hillsdale, NJ: Erlbaum.

Tronick, E. Z., Winn, S., & Morelli, G. A. (1985). Multiple caretaking in the context of human evolution: Why don't the Efé know the Western prescription for child care? In M. Reite & T. Field (Eds.), *The psychobiology of attachment and separation* (pp. 293–322). New York: Academic Press.

Turkheimer, M., Bakeman, R., & Adamson, L. B. (1989). Do mothers support and peers inhibit skilled object play in infancy? *Infant Behavior and Development, 12,* 37–44.

Urwin, C. (1986). Developmental psychology and psychoanalysis: Splitting the difference. In M. Richards & P. Light (Eds.), *Children of social worlds: Development in a social context* (pp. 257–286). Cambridge, MA: Harvard University Press.

Užgiris, I. Č., Benson, J. B., Kruper, J. C., & Vasek, M. (1989). Contextual influences on imitative interactions between mothers and infants. In J. J. Lockman & N. L. Hazen (Eds.), *Action in social context: Perspectives on early development* (pp. 103–127). New York: Plenum.

Užgiris, I. Č., & Kruper, J. C. (1992). The links between imitation and social referencing. In S. Feinman (Ed.), *Social referencing and the social construction of reality in infancy* (pp. 115–148). New York: Plenum.

Valsiner, J. (1987). *Culture and the development of children's action: A cultural-historical theory of developmental psychology.* Chichester, England: Wiley.

Vandell, D. L., & Wilson, K. S. (1987). Infants' interactions with mother, sibling, and peer: Contrasts and relations between interaction systems. *Child Development, 58,* 176–186.

Vandell, D. L., Wilson, K. S., & Buchanan, N. R. (1980). Peer interaction in the first year of life: An examination of its structure, content, and sensitivity to toys. *Child Development, 51,* 481–488.

Vedeler, D. (1987). Infant intentionality and the attribution of intentions to infants. *Human Development, 30,* 1–17.

Vibbert, M., & Bornstein, M. H. (1989). Specific associations between domains of mother–child interaction and toddler referential language and pretense play. *Infant Behavior and Development, 12,* 163–184.

Volterra, V., & Erting, C. J. (Eds.). (1990). *From gesture to language in hearing and deaf children.* New York: Springer-Verlag.

Vygotsky, L. S. (1978). *Mind in society: The development of higher psychological processes.* Cambridge, MA: Harvard University Press.

Vygotsky, L. S. (1981). The genesis of higher mental functions. In J. V. Wertsch (Ed.), *The concept of activity in Soviet psychology* (pp. 144–188). Armonk, NY: Sharpe.

Walden, T. A., & Baxter, A. (1989). The effect of context and age on social referencing. *Child Development, 60,* 1511–1518.

Walden, T. A., & Ogan, T. A. (1988). The development of social referencing. *Child Development, 59,* 1230–1240.

Walker, H., Messinger, D., Fogel, A., & Karns, J. (1992). Social and communicative development in infancy. In V. B. Van Hasselt & M. Hersen (Eds.), *Handbook of social development: A lifespan perspective* (pp. 157–181). New York: Plenum.

Walker-Andrews, A. S. (1988). Infants' perception of the affordances of expressive behaviors. In C. Rovee-Collier & L. P. Lipsitt (Eds.), *Advances in infancy research* (Vol. 5, pp. 173–221). Norwood, NJ: Ablex.

Walton, G. E., Bower, N. J. A., & Bower, T. G. R. (1992). Recognition of familiar faces by newborns. *Infant Behavior and Development, 15*, 265–270.

Watson, J. B. (1913). Psychology as the behaviorist views it. *Psychological Review, 20*, 158–177.

Watson, J. S. (1972). Smiling, cooing, and "the game." *Merrill-Palmer Quarterly, 18*, 323–339.

Watson, J. S. (1985). Contingency perception in early social development. In T. M. Field & N. A. Fox (Eds.), *Social perception in infants* (pp. 157–176). Norwood, NJ: Ablex.

Watzlawick, P., Beavin, J. H., & Jackson, D. D. (1967). *Pragmatics of human communication*. New York: Norton.

Waugh, L. R. (1976). *Roman Jakobson's science of language*. Lisse: Peter de Ridder Press.

Wedell-Monnig, J., & Lumley, J. (1980). Child deafness and mother–child interaction. *Child Development, 51*, 766–774.

Werker, J. F. (1989). Becoming a native listener. *American Scientist, 77*, 54–59.

Werker, J. F., & Lalonde, C. E. (1988). Cross-language speech perception: Initial capabilities and developmental change. *Developmental Psychology, 24*, 672–683.

Werker, J. F., & Tees, R. C. (1984). Cross-language speech perception: Evidence for perceptual reorganization during the first year of life. *Infant Behavior and Development, 7*, 49–63.

Werner, H. (1948). *Comparative psychology of mental development*. New York: International Universities Press.

Werner, H. (1957). The concept of development from a comparative and organismic point of view. In D. Harris (Ed.), *The concept of development* (pp. 125–148). Minneapolis: University of Minnesota Press.

Werner, H., & Kaplan, B. (1963). *Symbol formation*. New York: Wiley.

White, B. L. (1971). *Human infants: Experience and psychological development*. Englewood Cliffs, NJ: Prentice-Hall.

Whitehurst, G., Fischell, J., Arnold, D., & Lonigan, C. (1992). Evaluating outcomes with children with expressive language delay. In S. Warren & J. Reichle (Eds.), *Causes and effects in communication and language intervention* (pp. 277–314). Baltimore: Brookes.

Whiten, A. (Ed.). (1991). *Natural theories of mind: Evolution, development and simulation of everyday mindreading*. Cambridge, MA: Blackwell.

Whiting, B. B., & Edwards, C. P. (1988). *Children of different worlds: The formation of social behavior*. Cambridge, MA: Harvard University Press.

Wilkinson, L. C., & Rembold, K. L. (1981). The form and function of children's gestures accompanying verbal directives. In P. S. Dale & D. Ingram (Eds.), *Child language: An international perspective* (pp. 175–190). Baltimore: University Park Press.

Wolff, P. H. (1966). The causes, controls and organization of behavior in the neonate. *Psychological Issues Monograph Series, 5*. New York: International Universities Press.

Wolff, P. H. (1968). The serial organization of sucking in the young infant. *Pediatrics, 42*, 943–956.

Wolff, P. H. (1969). The natural history of crying and other vocalizations in early infancy. In B. M. Foss (Ed.), *Determinants of infant behavior* (Vol. 4, pp. 81–115). London: Methuen.

Wolff, P. H. (1985). Epilogue. In B. M. Lester & C. F. Z. Boukydis (Eds.), *Infant crying: Theoretical and research perspectives* (pp. 349–354). New York: Plenum.

Wolff, P. H. (1987). *The development of behavioral states and the expression of emotions in early infancy.* Chicago: University of Chicago Press.

Wood, D. (1989). Social interaction as tutoring. In M. H. Bornstein & J. Bruner (Eds.), *Interaction in human development* (pp. 59–80). Hillsdale, NJ: Erlbaum.

Wood, D., Bruner, J. S., & Ross, G. (1976). The role of tutoring in problem solving. *Journal of Child Psychology and Psychiatry, 17*, 89–100.

Yoder, P. J., & Farran, D. C. (1986). Mother–infant engagements in dyads with handicapped and nonhandicapped infants: A pilot study. *Applied Research in Mental Retardation, 7*, 51–58.

Zarbatany, C., & Lamb, M. E. (1985). Social referencing as a function of information source: Mothers versus strangers. *Infant Behavior and Development, 8*, 25–33.

Zeskind, P. S. (1985). A developmental perspective of infant crying. In B. M. Lester & C. F. Z. Boukydis (Eds.), *Infant crying: Theoretical and research perspectives* (pp. 159–185). New York: Plenum.

Zeskind, P. S., & Lester, B. M. (1981). Cry features of newborns with differential patterns of fetal growth. *Child Development, 52*, 207–212.

Zeskind, P. S., & Marshall, T. R. (1988). The relation between variations in pitch and maternal perceptions of infant crying. *Child Development, 59*, 193–196.

INDEX